WALKABLE CITY

ALSO BY JEFF SPECK

*Suburban Nation: The Rise of Sprawl and
the Decline of the American Dream*
(coauthor with Andres Duany
and Elizabeth Plater-Zyberk)

The Smart Growth Manual
(coauthor with Andres Duany)

WALKABLE CITY

HOW DOWNTOWN CAN SAVE AMERICA,
ONE STEP AT A TIME

JEFF SPECK

FARRAR, STRAUS AND GIROUX

NEW YORK

Farrar, Straus and Giroux
18 West 18th Street, New York 10011

Distributed in Canada by D&M Publishers, Inc.
Printed in the United States of America
First edition, 2012

Grateful acknowledgment is made to Charles Marohn
for permission to use an excerpt from *Grist*.

Library of Congress Cataloging-in-Publication Data
Speck, Jeff.
    Walkable city : how downtown can save America, one step at a
time / Jeff Speck.
      p. cm.
    Includes bibliographical references and index.
    ISBN 978-0-374-28581-4 (alk. paper)
    1. Central business districts—United States—Planning.
2. Pedestrian areas—United States—Planning.   3. Urban renewal—
United States.   4. City planning—United States.   I. Title.

HT175 .S64 2012
307.1'2160973—dc23

                                 2012018934

Designed by Jonathan D. Lippincott

www.fsgbooks.com

5   7   9   10   8   6   4

For Alice

CONTENTS

WALKABLE CITY

PROLOGUE

This is not the next great book on American cities. That book is not needed. An intellectual revolution is no longer necessary. What characterizes the discussion on cities these days is not a wrongheadedness or a lack of awareness about what needs to be done, but rather a complete disconnect between that awareness and the actions of those responsible for the physical form of our communities.

We've known for three decades how to make livable cities—after forgetting for four—yet we've somehow not been able to pull it off. Jane Jacobs, who wrote in 1960, won over the planners by 1980. But the planners have yet to win over the city.

Certain large cities, yes. If you make your home in New York, Boston, Chicago, San Francisco, Portland, or in a handful of other special places, you can have some confidence that things are on the right track. But these locations are the exceptions. In the small and midsized cities where most Americans spend their lives, the daily decisions of local officials are still, more often than not, making their lives worse. This is not bad planning but the absence of planning, or rather, decision-making disconnected from planning. The planners were so wrong for so many years that now that they are mostly right, they are mostly ignored.

But this book is not about the planning profession, nor is it an argument for more planning per se. Instead, it is an attempt to simply delineate what is wrong with most American cities and how to fix it. This book is not about why cities work or how cities work, but about what works in cities. And what works best in the best cities is walkability.

Walkability is both an end and a means, as well as a measure. While the physical and social rewards of walking are many, walkability is perhaps most useful as it contributes to urban vitality and most meaningful as an indicator of that vitality. After several decades spent redesigning pieces of cities, trying to make them more livable and more successful, I have watched my focus narrow to this topic as the one issue that seems to both influence and embody most of the others. Get walkability right and so much of the rest will follow.

This discussion is necessary because, since midcentury, whether intentionally or by accident, most American cities have effectively become no-walking zones. In the absence of any larger vision or mandate, city engineers—worshiping the twin gods of Smooth Traffic and Ample Parking—have turned our downtowns into places that are easy to get to but not worth arriving at. Outdated zoning and building codes, often imported from the suburbs, have matched the uninviting streetscape with equally antisocial private buildings, completing a public realm that is unsafe, uncomfortable, and just plain boring. As growing numbers of Americans opt for more urban lifestyles, they are often met with city centers that don't welcome their return. As a result, a small number of forward-thinking cities are gobbling up the lion's share of post-teen suburbanites and empty nesters with the wherewithal to live wherever they want, while most midsized American cities go hungry.

How can Providence, Grand Rapids, and Tacoma compete with Boston, Chicago, and Portland? Or, more realistically, how can these typical cities provide their citizens a quality of life that makes them want to stay? While there are many answers to that question, perhaps none has been so thoroughly neglected as design, and how a comprehensive collection of simple design fixes can reverse decades of counterproductive policies and practices and usher in a new era of street life in America.

These fixes simply give pedestrians a fighting chance, while also embracing bikes, enhancing transit, and making downtown living attractive to a broader range of people. Most are not expensive—some require little more than yellow paint. Each one individually makes a difference; collectively, they can transform a city and the lives of its residents.

Even New York and San Francisco still get some things wrong, but they will continue to poach the country's best and brightest unless our other, more normal cities can learn from their successes while avoiding their mistakes. We planners are counting on these typical places, because America will be finally ushered into "the urban century" not by its few exceptions, but by a collective movement among its everyday cities to do once again what cities do best, which is to bring people together—on foot.

A GENERAL THEORY OF WALKABILITY

As a city planner, I make plans for new places and I make plans for making old places better. Since the late eighties, I have worked on about seventy-five plans for cities, towns, and villages, new and old. About a third of these have been built or are well under way, which sounds pretty bad, but is actually a decent batting average in this game. This means that I have had my fair share of pleasant surprises as well as many opportunities to learn from my mistakes.

In the middle of this work, I took four years off to lead the design division at the National Endowment for the Arts. In this job, I helped run a program called the Mayors' Institute on City Design, which puts city leaders together with designers for intensive planning sessions. Every two months, somewhere in the United States, we would gather eight mayors and eight designers, lock ourselves in a room for two days, and try to solve each mayor's most pressing city-planning challenge.[*] As might be imagined, working side by side with a couple hundred mayors, one mayor at a time, proved a greater design education than anything I have done before or since.

[*] This program, now in its twenty-sixth year, has served nearly one thousand mayors, with dramatic results. More information can be found at micd.org.

I specialize in downtowns, and when I am hired to make a downtown plan, I like to move there with my family, preferably for at least a month. There are many reasons to move to a city while you plan it. First, it's more efficient in terms of travel and setting up meetings, something that can become very expensive. Second, it allows you to truly get to know a place, to memorize every building, street, and block. It also gives you the chance to get familiar with the locals over coffee, dinners in people's homes, drinks in neighborhood pubs, and during chance encounters on the street. These nonmeeting meetings are when most of the real intelligence gets collected.

These are all great reasons. But the main reason to spend time in a city is to live the life of a citizen. Shuttling between a hotel and a meeting facility is not what citizens do. They take their kids to school, drop by the dry cleaners, make their way to work, step out for lunch, hit the gym or pick up some groceries, get themselves home, and consider an evening stroll or an after-dinner beer. Friends from out of town drop in on the weekend and get taken out for a night on the main square. These are among the many normal things that nonplanners do, and I try to do them, too.

A couple of years ago, while I was working on a plan for Lowell, Massachusetts, some old high-school friends joined us for dinner on Merrimack Street, the heart of a lovely nineteenth-century downtown. Our group consisted of four adults, one toddler in a stroller, and my wife's very pregnant belly. Across the street from our restaurant, we waited for the light to change, lost in conversation. Maybe a minute passed before we saw the push-button signal request. So we pushed it. The conversation advanced for another minute or so. Finally, we gave up and jaywalked. About the same time, a car careened around the corner at perhaps forty-five miles per hour, on a street that had been widened to ease traffic.

The resulting near-miss fortunately left no scars, but it will not be forgotten. Stroller jaywalking is a surefire way to feel like a bad parent, especially when it goes awry. The only consolation this time was that I was in a position to do something about it.

As I write these words, I am again on the road with my family, this time in Rome. Now the new baby is in a sling, and the toddler alternates between a stroller and his own two feet, depending on the terrain and his frame of mind. It is interesting to compare our experience in Rome with the one in Lowell, or, more to the point, the experience of walking in most American cities.

Rome, at first glance, seems horribly inhospitable to pedestrians. So many things are wrong. Half the streets are missing sidewalks, most intersections lack crosswalks, pavements are uneven and rutted, handicap ramps are largely absent. Hills are steep and frequent (I hear there are seven). And need I mention the drivers?

Yet here we are among so many other pedestrians—tourists and locals alike—making our way around Trastevere . . . on our toes, yes, but enjoying every minute of it. This anarchic obstacle course is somehow a magnet for walkers, recently selected by readers of *Lonely Planet* travel guides as one of the world's "Top Ten Walking Cities." Romans drive a fraction of the miles that Americans do. A friend of ours who came here to work in the U.S. embassy bought a car when he arrived, out of habit. Now it sits in his courtyard, a target for pigeons.

This tumultuous urban landscape, which fails to meet any conventional American measure of "pedestrian friendliness," is a walker's paradise. So what's going on here? Certainly, in competing for foot traffic, Anatole Broyard's "poem pressed into service as a city" began with certain advantages. The *Lonely Planet* ranking is likely more a function of spectacle than pedestrian comfort. But the same monuments, arranged in a more modern American way, would hardly compete. (Think Las Vegas, with its

Walk Score of 54*.) The main thing that makes Rome—and the other winners: Venice, Boston, San Francisco, Barcelona, Amsterdam, Prague, Paris, and New York—so walkable is what we planners call "fabric," the everyday collection of streets, blocks, and buildings that tie the monuments together. Despite its many technical failures, Rome's fabric is superb.

Yet fabric is one of several key aspects of urban design that are missing from the walkability discussion in most places. This is because that discussion has largely been about creating adequate and attractive pedestrian facilities, rather than walkable cities. There is no shortage of literature on this subject and even a fledgling field of "walkability studies" that focuses on impediments to pedestrian access and safety, mostly in the Toronto suburbs.■ These efforts are helpful, but inadequate. The same goes for urban beautification programs, such as the famous "Five B's" of the eighties—bricks, banners, bandstands, bollards, and berms—that now grace many an abandoned downtown.[1]

Lots of money and muscle have gone into improving sidewalks, crossing signals, streetlights, and trash cans, but how important are these things, ultimately, in convincing people to walk? If walking was just about creating safe pedestrian zones, then why did more than 150 Main Streets pedestrianized in the sixties and seventies fail almost immediately?[2] Clearly, there is more to walking than just making safe, pretty space for it.

The pedestrian is an extremely fragile species, the canary in the coal mine of urban livability. Under the right conditions, this creature thrives and multiplies. But creating those conditions requires attention to a broad range of criteria, some more easily satisfied than others. Enumerating and understanding these criteria is a project for a lifetime—it has become mine—and is forever a work in progress. It is presumptuous to claim to have

*54 out of 100. See below for more on Walk Score.
■See janeswalk.net.

figured it out, but since I have spent a lot of time trying, I reckon it is worth communicating what I have learned so far. Since it tries to explain so much, I call this discussion the General Theory of Walkability.

The General Theory of Walkability explains how, to be favored, a walk has to satisfy four main conditions: it must be useful, safe, comfortable, and interesting. Each of these qualities is essential and none alone is sufficient. *Useful* means that most aspects of daily life are located close at hand and organized in a way that walking serves them well. *Safe* means that the street has been designed to give pedestrians a fighting chance against being hit by automobiles; they must not only be safe but *feel* safe, which is even tougher to satisfy. *Comfortable* means that buildings and landscape shape urban streets into "outdoor living rooms," in contrast to wide-open spaces, which usually fail to attract pedestrians. *Interesting* means that sidewalks are lined by unique buildings with friendly faces and that signs of humanity abound.

These four conditions are mostly a way of thinking about a series of specific rules that are further organized into what I call the Ten Steps of Walkability. These will be explored later. Together, I believe that they add up to a complete prescription for making our cities more walkable.

But first, we must understand that the walkable city is not just a nice, idealistic notion. Rather, it is a simple, practical-minded solution to a host of complex problems that we face as a society, problems that daily undermine our nation's economic competitiveness, public welfare, and environmental sustainability. For that reason, this book is less a design treatise than an essential call to arms. Why we need walkability so badly is the subject of the next section.

PART I

WHY WALKABILITY?

While battle was never declared, many American cities seem to have been made and remade with a mandate to defeat pedestrians. Fattened roads, emaciated sidewalks, deleted trees, fry-pit drive-thrus, and ten-acre parking lots have reduced many of our streetscapes to auto zones in which pedestrian life is but a theoretical possibility.

The causes of this transformation are sometimes surprising. In Miami, for example, people wonder why intersections in residential neighborhoods are often so fat: two relatively narrow streets will meet in a sweeping expanse of asphalt that seems to take hours to walk across. The answer is that the firefighters' union once struck a deal that no truck would ever be sent out with fewer than four firemen on it. That's good for safety and even better for job security, but the only truck that seated four was the hook and ladder. So, for many years, one-story residential neighborhoods in Miami had to be designed around the lumbering turning radius of a truck built for tall-building fires.[1]

The above anecdote is far from unusual in today's landscape of disassociated professions and special interests that determine the shape of our communities. The modern world is full of experts who are paid to ignore criteria beyond their professions. The school and parks departments will push for fewer, larger facilities, since these are easier to maintain—and show off. The public works department will insist that new neighborhoods be designed principally around snow and trash removal. The department of transportation will build new roads to ease traffic generated by the very sprawl that they cause. Each of these approaches may seem correct in a vacuum, but is wrong in a city.

If they are to function properly, cities need to be planned by generalists, as they once were. Generalists understand that consolidating parks means that fewer people can walk to them. Generalists understand that infrastructure organized in service of big trucks is not always inviting to small people. And generalists, finally, are coming to understand that more lanes usually just lead to more traffic.

Most significantly, generalists—such as planners and, one hopes, mayors—ask the big-picture questions that are so often forgotten among the day-to-day shuffle of city governance. Questions like: What kind of city will help us thrive economically? What kind of city will keep our citizens not just safe, but healthy? What kind of city will be sustainable for generations to come?

These three issues—wealth, health, and sustainability—are, not coincidentally, the three principal arguments for making our cities more walkable.

WALKING, THE URBAN ADVANTAGE

The walking generation; A demographic perfect storm;
The walkability dividend

Many of my client cities ask me the same question: "How can we attract corporations, citizens, and especially young, entrepreneurial talent?" In Grand Rapids, Michigan, where I am employed by the city's leading philanthropists, they ask it differently: "How can we keep our children from leaving? How can we keep our grandchildren from leaving?"

The obvious answer is that cities need to provide the sort of environment that these people want. Surveys—as if we needed them—show how creative-class citizens, especially millennials, vastly favor communities with *street life*, the pedestrian culture that can only come from walkability.

A lack of street life was one reason why the leadership at Wolverine World Wide, the manufacturers of Merrell and Patagonia Footwear, was having trouble keeping new creative workers from jumping ship from their suburban West Michigan headquarters. The problem was not the company, but the impression among newly arrived spouses that they had no way to break into the social scene . . . even though West Michiganders are known for their openness and hospitality. So what was going on? It turns out that this social scene could only be accessed by car and thus by invitation. With no pedestrian culture, there were no opportunities for the chance encounters that turn into friendships.

When it came time to launch a new apparel division, they decided to base it in Portland, Oregon.

Since that time, Wolverine has set up a new innovation center along with three other top West Michigan companies in downtown Grand Rapids. According to Blake Krueger, Wolverine's president and CEO, the company needed "an urban hub that attracts and retains the millennial creative class. You need a vibrant city heartbeat for these people. Downtown, they're in a more creative live/work/play environment than if they are stuck out here in suburbia." This facility now includes designers and product developers across a dozen different brands.

For many companies, an urban satellite is not enough. Brand Muscle, formerly of leafy Beachwood, Ohio, recently relocated all of its 150 employees to downtown Cleveland, thanks in part to the desires of a largely twentysomething workforce. Now staffer Kristen Babjack brags about her urban lifestyle: "We can leave our apartment and walk five feet to a restaurant to get something to eat, or to go shopping. We have all of our arenas and sporting areas and concerts all in one pretty much walkable area."[•] Similar stories are making the news in Saint Louis, Buffalo, and even in beleaguered Detroit.

The economic advantage that has already begun to accrue to walkable places can be attributed to three key factors. First, for certain segments of the population, chief among them young "creatives," urban living is simply more appealing; many wouldn't be caught dead anywhere else. Second, massive demographic shifts occurring right now mean that these pro-urban segments of the population are becoming dominant, creating a spike in demand that is expected to last for decades. Third, the choice to live the walkable life generates considerable savings for these households,

---

[•]David Barnett, "A Comeback for Downtown Cleveland." United Airlines just moved thirteen hundred of its employees to downtown Chicago from suburban Elk Grove Township, Illinois (Fran Spielman, "1300 More United Jobs Downtown").

and much of these savings are spent locally. I will address each of these factors in turn.

THE WALKING GENERATION

When I worked for the town planning firm DPZ* in Miami in the nineties, everyone drove to the office, without exception. Taking transit or bicycling made no sense at all, as the buses took forever and the biking was worse than perilous. In more recent visits, I learned that a significant segment of the young designer workforce now bikes or rides the bus, even though the conditions for either are hardly better.

These are the same folks who have put a composting bin in the office kitchen . . . so are they just the exceptions to the rule?

It turns out that since the late nineties, the share of automobile miles driven by Americans in their twenties has dropped from 20.8 percent to just 13.7 percent. And if one looks at teens, future shifts seem likely to be greater. The number of nineteen-year-olds who have opted out of earning driver's licenses has almost tripled since the late seventies, from 8 percent to 23 percent.[1] This statistic is particularly meaningful when one considers how the American landscape has changed since the seventies, when most American teens could walk to school, to the store, and to the soccer field, in stark contrast to the realities of today's auto-centric sprawl.

This trend began well before the recession of 2008 and subsequent fuel spikes, and is seen as cultural, not economic. Market researchers J. D. Power—hardly part of the anticar lobby—report that "online discussions by teens indicate shifts in perceptions regarding the necessity of and desire to have cars."[2] In

---

*DPZ stands for Duany-Plater Zyberk & Company, the firm founded by Andres Duany and Elizabeth Plater-Zyberk, my coauthors on *Suburban Nation*.

"The Great Car Reset," Richard Florida observes: "Younger people today . . . no longer see the car as a necessary expense or a source of personal freedom. In fact, it is increasingly just the opposite: not owning a car and not owning a house are seen by more and more as a path to greater flexibility, choice, and personal autonomy."[3] These driving trends are only a small part of a larger picture that has less to do with cars and more to do with cities, and specifically with how young professionals today view themselves in relation to the city, especially in comparison to previous generations.

Born as the baby boom ended, I grew up watching three television shows almost daily: *Gilligan's Island*, *The Brady Bunch*, and *The Partridge Family*. While *Gilligan's Island* may have had little to say about urbanism, the other two were extremely instructive. They idealized the mid-twentieth-century suburban standard of low-slung houses on leafy lots, surrounded by more of the same. This was normal and good. As a would-be architect, I was particularly susceptible to the charms of Mike Brady's self-built split-level. This is not to say that there were no urban shows on my television set. I saw a good amount of four: *Dragnet*, *Mannix*, *The Streets of San Francisco*, and *Hawaii 5-0*—all focused on one subject: crime.•

Now, contrast my experience growing up in the seventies with that of a child growing up in or around the nineties, watching *Seinfeld*, *Friends*, and, eventually, *Sex and the City*. In these shows, the big city (in all cases New York) was lovingly portrayed as a largely benevolent and always interesting force, often a character and coconspirator in its own right. The most urban of American cities was the new normal, and certainly good.

The first thing that I take away from this comparison is that I watched far too much television as a child. But the real point

---

• To be fair, I also caught occasional episodes of *The Honeymooners* and *The Lucille Ball Show*, in which the city took the form of a vague, sooty presence outside the window of a cramped apartment—unthreatening but also uninviting. The only memorable exception was *The Mary Tyler Moore Show*. We'll talk about her later.

here is that today's young professionals grew up in a mass culture—of which TV was only one part—that has predisposed them to look favorably upon cities; indeed, to aspire to live in them. I grew up in the suburbs watching shows about the suburbs. They grew up in the suburbs watching shows about the city. My complacency has been replaced by their longing.

This group, the *millennials*, represent the biggest population bubble in fifty years. Sixty-four percent of college-educated millennials choose first where they want to live, and only then do they look for a job.[4] Fully 77 percent of them plan to live in America's urban cores.[5]

A DEMOGRAPHIC PERFECT STORM

Meanwhile, the generation raised on *Friends* is not the only major cohort looking for new places to live. There's a larger one: the millennials' parents, the front-end boomers. They are citizens that every city wants—significant personal savings, no schoolkids.

And according to Christopher Leinberger, the Brookings Institution economist who first brought my attention to the *Brady Bunch/Friends* phenomenon, empty nesters want walkability:

At approximately 77 million Americans, they are fully one-quarter of the population. With the leading edge of the boomers now approaching sixty-five years old, the group is finding that their suburban houses are too big. Their child-rearing days are ending, and all those empty rooms have to be heated, cooled, and cleaned, and the unused backyard maintained. Suburban houses can be socially isolating, especially as aging eyes and slower reflexes make driving everywhere less comfortable. Freedom for many in this generation means living in walkable, accessible communities with convenient transit linkages and good public services like libraries, cultural activities, and health care.[6]

In the 1980s, my city-planning colleagues and I began hearing from sociologists about something called a NORC, a naturally occurring retirement community. Over the past decade, I have watched a growing number of my parents' generation abandon their large-lot houses to resettle in mixed-use urban centers. My own parents finally jumped ship last year, moving from leafy Belmont Hill, Massachusetts, to only-slightly-less-leafy but much more walkable Lexington Center. For them, that increased walkability means all the difference between an essentially housebound existence and what we all hope will be several decades of continued independence.

On the cusp of their eighties, my parents could be considered late adopters. But as pre-boomers, they represent a trickle of what is to become a torrent. Leinberger notes how, starting now, an average of 1.5 million Americans will be turning sixty-five every year, quadruple the rate of a decade ago.[7] This rate will not begin to plateau until 2020 and we will not see it return to current levels until 2033.

In combination with their independent children, these retiring boomers will numerically overwhelm those families of child-rearing age who typically prefer the suburbs. This upcoming convergence represents "the biggest demographic event since the baby boom itself."[8] Of the 101 million new households expected to take shape between now and 2025, fully 88 percent are projected to be childless. This is a dramatic change from 1970, when almost half of all households included children.* These new adults-only households won't give a hoot about the quality of

---

*Christopher B. Leinberger, *The Option of Urbanism*, 89–90. Leinberger's book is a central source for this section, as it lays out many of the arguments and statistics surrounding the demand for walkable cities. While 4 million Americans lived alone in 1950, that number now tops 31 million (Nathan Heller, "The Disconnect," 110). According to *USA Today*, there are now more households with dogs than children (Haya El Nasser, "In Many Neighborhoods, Kids Are Only a Memory").

local schools or the size of their backyards. "This fact will open up many possibilities," Leinberger observes.[9]

As that current statistical oddity, a parent of young children, I often advocate for stronger public schools and neighborhood parks to benefit families. I remind people that a community cannot fully thrive in the absence of any generational cohort, since we all support one another. I like to quote David Byrne: "If we can build a successful city for children, we can build a successful city for all people."[10] This is true enough, but I am often reminded that I lived comfortably for a full decade in one of the most extreme exceptions to that rule, Miami's South Beach, where I could easily go for a month at a time without a stroller sighting. Not one adult in my neighborhood appeared to be between thirty-five and fifty-five, and none seemed (productively) fertile. Yet South Beach was and remains a great place physically, socially, and economically. Demographically speaking, South Beach is the future of many American cities.

That seems to be the case in walkable Washington, D.C., where the past decade has seen a 23 percent uptick in the number of residents between twenty and thirty-four, simultaneous with an increased number of adults in their fifties and early sixties. Meanwhile, the number of children under fifteen has dropped by 20 percent.[11]

Clearly, Leinberger is optimistic about the larger impact of these population trends on cities. Writing in *Grist*, he concludes that "meeting the pent-up demand for walkable urban development will take a generation. It will be a boon to the real estate industry and put a foundation under the American economy for decades, just as the construction of low-density suburbs did during the last half of the 20th century."[12] Whether or not it can salvage our struggling economy, he makes a convincing case that people will be moving back to the city.

The question that remains is: Will they be moving back to your city, or to someone else's? The answer may well lie in its walkability.

Christopher Leinberger was once the owner of Robert Charles Lesser & Co., the largest real estate advisory firm in the United States, which means that he helped to build a lot of sprawl. He is now convinced that much of suburbia is poised to become "The Next Slum."[13]

In order to study real estate performance, Leinberger divides the American built environment into two categories: *walkable urbanism* and *drivable sub-urbanism.** In the Detroit region, he finds that housing in walkable urbanism fetches a 40 percent price premium over similar housing in drivable sub-urbanism; in the Seattle region, that premium is 51 percent; in Denver, it's 150 percent. New York City, unsurprisingly, tops the list at 200 percent—that is to say, people are paying three times as much per square foot for apartments in walkable neighborhoods as for comparable suburban houses. In most markets, the demand for walkable urbanism dramatically outpaces the supply: in Atlanta, only 35 percent of poll respondents who want to live in a walkable urban place are able to find and afford it.[14]

A similar dynamic can be found at work for commercial properties. In Washington, D.C., walkable office space recently leased at a 27 percent premium over drivable suburban office space and had single-digit rather than double-digit vacancy rates. *The Wall Street Journal* has confirmed similar trends nationwide: while the suburban office vacancy rate has jumped 2.3 points since 2005, occupancy in America's downtowns has held steady.[15]

Looking at these numbers, Leinberger concludes:

> The metropolitan area that does not offer walkable urbanism is probably destined to lose economic development opportunities; the creative class will gravitate to

---

*These categories are slightly misleading, since walkable urbanism is still drivable, while drivable sub-urbanism is not walkable. Or, more accurately, in walkable urbanism, driving remains a viable option for those people with disposable income and time to spend in traffic, while in drivable sub-urbanism, walking is a practice undertaken only by the least advantaged people with no choice.

those metro areas that offer multiple choices in living arrangements. . . . As consumer surveys in downtown Philadelphia and Detroit in 2006 have shown, this seems to be particularly true for the well-educated, who seem to have a predilection for living in walkable urban places.[16]

This growing demand for pedestrian-friendly places is reflected in the runaway success of Walk Score, the website that calculates neighborhood walkability.• It was started on a lark in 2007 by Matt Lerner, Mike Mathieu, and Jesse Kocher, three partners in a software company with the incongruously automotive name of Front Seat. "I had heard a story on NPR about food miles in England—labeling food with how far it had to travel to get to you," Lerner told me recently, "and I thought, why not instead measure house miles: how many miles from your house you had to go for daily errands."

Addresses are ranked in five categories, with a score of 50 needed to cross the threshold from *car dependent* to *somewhat walkable*. Seventy points earns a *very walkable* ranking, and anything above 90 qualifies as a *walker's paradise*. San Francisco's Chinatown earns a 100, as does NYC's Tribeca, while Los Angeles's Mulholland Drive rates a 9. South Beach in Miami gets a 92. Nike's headquarters in Beaverton, Oregon, comes in at a *car dependent* 42, while the street address of the nationally acclaimed "Walking Guru" Leslie Sansone, of New Castle, Pennsylvania, has a Walk Score of 37.■

•According to Lerner, once a crude version was up and running, "I emailed twenty people about the site, and we had 150,000 unique visitors the next day." Walk Score now serves up more than 4 million scores daily.

■One of the fascinating things about Walk Score is how accurate it is, despite the fact that it currently measures only one aspect of walkability: proximity to daily destinations. Specifically, the algorithm asks how far one is (as the crow flies) from nine different "amenity categories," including shopping, dining, coffee, parks, and schools. As will be discussed ahead, true walkability depends dramatically upon so many other factors that Walk Score doesn't measure—such as the size of the blocks and the speed of the cars—but its failure (so far) to measure these attributes doesn't hurt it too much due to a convenient coincidence: almost all of the places in America with many different uses

Tellingly, Walk Score has become a big hit with real estate agents. Driven by their demand, the Front Seat team has recently developed Walk Score Professional, a subscription site that already boasts links from more than ten thousand other websites, most of them belonging to realtors.

I spoke with one of these agents, Eva Otto, whose face adorns a testimonial on the Walk Score homepage. She is confident that "in a place like Seattle, walkability is the make or break for some buyers. It can add 5 to 10 percent to a person's willingness to pay for a house." For each property she handles, she places the Walk Score website amenity map inside the house in an obvious place. She comments that her buyers are increasingly aware of "how surprising and delightful your quality of life can be when you don't have to get into a car to go every place in your life besides home."

If Walk Score is so useful in helping people decide where to live, then it can also help us determine how much they value walkability. Now that it has been around for a few years, some resourceful economists have had the opportunity to study the relationship between Walk Score and real estate value, and they

---

in close proximity tend to possess smaller blocks and slower-speed traffic. Mixed uses and pedestrian-friendly streets are both part of one common model (the traditional urban neighborhood), while isolated uses and unwalkable streets constitute the other (sprawl). Where the algorithm begins to fail is in high-intensity, commercial edge cities. Here, a preponderance of retail outlets cranks up the score, despite the fact that the only walking occurs in gigantic parking lots. For this reason, sprawl poster child Tysons Corner, Virginia—straight from the cover of Joel Garreau's book *Edge City*—earns an impressive 87. This puts it two points ahead of my own U Street neighborhood in Washington, D.C., even though half my neighbors don't own cars and walk to everything. Living car-free in Tysons Corner, if not actually illegal, is still a preposterous concept.

Happily, the developers are hard at work refining the algorithm. A new version called Street Smart impressively manages to take block size, street width, and vehicle speed into account. This new version will eventually replace the original one—perhaps by the time you are reading this. But Lerner and his team are wary of moving too quickly: "When we make the change over to Street Smart, a lot of people's scores will change, so we want to have a long beta period to work out any issues."

have put a price on it: five hundred to three thousand dollars *per point.*

In his white paper for CEOs for Cities, "Walking the Walk: How Walkability Raises Home Values in U.S. Cities," Joe Cortright looked at data for ninety thousand distinct home sales in fifteen markets nationwide, places like Chicago, Dallas, and Jacksonville. After controlling for all other factors that are known to impact house price, he found a clear positive correlation in all but two of those markets.[*] In a typical example, Charlotte, North Carolina, Cortright found that an increase in Walk Score from the metropolitan average of 54 (*somewhat walkable*) to 71 (*very walkable*) correlated with an increase in average house price from $280,000 to $314,000.[17] That's two thousand dollars per point, or two hundred thousand dollars across the full scale. Interestingly, two hundred thousand dollars is about the minimum price you can pay for an empty buildable lot in the more walkable parts of Washington, D.C.

Of course, it's generally useful to back up the data by asking real humans what they want. The market-research firm Belden Russonello & Stewart polled several thousand American adults for the National Association of Realtors, and found the following: "When selecting a community, nearly half of the public (47 percent) would prefer to live in a city or a suburban neighborhood with a mix of houses, shops, and businesses. . . . Only one in ten say they would prefer a suburban neighborhood with houses only."[18] Given that the vast majority of the American built environment is currently the latter, it is no surprise that the demand

---

[*]The outliers were Las Vegas and Bakersfield, California, two cities almost entirely lacking in traditional urbanism (Cortright, "Walking the Walk," 2). In a more recent study of the Washington, D.C., region, Chris Leinberger and Mariela Alfonzo found a positive correlation across all market segments. Referring to Walk Score's five categories, they state that "each step up the walkability ladder adds $9 per square foot to annual office rents, $7 per square foot to retail rents, more than $300 per month to apartment rents, and nearly $82 per square foot to home values" (Christopher B. Leinberger, "Now Coveted: A Walkable, Convenient Place").

for walkable urbanism already outpaces the supply. This disparity is only going to get bigger.

THE WALKABILITY DIVIDEND

In 2007, Joe Cortright, the fellow responsible for the Walk Score value study cited above, published a report called "Portland's Green Dividend," in which he asked the question: What does Portland get for being walkable? Quite a lot, it turns out.

To set the stage, we should describe what makes Portland different. Clearly, it is not Manhattan. It is not particularly big or particularly small and its residential density, by American standards, is pretty normal. It has attracted a good amount of industry lately, but has shown no great historical predisposition to do so, nor is it gifted with mineral wealth. It rains a lot in Portland and, interestingly, locals pride themselves on not using umbrellas. Perhaps most fascinating is the way that Portlanders refuse to disobey DON'T WALK signs, even if it's 1:00 a.m. on a tiny two-lane street swathed in utter silence . . . and even if a blithe east-coaster is striding happily into the intersection (I'm not naming names here).

But what really makes Portland unusual is how it has chosen to grow. While most American cities were building more highways, Portland invested in transit and biking. While most cities were reaming out their roadways to speed traffic, Portland implemented a Skinny Streets program. While most American cities were amassing a spare tire of undifferentiated sprawl, Portland instituted an urban growth boundary. These efforts and others like them, over several decades—a blink of the eye in planner time—have changed the way that Portlanders live.•

• To be accurate, Portland has not been spared its spare tire of sprawl. But thanks to the urban growth boundary, this area is smaller and more contiguous than it would have been otherwise.

This change is not dramatic—were it not for the roving hordes of bicyclists, it might be invisible—but it is significant. While almost every other American city has seen its residents drive farther and farther every year and spend more and more of their time stuck in traffic, Portland's vehicle miles traveled per person peaked in 1996. Now, compared to other major metropolitan areas, Portlanders on average drive 20 percent less.[19]

Small change? Not really: according to Cortright, this 20 percent (four miles per citizen per day) adds up to $1.1 billion of savings each year, which equals fully 1.5 percent of all personal income earned in the region. And that number ignores time not wasted in traffic: peak travel times have actually fallen from 54 minutes per day to 43 minutes per day.[20] Cortright calculates this improvement at another $1.5 billion. Add those two dollar amounts together and you're talking real money.

What happens to these savings? Portland is reputed to have the most independent bookstores per capita and the most roof racks per capita. The city is also said to have the most strip clubs per capita. These claims are all exaggerations, but they reflect a documented above-average consumption of recreation of all kinds. Portland has more restaurants per capita than all other large cities except Seattle and San Francisco. Oregonians also spend considerably more than most Americans on alcohol,[21] which could be a good thing or a bad thing, but in any case makes you glad they are driving less.

More significantly, whatever they are used for, these savings are more likely to stay local than if spent on driving. Almost 85 percent of money expended on cars and gas leaves the local economy[22]—much of it, of course, bound for the pockets of Middle Eastern princes. A significant amount of the money saved probably goes into housing, since that is a national tendency: families that spend less on transportation spend more on their homes,[23] which is, of course, about as local as it gets.

The housing and driving connection is an important one,

and has been the subject of much recent study, especially since transportation costs have skyrocketed. While transportation used to absorb only one-tenth of a typical family's budget (1960), it now consumes more than one in five dollars spent.* All told, the average American family now spends about $14,000 per year driving multiple cars.[24] By this measure, this family works from January 1 until April 13 just to pay for its cars. Remarkably, the typical "working" family, with an income of $20,000 to $50,000, pays more for transportation than for housing.[25]

This circumstance exists because the typical American working family now lives in suburbia, where the practice of drive-'til-you-qualify reigns supreme. Families of limited means move farther and farther away from city centers in order to find housing that is cheap enough to meet bank lending requirements. Unfortunately, in doing so, they often find that driving costs outweigh any housing savings.[26] This phenomenon was documented in 2006, when gasoline averaged $2.86 per gallon. At that time, households in the auto zone were devoting roughly a quarter of their income to transportation, while those in walkable neighborhoods spent well under half that amount.[27]

No surprise, then, that as gasoline broke $4.00 per gallon and the housing bubble burst, the epicenter of foreclosures occurred at the urban periphery, "places that required families to have a fleet of cars in order to participate in society, draining their mortgage carrying capacity," as Chris Leinberger notes. "Housing prices on the fringe tended to drop at twice the metropolitan average while walkable urban housing tended to maintain [its] value and [is] coming back nicely in selected markets today."[28] Not only have city centers fared better than suburbs, but walkable cities have fared better than drivable ones. Catherine Lutz and Anne Lutz Fernandez note that "the cities with the largest drops in housing value (such as Las Vegas, down

---

*Catherine Lutz and Anne Lutz Fernandez, *Carjacked*, 80. Vehicle miles traveled per household increased 70 percent from 1969 to 2001 (Chuck Kooshian and Steve Winkelman, "Growing Wealthier," 3).

37 percent) have been the most car-dependent, and the few cities with housing prices gains . . . have good transit alternatives."[29]

This is bad news for Orlando and Reno, but it's good news for Portland . . . and also for Washington, D.C., which continues to benefit from earlier investments in transit. From 2005 to 2009, as the District's population grew by 15,862 people, car registrations fell by almost 15,000 vehicles.* The National Building Museum, in its Intelligent Cities Initiative, notes that this reduction in auto use results in as much as $127,275,000 being retained in the local economy each year.▪

Those are the economic benefits of not driving. Are there additional economic benefits of walking, biking, and taking transit instead? The evidence here is a little more scarce, but the indications are positive. Ignoring the health benefits, there is a clear distinction to be made in the category of job creation. Road and highway work, with its big machines and small crews, is notoriously bad at increasing employment. In contrast, the construction of transit, bikeways, and sidewalks performs 60 percent to 100 percent better. A study of President Obama's American Recovery and Reinvestment Act documented a 70 percent employment premium for transit over highways. By this measure, that job-creation program would have created fifty-eight thousand more jobs if its road-building funds had gone to transit instead.▲

*National Building Museum Intelligent Cities Initiative poster. By my estimate, this all occurred on January 20, 2009, when 15,000 Bushies were replaced by 30,000 Obamans. Many Bush staffers, as a point of pride, lived "beyond the beltway" in red-state Virginia.
▪Ibid. In Australia, a similar study determined that living in a transit-oriented neighborhood was likely to save a total of about $750,000 over a lifetime, most of which would be spent locally (Peter Newman, Timothy Beatley, and Heather Boyer, *Resilient Cities*, 120). And since each car removed from the typical household budget allows that family to afford a $135,000 larger mortgage, it's easy to see why Washington real estate prices have dropped only 20 percent from their peak, while housing beyond the beltway has lost half its value.
▲A study of expenditures in Baltimore showed that while each million spent on roads created about seven jobs, each million spent on pedestrian facilities generated eleven jobs, and each million spent on bike lanes created more than fourteen jobs (Heidi Garrett-Peltier, "Estimating the Employment Impacts of Pedestrian, Bicycle, and Road Infrastructure," 1–2).

How does this translate at the local level? Portland has spent roughly $65 million on bicycle facilities over the past several decades. That is not a lot of money by infrastructure standards—it cost more than $140 million to rebuild just one of the city's freeway interchanges.[30] Yet, in addition to helping to boost the number of bicyclists from near normal to fifteen times the national average,* this investment can be expected to have created close to nine hundred jobs, about four hundred more than would have come from spending it on road building.

But the real Portland story is neither its transportation savings nor its bikeway employment, but something else: young, smart people are moving to Portland in droves. According to Cortright and coauthor Carol Coletta, "Over the decade of the 1990s, the number of college-educated 25 to 34 year-olds increased 50 percent in the Portland metropolitan area—five times faster than in the nation as a whole, with the fastest increase in this age group being recorded in the city's close-in neighborhoods."■ There is another kind of walkability dividend, aside from resources saved and resources reinvested: resources attracted by being a place where people want to live. This has certainly been the case in San Francisco, where headhunters for companies like Yelp and Zynga (the social-gaming developers who created FarmVille) actively use urbanism as a recruiting tool. "We're able to attract creative and tech talent because we are in the city," acknowledges Colleen McCreary, Zynga's head of human resources.[31]

Ultimately, though, it would seem that urban productivity has even deeper causes. There is mounting evidence that dense,

---

*According to the census, Portland's bicycling mode share is 5.8 percent, and local studies place it at just under 8 percent. The national average is 0.4 percent.

■"The Young and the Restless," 34. As the number of college graduates in a metropolitan area increases by 10 percent, individuals' earnings increase by 7.7. This applies even to non–college graduates in the city because their productivity rises, too (David Brooks, "The Splendor of Cities").

walkable cities generate wealth by sheer virtue of the propinquity that they offer. This is a concept that is both stunningly obvious—cities exist, after all, because people benefit from coming together—and tantalizingly challenging to prove.* This hasn't kept it from the lips of some of our leading thinkers, including Stewart Brand, Edward Glaeser, David Brooks, and Malcolm Gladwell.

Speaking at the Aspen Institute, David Brooks pointed out how most U.S. patent applications, when they list similar patents that influenced them, point to other innovators located less than twenty-five miles away.* He also mentioned a recent experiment at the University of Michigan, where "researchers brought groups of people together face to face and asked them to play a difficult cooperation game. Then they organized other groups and had them communicate electronically. The face-to-face groups thrived. The electronic groups fractured and struggled."[32]

Face-to-face collaboration is, of course, possible in any setting. But it is easier in a walkable city. Susan Zeilinski, managing director of the University of Michigan's SMART Center, puts it this way: "In Europe you can get five good meetings done in a day. In Australia, maybe three, and in Atlanta, maybe two, because you've gone way, way farther and way, way faster but you haven't been in an accessible place that allows a lot to happen. You've spent a lot of time sitting in traffic."[33] This discussion raises a larger theoretical question that scientists have just begun to take on: are there underlying universal rules that govern the success of a place?

The theoretical physicists Geoffrey West and Luis Bettencourt believe so. They do not believe in urban theory—"a field without principles"—they are interested only in math. "What

---

*More than twenty-five years ago, William Whyte's research tracked the stock performance of thirty-eight New York City companies that chose to relocate to the suburbs, and found that they appreciated at less than half the rate of thirty-five similar companies that had stayed put (Whyte, *City: Rediscovering the Center*, 294–95).

the data clearly shows," West notes, "is that when people come together they become much more productive."[34] Do the same physical laws work in reverse? Writing about West's research in *The New York Times Magazine*, Jonah Lehrer notes:

> In recent decades, though, many of the fastest-growing cities in America, like Phoenix and Riverside, Calif., have given us a very different urban model. These places have traded away public spaces for affordable single-family homes, attracting working-class families who want their own white picket fences. West and Bettencourt point out, however, that cheap suburban comforts are associated with poor performance on a variety of urban metrics. Phoenix, for instance, has been characterized by below-average levels of income and innovation (as measured by the production of patents) for the last 40 years.[35]

These findings align with a recent Environmental Protection Agency study that found, state by state, an inverse relationship between vehicle travel and productivity: the more miles that people in a given state drive, the weaker it performs economically.* Apparently, the data are beginning to support the city planners' bold contention that time wasted in traffic is unproductive.

In contrast, the Portland metro area is now home to more than twelve hundred technology companies. Like Seattle and San Francisco, it is one of the places where educated millennials are heading in disproportionate numbers. This phenomenon is what the demographer William Frey has in mind when he says:

---

*Kooshian and Winkelman, "Growing Wealthier," 2. This correlation seems especially meaningful, since wealthier people have the disposable income that would allow them to drive more.

"A new image of urban America is in the making. What used to be white flight to the suburbs is turning into 'bright flight' to cities that have become magnets for aspiring young adults who see access to knowledge-based jobs, public transportation and a new city ambiance as an attraction."[36]

The conventional wisdom used to be that creating a strong economy came first, and that increased population and a higher quality of life would follow. The converse now seems more likely: creating a higher quality of life is the first step to attracting new residents and jobs. This is why Chris Leinberger believes that "all the fancy economic development strategies, such as developing a biomedical cluster, an aerospace cluster, or whatever the current economic development 'flavor of the month' might be, do not hold a candle to the power of a great walkable urban place."[37]

WHY JOHNNY CAN'T WALK

The obesity bomb; Clearing the air; American car-nage; Tense and lonely

The best day for being a city planner in America was July 9, 2004. That's when Howard Frumkin, Lawrence Frank, and Richard Jackson published their book *Urban Sprawl and Public Health*.

Until that day, the main arguments for building walkable cities were principally aesthetic and social. More significantly, almost nobody but the planners was making them. But it turns out that while we were shouting into the wilderness about the frustrations, anomie, and sheer waste of suburban sprawl, a small platoon of physicians was quietly doing something much more useful: they were documenting how our built environment was killing us.

For Dr. Jackson, the epiphany came in 1999, when he was driving on Atlanta's Buford Highway—voted by the Congress for the New Urbanism as one of the ten "Worst Streets in America"[1]—a seven-laner flanked by low-income garden apartments, "with no sidewalks and two miles between traffic lights."[2] There, by the side of the road, in the ninety-five-degree afternoon, he saw a woman in her seventies, struggling under the burden of two shopping bags. He tried to relate her plight to his own work as an epidemiologist:

> If that poor woman had collapsed from heat stroke, we docs would have written the cause of death as heat stroke

and not lack of trees and public transportation, poor urban form, and heat-island effects. If she had been killed by a truck going by, the cause of death would have been "motor-vehicle trauma," and not lack of sidewalks and transit, poor urban planning, and failed political leadership. That was the "aha!" moment for me. Here I was focusing on remote disease risks when the biggest risks that people faced were coming from the built environment.[3]

Jackson, who has more recently served as former California governor Arnold Schwarzenegger's state public health adviser, spent the next five years quantifying how so much of what ails us can be attributed directly to the demise of walkability in the auto age. The resulting book finally put some technical meat on the bones of the planning profession's admonitions against sprawl.

And the numbers are compelling. Despite spending one dollar out of six on health care, the United States has some of the worst health statistics in the developed world. According to the U.S. Centers for Disease Control (CDC), fully one-third of American children born after 2000 will become diabetics. This is due partly to diet, but partly to planning: the methodical eradication from our communities of *the useful walk* has helped to create the least active generation in American history. This insult is compounded by the very real injuries that result from car crashes—the greatest killer of children and young adults nationwide—as well as an asthma epidemic tied directly to vehicle exhaust. Comparison of walkable cities and auto-dependent suburbs yields some eye-opening statistics—for example, that transit users are more than three times as likely as drivers to achieve their CDC-recommended thirty minutes of daily physical activity.[4] Increasingly, it is becoming clear that the American healthcare crisis is largely an urban-design crisis, with walkability at the heart of the cure.

Particularly affected have been our children. While fully 50 percent walked to school in 1969, fewer than 15 percent do now.* And sometimes when children do walk to school, their parents are visited by the police: a Salt Lake City newspaper carried in December 2010 the story of Noah Talbot, of South Jordan, who was picked up by the police on the way to school and his mother issued a citation for child neglect.[5] Jackson and his coauthors note how "children are increasingly medicated for inattentiveness or hyperactivity, even as many are losing their opportunities for exercise at school or in the neighborhood. There are third-grade classes in which as many as a third of the boys are on Ritalin or similar medications."[6]

To summarize the findings of *Urban Sprawl and Public Health*—which are echoed by a growing number of epidemiologists nationwide—the inactivity-inducing convenience, often violent speed, and toxic exhaust of our cars have contributed mightily to the circumstance that "for the first time in history, the current generation of youth will live shorter lives than their parents."[7]

THE OBESITY BOMB

In any meaningful discussion about American health (and health care), obesity has to be front and center.■ In the mid-1970s, only about one in ten Americans was obese, which put us where much of Europe is right now. What has happened in the intervening

* Neal Peirce, "Biking and Walking: Our Secret Weapon?" Similarly, the number of elementary school–aged children driven to school in private vehicles has risen from 12 percent in 1969 to 44 percent in 2009 (Poster, Intelligent Cities Initiative, National Building Museum).

■ All told, obesity has been blamed for about one-eighth of the recent increase in health-care costs (Jeff Mapes, *Pedaling Revolution*, 230). Medicare reports that it pays 15 percent more expenses for obese beneficiaries. Obese employees take twelve times as many sick days as their trimmer colleagues. General Motors reports $286 million in medical expenses per year due to obesity (Thomas Gotschi and Kevin Mills, "Active Transportation for America," 29). As urban affairs writer Neal Peirce puts it, "if the fat crisis can't be dealt with, rising levels of heart disease and diabetes will assuredly swamp the nation's efforts to reduce spiraling health costs" (Peirce, "Biking and Walking: Our Secret Weapon?").

thirty years is astonishing: by 2007, that rate had risen to one in three,[8] with a second third of the population "clearly over-weight."[9] The childhood obesity rate has almost tripled since 1980 and the rate for adolescents has more than quadrupled.[10] According to the rules of the U.S. military, 25 percent of young men and 40 percent of young women are too fat to enlist.•

As recently as 1991, no states had adult obesity rates over 20 percent. By 2007, only one state, Colorado, was *under* 20 percent.[11] Projecting current trends forward, it would seem that 100 per-cent of the population will be obese by 2080, a year that my chil-dren will probably live to see—but perhaps not if they are obese.

In terms of actual weight, men are now seventeen pounds heavier than they were in the late 1970s, and women nineteen pounds heavier. This means that, independent of population growth, as a nation we have gained 5.5 billion pounds. The real problem, of course, is not obesity itself, but all the other mala-dies that obesity causes or makes worse.• These include coronary disease, hypertension, a variety of cancers—including colorectal and endometrial—gallstones, and osteoarthritis. Excessive weight now kills more Americans than smoking.[12]

Over the past decade, there has been a series of studies that attribute obesity and its related illnesses directly to the automo-

---

•Writing for *The New Yorker*, Elizabeth Kolbert notes, "Hospitals have had to buy spe-cial wheelchairs and operating tables to accommodate the obese, and revolving doors have widened—the typical door went from about ten feet to about twelve feet across. An Indiana company called Goliath Casket has begun offering triple-wide coffins with reinforced hinges that can hold up to eleven hundred pounds. It has been estimated that Americans' extra bulk costs the airlines a quarter of a billion dollars' worth of jet fuel annually" (Kolbert, "XXXL: Why Are We So Fat?").

•Even gout, once called the "disease of kings," is staging a painful comeback among the middle class. But the biggest threat, both physically and financially, has to be diabetes, the sixth-leading cause of death in the United States. More than 21 million Americans—that's 7 percent of the population—have type 2 diabetes and it currently consumes about 2 percent of the gross national product. Obesity is the number one risk factor for diabetes, increasing one's odds of contracting the disease by as much as forty times (Howard Frumkin, Lawrence Frank, and Richard Jackson, *Urban Sprawl and Public Health*, xi).

tive lifestyle and, better yet, to the automotive landscape.[*] One effort found that for every additional five minutes Atlanta-area residents drove each day, they were 3 percent more likely to be obese.[13] Another showed that drivers who switch to public transit drop an average of five pounds.[14] A third, in San Diego, reported that 60 percent of residents in a "low-walkable" neighborhood were overweight, compared to only 35 percent in a "high-walkable" neighborhood.[15] Another Atlanta study found that "the proportion of obese white males declined from 23 percent to 13 percent as neighborhood residential density increased from less than two to more than eight dwellings per acre."[16] These are careful academic studies that control for age, income, and the other factors that correlate with body mass.

Finally, a six-year analysis of 100,000 Massachusetts residents found that the lowest body mass index averages were located in

---

[*]Much has been written, almost all of it convincing, about the absurdity of the American corn-syrup-based diet and its contribution to our national girth. Since our diets are so notoriously bad, is it fair to blame inactivity for our expanding waistlines? No American study seems to directly compare these competing factors, but the *British Medical Journal* took them on in an article that asked "gluttony or sloth?" The study compared obesity rates with data on diet and inactivity, and found a much stronger correlation with the latter. Specifically, "from 1950 to 1990, obesity steadily increased, even as gluttony peaked and declined in England. Sloth, on the other hand, increased in tandem with obesity, suggesting an important causal role" (Frumkin et al., *Urban Sprawl and Public Health*, 95).

Whatever the evidence, it is clear that our weight, independent of genetics, is a function of two primary factors: calories in and calories out. It would be wrong to ignore either of those two inputs, and the medical establishment, until recently focused principally on the former, is now giving physical activity its due. A 2007 UCLA study, investigating why so many diet regimes were unsuccessful, concluded that the "real key to slimming down appears to be not the cleverness of the food plan, but the amount of physical activity" (Mapes, *Pedaling Revolution*, 231).

Meanwhile, at the Mayo Clinic, Dr. James Levine put test subjects in motion-detecting underwear, placed them all on the same diet, and then began to stuff them with additional calories. As anticipated, some subjects gained weight while others didn't. Expecting to find a metabolic factor at work, he learned instead that the outcome was entirely attributable to physical activity. The people who got fatter made fewer unconscious motions and, indeed, spent (on average) two more hours per day sitting down (James Vlahos, "Is Sitting a Lethal Activity?").

Boston and its inner-ring suburbs, while the highest could be found in the "car-dependent" outer ring surrounding Interstate 495. *The Boston Globe* noted that "health officials suggest these higher rates are due, in part, to a lack of opportunities for everyday recreation and the time-squeezed lifestyle of many residents who have long commutes."[17]

I am wary of confusing causality with correlation, and it would be fair to say that heavier people are probably more likely to prefer driving over walking, and are therefore also more likely to prefer sprawl over urban neighborhoods. It is theoretically possible that, rather than suburbs making people fat, fat people make suburbs. But only a soulless pundit funded by the automotive industry—and there are several*—would claim that people are not more likely to be healthy in environments that invite walking.

You can tell that an idea has reached its tipping point when it makes enemies, and the sprawl-obesity connection finally has. The American Dream Coalition ("Protecting Freedom, Mobility, and Affordable Homeownership"), a consortium of automotive and sprawl-building interests, has come up with the fairly hilarious concept of the *Compactorizer.* As celebrated on their website in the (stereotypically effeminate) voice of the fictional Biff Fantastic:

> Urban planners and metrosexuals agree that suburbs make you fat! With the *Compactorizer,* you'll move out of boring and subtly racist suburban homes and into smallish apartments in high-density transit-oriented developments.

*Wendell Cox and Randall O'Toole. Skipping right past obesity to its outcomes, doctors have found that physical inactivity is associated with a "30 to 50 percent increase in coronary heart disease, a 30 percent increase in hypertension, and a 20 to 50 percent increase in strokes [as well as a] 30 to 40 percent increase in the risk of colon cancer and a 20 to 30 percent increase in the risk of breast cancer" (Vlahos, "Is Sitting a Lethal Activity?"). The United States' annual medical costs of physical inactivity have been estimated at between $76 billion and $117 billion, which is more than 10 percent of all medical expenses (Gotschi and Mills, "Active Transportation for America," 47–48).

Only the *Compactorizer* uses a patented planning doctrine to create noisy nights, random crimes, and panhandler harassment, triggering the high-stress and abnormal dietary patterns so important for rapid weight loss.[18]

As both an urban planner and a purported metrosexual, I can feel my credibility tanking here. But I have to admit that this piece is funnier than it is offensive and it appropriately pokes fun at an antisuburban snobbery that I probably share. But, ultimately, I have to ask myself: whom do I trust more: the doctors—who have nothing to gain either way—or the sprawl-builders? I'm going with the doctors.

CLEARING THE AIR

During the 1996 Olympics, more than 2 million visitors descended on the city of Atlanta, effectively increasing the city's population by 50 percent. Most of these visitors—I was among them—spent many hours huffing around the hot, crowded sports venues. Yet, during this time, asthma hospitalizations surprisingly declined by a full 30 percent.[19] What happened?

The difference was walking. Warned of the impossibility of motoring around the downtown during the games, many driving commuters took transit and walked instead. At a time when Atlanta was "one of the nation's worst violators of federal standards for ground-level ozone, with most of the problem caused by motor vehicle emissions,"[20] pollution levels dropped precipitously.•

•Sadly, the respite was only temporary, ending with the games' closing ceremony. Atlanta got a second breather in 1998, when the city's legendary highway-building binge was put on hold for two years thanks to its repeated violation of the federal Clean Air Act. But those were the exceptions, and by 2002, Atlanta was named "America's Unhealthiest City for Men" by *Men's Health* magazine, thanks to its forty-five days a year of "stay inside" warnings (Doug Monroe, "Taking Back the Streets," 89).

Pollution isn't what it used to be. American smog now comes principally from tailpipes, not factories. It is considerably worse than it was a generation ago, and it is unsurprisingly worst in our most auto-dependent cities, like Los Angeles and Houston. Phoenix put Atlanta to shame in 2007, with three full months of days in which it was deemed unhealthy for the general public to leave their homes.[21]

For this reason, asthma is dramatically on the rise. Almost one in fifteen Americans suffers from asthma, and the economic costs of the disease are estimated at $18.2 billion annually. About fourteen Americans die each day from asthma attacks, which is three times the rate of 1990.[22]

Of course, a community's auto dependence is not the only factor that contributes to asthma. But the 2011 WebMD list of the best and worst cities for asthma[23] speaks to a connection between walkability and breathing easier: residents of the five "worst" cities (Richmond, Knoxville, Memphis, Chattanooga, and Tulsa) drive 27 percent farther each day than residents of the five "best" (Portland, San Francisco, Colorado Springs, Des Moines, and Minneapolis).•

AMERICAN CAR-NAGE

Even if we were to dispute the notion that walking is good for you, it is indisputable that cars kill a lot of people. Car crashes have killed over 3.2 million Americans, considerably more than all of our wars combined.[24] They are the leading cause of death for all Americans between the ages of one and thirty-four,[25] and their monetary cost to the nation is estimated to be hundreds of billions of dollars annually.▪

• This calculation is based on data found in the Brookings Institution's ranking of U.S. metropolitan areas by vehicle miles traveled.
▪ The math used by different analysts is so varied that I hesitate to be more specific. The authors of *Carjacked* put it at "as high as $433 billion" (91).

Most people take the risks of driving for granted, as if they were some inevitable natural phenomenon. We don't bother with hand-wringing over the half-a-percent chance that our lives will end in a car crash[26] or the roughly one-in-three chance that we will eventually be seriously injured in one,* since these risks seem unavoidable. But the numbers from other developed nations tell a different story. While the United States in 2004 suffered 14.5 traffic fatalities per 100,000 population, Germany, with its no-speed-limit autobahns, suffered only 7.1. Denmark rated a 6.8, Japan a 5.8, and the U.K. hit 5.3.[27] And who beat them all? New York City, with a rate of 3.1. Indeed, since September 11, 2001, New York has saved more lives in traffic than it lost on 9/11.▪

If our entire country shared New York City's traffic statistics, we would prevent more than twenty-four thousand deaths a year.▲ San Francisco and Portland both compete with New York, with rates of 2.5 and 3.2 deaths per 100,000 population, respectively. Meanwhile, Atlanta comes in at 12.7, and anti-urban Tampa at a whopping 16.2.[28] Clearly, it's not just how much you drive, but where you drive and, more accurately, how those places were designed. Older, denser cities have much lower automobile fatality rates than newer, sprawling ones. It is the places shaped around automobiles that seem most effective at smashing them into each other.

I provide all this information to communicate the point that, while we Americans may take our great risk of automobile injury for granted, it is actually something that is well within our

---

*The injury statistic is calculated based on the fact that recent years have seen about seventy times as many reportable traffic injuries as traffic deaths.

▪Richard Jackson, "We Are No Longer Creating Wellbeing." New York suffered fewer than 1 death per 30,000 population in 2004 versus the 2010 U.S. rate of more than 4 deaths per 30,000. The difference between these two rates across a city population of 8 million amounts to more than 270 deaths averted annually.

▲Are New Yorkers (and Europeans) better drivers than the rest of us? Probably not. As you might expect, the difference in death rates comes, in part, from a difference in miles driven. But it's only in part. Here's something interesting: residents of the five

control—in the long term, as a function of how we design places, and in the short term, as a function of where we choose to live. This discussion becomes particularly ironic when we consider how many people through the decades have decamped from the city into the suburbs ostensibly for the safety of their families. Dr. Jackson is famously fond of asking his audiences "In what kind of community are you most likely to end up dead in a pool of blood?"[29] He points to the work of Alan Durning, who analyzed the combined risk of dying from two causes—traffic crashes and crime—in Seattle, Portland, and Vancouver, British Columbia. He found that, on average, if you add the two factors together, you are 19 percent safer in the inner city than in the outer suburbs.*

More recently, several more thorough studies have been completed by William Lucy at the University of Virginia, looking at auto accidents and murder by strangers. In one, he found that the ten safest places in the state of Virginia were eight of its most densely populated cities and the two counties abutting Washing-

---

most dangerous states drove 64 percent more miles in 2003 than residents of the five least dangerous states. If traffic fatalities simply increased with miles traveled, then we would expect the five most dangerous states to have experienced 64 percent more traffic deaths per capita than the five safest. But, shockingly, they experienced 243 percent more traffic deaths per capita. Each mile driven in a least-safe state was more than twice as deadly as a mile in a most-safe state. (This calculation is based on state traffic fatality data collected by Drive and Stay Alive, Inc., and state VMT data from the U.S. Research and Innovative Technology Administration.)

It turns out that the four safest American states, in addition to New York, are all in the Northeast: Massachusetts (which beats New York), Connecticut, New Jersey, and Rhode Island. The four most dangerous are largely rural: Wyoming, Mississippi, Montana, and South Dakota. The principal distinction between these states, much more than miles driven, is urbanization. The five safest states average eighteen times the residential density of the five most deadly (data from U.S. Census Bureau). They are also considerably older, and were therefore extensively developed according to the more walkable pre–World War II model, rather than the higher-speed paradigm that followed. This is why a mile driven in South Dakota is about three times as likely to kill you as a mile driven in Massachusetts.

*James Gerstenang, "Cars Make Suburbs Riskier Than Cities, Study Says," A1, A20. It is worth noting that this study was completed almost two decades ago, when the murder rate in many American cities was three times what it is today (Kevin Johnson, Judy Keen, and William M. Welch, "Homicides Fall in Large American Cities").

ton, D.C., while the ten most dangerous places were all low-population counties.[30] In another, he compared crash and crime statistics in eight large American cities between 1997 and 2000. Here the data produced more subtle results. The basic theory held true: car crashes far outweighed murder by strangers as a cause of death in all locations and, in older cities like Pittsburgh, the inner cities were considerably safer overall. But in more modern places like Dallas and Houston, where the downtowns are largely unwalkable, the city car-crash statistics were almost as bad as in the suburbs. Even with its fourteen annual traffic deaths per 100,000 population, however, Dallas was still safer overall than half of its surrounding counties.*

TENSE AND LONELY

Jacqueline McFarland is a licensed clinical social worker who specializes in the driving stresses of Atlanta commuters. She teaches her patients what are called Emotional Freedom Techniques (EFT) to help them calm down in traffic. "Basically, it's

---

*Jane Ford, "Danger in Exurbia." If people knew these statistics, would it impact their choices about where to live? Probably not. The illusion of control that we have while driving gives us confidence that we are the masters of our own fate on the road. After all, in another study, 85 percent of drivers who were in the hospital recovering from accidents *that they themselves caused* rated their driving skills as "above average" (National Public Radio, July 20, 2010). But, individual drivers aside, it would be nice to see these numbers have some impact on government policy, especially at the state and federal levels. Given the tremendous economic and human cost of car crashes, and the increased death toll found in unwalkable areas, it would make tremendous sense to invest a bit in walkability. In response to September 11, we have more than doubled the size of our national intelligence apparatus; indeed, almost 1 percent of all Americans now hold confidential, secret, or top-secret security clearance (Jane Mayer, "The Secret Sharer," 48). Four hundred thousand driving deaths later, how have our leaders responded? There may be hope for a correction over time. This is of course the same federal government that in 1970 made the pronouncement that "the possible benefits of required seat belts would not justify the costs to the manufacturers and the public" (National Highway Traffic Safety Administration).

tapping on acupressure points on the body, which clears up emotional issues."[31]

Let's hope it works. A German study found that "an unusually high percentage of people having heart attacks had spent time in traffic congestion on the day they were stricken." The study concluded that an hour spent driving triples your risk of heart attack in the hours that follow.[32] A Belgian paper published in *The Lancet* found that traffic exposure accounts for more heart attacks worldwide than any other activity, even including physical exertion.[33]

Closer to home, a Miami study found that "after driving their cars across the city for forty-five minutes, university students had higher blood pressure, higher heart rates, and lower frustration tolerance." This study is mentioned in *Urban Sprawl and Public Health*, where Dr. Jackson and his colleagues go on at length about driving stress, road rage, and their significant impacts on our national well-being. And the numbers are not insignificant—but let's step back from health for a minute and talk about happiness. Is motoring around and around really how we want to be spending so much of our time?

While many of us love driving, we hate commuting. Unsurprisingly, people with longer commutes report "lower satisfaction with life" than those who drive less.[34] One study found that "a 23-minute commute had the same effect on happiness as a 19 percent reduction in income." And twenty-three minutes is hardly a long commute—it's a bit below the national average. In another poll, 5 percent of respondents said that they would be "willing to divorce their spouse if that meant they could stop commuting and work from home instead."[35]

The Princeton psychologist Daniel Kahneman reports that commuting ranks as people's least favorite regular activity, less favored than housework or child care. "Intimate relations" scored highest—big surprise there—followed closely by socializing after work.[36]

Commuting unfortunately cuts into both. In his book *Bowl-*

ing Alone, the Harvard professor Robert Putnam documents a marked decline in American social capital, and notes that commute time is more predictive than almost any other variable he measured in determining civic engagement. He states that "each ten additional minutes in daily commuting time cuts involvement in community affairs by ten percent—fewer public meetings attended, fewer committees chaired, fewer petitions signed, fewer church services attended, and so on."[37]

This finding seems perfectly logical—there's only so much time in the day, after all—but it is only one part of a much larger picture that includes not only how long it takes to get home, but also in what sort of neighborhood that home is located. Much civic engagement is physical, grown from interaction on the street. Jane Jacobs put it this way: "Lowly, unpurposeful, and random as they may appear, sidewalk contacts are the small change from which a city's wealth of public life may grow."•

About now we could use some good news, so let's turn to Dan Buettner, the charismatic National Geographic host and bestselling author responsible for *The Blue Zones: Lessons for Living Longer from the People Who've Lived the Longest*. After a tour of the world's longevity hot spots, Buettner takes us through the *"Power Nine*: the lessons from the Blue Zones, a cross cultural distillation of the world's best practices in health and longevity." Lesson One? "Move Naturally." He explains: "Be active without having to think about it. . . . Longevity all-stars don't run marathons or compete in triathlons; they don't transform themselves

---

•*The Death and Life of Great American Cities*, 72. Putnam did not measure walkability, but a 2010 University of New Hampshire study did. The researchers first did their best to determine the more and less walkable neighborhoods of two cities, Manchester and Portsmouth, New Hampshire, each of which contains a charming mixed-use downtown and a girdle of sprawl. They then surveyed seven hundred residents of twenty neighborhoods, split between more and less walkable locations. They found that "those living in more walkable neighborhoods trusted their neighbors more; participated in community projects, clubs and volunteering more; and described television as their major form of entertainment less than survey participants living in less walkable neighborhoods" (Rogers et al., "Examining Walkability," 201–203).

into weekend warriors on Saturday morning. Instead, they engage in regular, low-intensity physical activity, often as a part of a daily work routine."• Buettner quotes Robert Kane, M.D., the director of the Minnesota Geriatric Education Center, who says, "Rather than exercising for the sake of exercising, try to make changes to your lifestyle. Ride a bicycle instead of driving. Walk to the store instead of driving. . . . Build that into your lifestyle."■

Like most writers on the subject, Buettner and his sources neglect to discuss how these "lifestyle" choices are inevitably a function of the design of the built environment. They may be powerfully linked to place—the Blue Zones are zones, after all—but there is scant admission that walking to the store is more possible, more enjoyable, and more likely to become habit in some places than in others. It is those places that hold the most promise for the physical and social health of our society.

Enrique Peñalosa, the former mayor of Bogotá, Colombia, sees things in a much simpler light: "God made us walking animals—pedestrians. As a fish needs to swim, a bird to fly, a deer to run, we need to walk, not in order to survive, but to be happy."[38] That thought is beautiful, perfectly obvious, and probably impossible to prove. But we do know that we need to be active in order to be healthy and that walking is the easiest way for most humans to be usefully active. Let's make it easier.

•*The Blue Zones*, 220. It's worth noting that Lesson Four is "buy a case of high-quality red wine," which certainly adds to the book's appeal (240).
■*The Blue Zones*, 223. According to *The New York Times*, "a recent meta-analysis of studies about exercise and mortality showed that, in general, a sedentary person's risk of dying prematurely from any cause plummeted by nearly 20 percent if he or she began brisk walking (or the equivalent) for 30 minutes five times a week" (Gretchen Reynolds, "What's the Single Best Exercise?").

THE WRONG COLOR GREEN

You can't spell carbon without CAR; Missing the forest for the trees;
Manhattan as Mecca; Happy urbanism

In 2001, Scott Bernstein, at the Center for Neighborhood Technology in inner-city Chicago, produced a set of maps that are still changing the way we think about our country. In these maps, remarkably, the red and the green switched places. This reversal, perhaps even more than the health discussion, threatens to make walkability relevant again.

By red and green, I am referring to carbon emissions. On typical carbon maps, areas with the greatest amounts of carbon output are shown in bright red, and those with the least are shown in green, with areas in between shown in orange and yellow. Basically, the hotter the color, the greater the contribution to climate change.

Historically, these maps had always looked like the night-sky satellite photos of the United States: hot around the cities, cooler in the suburbs, and coolest in the country. Wherever there are lots of people, there is lots of pollution. A typical carbon map, such as that produced in 2002 by the Vulcan Project at Purdue University, sends a very clear signal: countryside good, cities bad.

For a long time, these were the only maps of this type, and there is certainly a logic in looking at pollution from a location-by-location perspective. But this logic was based on an unconsidered assumption, which is that the most meaningful way to measure carbon is by the square mile. It isn't.

The best way to measure carbon is per person. Places should be judged not by how much carbon they emit, but by how much carbon they cause us to emit. There are only so many people in the United States at any given time, and they can be encouraged to live where they have the smallest environmental footprint. That place turns out to be the city—the denser the better.

For this reason, when Bernstein replaced carbon per square mile with carbon per household, the colors simply flipped. Now the hottest areas in each American metropolitan area—and their website shows hundreds, from Abilene to Yuma—are inevitably the outer suburbs. The coolest are smack-dab in the center of town.

To be accurate: Bernstein's maps have a limitation. They do not show full carbon output; they only show CO_2 from household automobile use—data that are much easier to collect. But this limitation turns out to be useful, for several reasons: first, because it causes us to confirm that automobile use is not only the single greatest contributor to our total carbon footprint, but also a reliable predictor of that total; and second, because limiting our greenhouse gas emissions, for many, is a much less pressing issue than our dependence on foreign oil.

YOU CAN'T SPELL CARBON WITHOUT CAR

At last measure, we are sending $612,500 overseas every minute in support of our current automotive lifestyle.[1] Cumulatively, over recent decades, this has amounted to a "massive, irreversible shift in wealth and power from the United States to the petro-states of the Middle East and energy-rich Russia."[2] This cash transfer, which is quickly working its way up to a third of a trillion dollars each year, is building some truly stunning metrorail systems in Dubai and Abu Dhabi—our cars are buying their trains. Add to this amount the significant chunk of our $700 billion military budget that is used to protect these questionable foreign interests,• and it's easy to see how our oil appetite could undo us economically long before the oil begins to run dry.

Do electric cars present an answer to this challenge? Certainly hybrids don't. Their marginally improved gas mileage mostly offers a feel-good way to drive more miles in increasingly larger vehicles. I always get angry when I see a "Hybrids Only" municipal parking space, knowing that it welcomes a 21-mpg Chevy Tahoe Hybrid but not a conventional 35-mpg Ford Fiesta.• You could (theoretically) drive two 1990 Geo Metros at once and still beat the Tahoe.

In contrast, the all-electric car seems to hold some real promise for curtailing our foreign oil addiction—but at what environmental cost? In most of the United States, an electric-powered car is essentially a coal-powered car,▲ and "clean coal" is of course an oxymoron.[3] Both in its extraction and its combustion—replacing a hydrocarbon with a pure carbon—coal can make oil look positively green.•

To be perfectly accurate, electric cars are currently a bit

•In *Carjacked*, Catherine Lutz and Anne Lutz Fernandez suggest that "10 to 25 percent of the annual military budget should be allocated to the line item of oil resource control" (96).

•The Tahoe data are also from *Carjacked*, whose authors note that the Tahoe costs nearly $13,000 more than its conventional twin and gets only four more miles per gallon (*Carjacked*, 88).

▲As of 2010, almost half of all U.S. electricity was generated by burning coal, which is about twice as much as came from the next most common source, natural gas (U.S. Energy Information Administration, "Net Generation by Energy Source").

•Moreover, thanks to meager federal commitment, a significant uptick in wind, solar, hydro, tidal, or even nuclear generation seems at least a generation away. It is almost inevitable that the path to energy independence, so important to our nation's security and solvency, will take us through a sooty valley of even greater carbon expulsion. As David Owen notes in *Green Metropolis*, "sometimes the invisible hand goes for the throat" (66). See also Daniel Gros, "Coal vs. Oil: Pure Carbon vs. Hydrocarbon," achangeinthewind.com, December 28, 2007. Electricity generation is also responsible for about 20 percent of all water consumption in the United States (John F. Wasik, *The Cul-de-Sac Syndrome*, 60).

greener than gasoline cars—*per mile*. Driving one hundred miles in a Nissan Altima results in the emission of 90.5 pounds of greenhouse gases. Driving the same distance in an all-electric Nissan Leaf emits 63.6 pounds of greenhouse gases—a significant improvement. But while the Altima driver pays fourteen cents a mile for fuel, the Leaf driver pays less than three cents per mile,[4] and this difference, thanks to the law of supply and demand, causes the Leaf driver to drive more.

How much more? We don't know. But we do know what happened in Sweden, where aggressive government subsidies have led to the world's highest per-capita sales of "clean" cars. The results are in, and, shockingly, "greenhouse gas emissions from Sweden's transportation sector are up."[5] As reported by Firmin DeBrabander:

> But perhaps we should not be so surprised. What do you expect when you put people in cars they feel good (or at least less guilty) about driving, which are also cheap to buy and run? Naturally, they drive them more. So much more, in fact, that they obliterate energy gains made by increased fuel efficiency.[6]

Electric vehicles are clearly the right answer to the wrong question. This fact becomes even clearer when we note that tailpipe emissions are only one part of the footprint of motoring. As described by the strategic consultant Michael Mehaffy, this footprint includes "the emissions from the construction of the vehicles; the embodied energy of streets, bridges and other infrastructure; the operation and repair of this infrastructure; the maintenance and repair of the vehicles; the energy of refining fuel; and the energy of transporting it, together with the pipes, trucks and other infrastructure that is required to do so." These add an estimated 50 percent more pollution to the atmosphere than emissions alone.[7]

But that's just the beginning. A much larger multiplier effect comes from the way that all of our other, nonautomotive consumption patterns expand as we drive. In *Green Metropolis*, David Owen puts it this way:

> The real problem with cars is not that they don't get enough miles per gallon; it's that they make it too easy for people to spread out, encouraging forms of development that are inherently wasteful and damaging. . . . The critical energy drain in a typical American suburb is not the Hummer in the driveway; it's everything else the Hummer makes possible—the oversized houses and irrigated yards, the network of new feeder roads and residential streets, the costly and inefficient outward expansion of the power grid, the duplicated stores and schools, the two-hour solo commutes.[8]

So, while I have gone to great efforts to explain how the way we move is more important than the way we live, it turns out that the way we move largely determines the way we live.

MISSING THE FOREST FOR THE TREES

When we built our new house in Washington, we too did our best to clear the shelves of the sustainability store. We put in bamboo floors, radiant heating, double-thick insulation, dual-flush toilets, a solar water heater, and a twelve-panel 2.5-kilowatt solar photovoltaic system. A pine log crackling in our high-tech wood-burning stove supposedly contributes less pollution to the atmosphere than if it were left to decompose in the forest.

Yet all these gadgets cumulatively contribute only a fraction of what we save by living in a walkable neighborhood. It turns out that trading all of your incandescent lightbulbs for energy savers conserves as much carbon per year as living in a walkable neighborhood does each week.[9] Why, then, is the vast majority of our national conversation on sustainability about the former and not the latter? Witold Rybczynski puts it this way:

> Rather than trying to change behavior to reduce carbon emissions, politicians and entrepreneurs have sold greening to the public as a kind of accessorizing. "Keep doing what you're doing," is the message, just add another solar panel, a wind turbine, a bamboo floor, whatever. But a solar-heated house in the suburbs is still a house in the suburbs, and if you have to drive to it—even in a Prius— it's hardly green.[10]

We planners have taken to calling this phenomenon *gizmo green*: the obsession with "sustainable" products that often have a statistically insignificant impact on the carbon footprint when compared to our location. And, as already suggested, our location's greatest impact on our carbon footprint comes from how much it makes us drive.

This point was pounded home in a recent EPA study, "Location Efficiency and Building Type—Boiling It Down to BTUs,"[11] that compared four factors: drivable versus walkable location; conventional construction versus green building; single-family versus multifamily housing; and conventional versus hybrid automobiles. The study made it clear that, while every factor counts, none counts nearly as much as walkability. Specifically, it showed how, in drivable locations, transportation energy use consistently tops household energy use, in some cases by more than 2.4 to 1. As a result, the most green home (with Prius) in sprawl still loses out to the least green home in a walkable neighborhood.[12]

It is important that the EPA is doing its best to share the good news on how location trumps building design, but who is listening? Certainly not the EPA. A mere month after releasing the above study, the agency announced that it was relocating its 672-employee Region 7 Headquarters from downtown Kansas City to the new far-flung suburb of Lenexa, Kansas (Walk Score 28). Why are they moving twenty miles out of town into a former Applebee's office park? Well, because the building is LEED* (green) certified, of course.[13]

Kaid Benfield, a long-serving environmental watchdog at the Natural Resources Defense Council, did some numbers, and he found that while "an average resident in the vicinity of the current EPA Region 7 headquarters emits 0.39 metric tons of carbon dioxide per month . . . the transportation carbon emissions associated with the new location are a whopping 1.08 metric tons per person per month . . . one and a half times the regional average."[14]

These numbers are, of course, just a stand-in for the actual increased carbon footprints of the EPA's staffers, most of whom will probably not move from their current homes. Presuming these employees' houses are distributed around Kansas City in the normal manner, the vast majority will have their commutes lengthened, many by twenty miles or more each way. Those who used to take transit to work will now have to get on the highway.

This would be funny if it weren't so sad. The carbon saved by the new building's LEED status, if any, will be a small fraction of the carbon wasted by its location.■ This missing the forest for the trees is what David Owen calls "LEED Brain." Many governments and corporations—and they are to be congratulated—have committed themselves to LEED-rated building construction, including the federal government, New York, Chicago, San Francisco, the District of Columbia, and a boatload of others. The list

*LEED refers to the now widely adopted standards of the U.S. Green Building Council, called "Leadership in Energy and Environmental Design."

■The downtown building, while not certified, is no energy hog (Kaid Benfield, "EPA Region 7: We Were Just Kidding About That Sustainability Stuff").

is getting longer every day and seems to have reached a tipping point where you can't get hired as an architect without becoming LEED accredited.

Urban location is indeed one of the factors that contributes to a LEED building rating, but it is only one of many factors, such that the overall carbon savings created by downtown locations are almost always undercounted. And because it's better than nothing, LEED—like the Prius—is a get-out-of-jail-free card that allows us to avoid thinking more deeply about our larger footprint. For most organizations and agencies, it is enough. Unfortunately, as the transportation planner Dan Malouff puts it, "LEED architecture without good urban design is like cutting down the rainforest using hybrid-powered bulldozers."[15]

MANHATTAN AS MECCA

If—in America—dense, transit-served cities are better, then New York is the best. This is the clear and convincing message of David Owen's *Green Metropolis*, certainly the most important environmental text of the past decade. This book deserves a bit more of our attention, so profound is the revolution in thinking that it represents.

As Owen himself notes, the environmental movement in the United States has historically been anti-city, as has so much American thought. This strain traces its roots back to Thomas Jefferson, who described large cities as "pestilential to the morals, the health, and the liberties of man." Not without a sense of humor, he went on: "When we get piled up upon one another in large cities, as in Europe, we shall become as corrupt as in Europe, and go to eating one another as they do there."[16]

Given that the U.S. population in 1780 was less than 1 percent of its current total, it is easy to understand why Jefferson did not see anything but good in its dispersal. With what must have seemed to be both infinite land area and resources, there was no reason not to stretch our legs, especially since the greatest by-product of transportation was fertilizer.

Unfortunately, over the next two hundred years, the American anti-urban ethos remained intact as everything else changed. The desire to be isolated in nature, adopted en masse, led to the quantities and qualities we now call sprawl, which somehow mostly manages to combine the traffic congestion of the city with the intellectual culture of the countryside.[17] Now that the full environmental impacts of suburban development are being measured, a new breed of thinkers is finally turning the old paradigm on its head. These include David Owen—like Jane Jacobs, a mere writer—and the economist Ed Glaeser, who puts it this way: "We are a destructive species, and if you love nature, stay away from it. The best means of protecting the environment is to live in the heart of a city."[18]

And no American city performs like New York. Owen's book, which was originally to be called *Green Manhattan*, is stuffed full of astounding data. The average New Yorker consumes roughly one-third the electricity of the average Dallas resident, and ultimately generates less than one-third the greenhouse gases of the average American. The average resident of Manhattan—New York at its most New Yorky—consumes gasoline "at a rate that the country as a whole hasn't matched since the mid-1920s."[19] And so on. We have already discussed the city's impressive traffic-safety record.

New York is our densest big city and, not coincidentally, the one with the best transit service. All the other subway stations in America put together would not outnumber the 468 stops of the MTA. In terms of resource efficiency, it's the best we've got. But why stop there? Other places, with a variety of densities and transit options, do much better. Sure, New York consumes half the gasoline of Atlanta (326 versus 782 gallons per person per year). But Toronto cuts *that* number in half again, as does Sydney—and most European cities use only half as much as those places. Cut Europe's number in half and you end up with Hong Kong.[20] If ten Hong Kongers were to move to New York with the goal of keeping their gasoline consumption unchanged, nine of them would have to stay at home.

These numbers become especially meaningful as we consider the impacts of peak oil prices in the years ahead. What city, or country, is likely to be the most competitive in the face of $200-per-barrel oil? Paris is one place that has determined that its future depends on reducing its auto dependence. The city has recently decided to create twenty-five miles of dedicated busways, introduced twenty thousand shared "city bikes" in 1,450 locations, and committed to removing fifty-five thousand parking spaces from the city every year for the next twenty years. These changes sound pretty radical, but they are supported by 80 percent of the population.[21]

HAPPY URBANISM

Stories and numbers like these are truly intimidating, and potentially demotivating. Why even bother trying, when other countries are so far ahead?

Back in 1991, the Sierra Club's John Holtzclaw studied travel habits in twenty-eight California communities of widely varying residential density. He found, as expected, an inverse relationship between urbanity and driving miles. But, perhaps not expected, he also found his data points distributed around a pretty sharp curve, with most of the gains in efficiency occurring early on. Increasing housing density at the suburban end of the scale had a much greater impact than at the urban end, such that the vast majority of the driving reduction occurred in the switch from large-lot sprawl to densities of ten to twenty units per acre. These densities represent a traditional urbanism of apartments, row houses, and, yes, some freestanding single-family homes. In contrast, the further concentration of households at higher densities—even above one hundred per acre—while helpful, produced less dramatic results.

He subsequently conducted similar studies in New York and Los Angeles, and found the data tracking along almost identical curves. In each case, increasing density from two units per acre to twenty units per acre resulted in about the same savings as the increase from twenty to two hundred.[22] To students of urban form, these outcomes are not that surprising, because ten to twenty units per acre is the density at which drivable sub-urbanism transitions into walkable urbanism. There are of course some (rather horrid tower-in-the-parking-lot) exceptions, but most communities with these densities are also organized as traditional, mixed-use, pedestrian-friendly neighborhoods, the sort of accommodating environment that entices people out of their cars. Everything above that is icing on the cake.

That means that, while Americans might have a long way to go to match European or Asian sustainability, a little effort can get us a lot closer. But not every American is motivated by concerns about climate change or peak oil and, even among those of us who are, it is not always easy to turn that intention into action. Certainly, unless we hit a national crisis of unprecedented severity, it is hard to imagine any argument framed in the language of sustainability causing many people to modify their behavior. So what will?

The gold standard of quality-of-life rankings is the Mercer Survey, which carefully compares global cities in the ten categories of political stability, economics, social quality, health and sanitation, education, public services, recreation, consumer goods, housing, and climate.

Its rankings shift slightly from year to year, but the top ten cities always seem to include a bunch of places where they speak

German (Vienna, Zürich, Düsseldorf, etc.), along with Vancouver, Auckland, and Sydney.[23] These are all places with compact settlement patterns, good transit, and principally walkable neighborhoods. Indeed, there isn't a single auto-oriented city in the top fifty. The highest-rated American cities in 2010, which don't appear until number 31, are Honolulu, San Francisco, Boston, Chicago, Washington, New York, and Seattle.•

The Economist magazine has its own ranking that, although it uses Mercer data, tends to turn out a bit differently. It has been criticized as favoring Anglophone countries, which—although no help to the United States—means that eight of its top ten cities are in Canada, Australia, and New Zealand. But all are still places that are better for walking than driving.

Whomever you want to believe, the message is clear. Our cities, which are twice as efficient as our suburbs, burn twice the fuel of these European, Canadian, and Aussie/Kiwi places. Yet the quality of life in these foreign cities is deemed higher than ours, by a long shot. This is not to say that quality of life is directly related to sustainability, but merely that many Americans, by striving for a better life, might find themselves moving to places that are more like the winners—or better yet, might try transforming their cities to resemble the winners. This sort of transformation could include many things, but one of them would certainly be walkability.

Vancouver, British Columbia, number one in *The Economist*'s ranking, proves a useful model. By the mid-twentieth century, it was fairly indistinguishable from a typical U.S. city. Then, beginning in the late 1950s, when most American cities were building highways, planners in Vancouver began advocating for high-rise housing downtown. This strategy, which included stringent requirements for green space and transit, really hit its stride

---

•Mercer, "2010 Quality of Living Worldwide City Rankings," Mercer.com. Incidentally, the biggest loser was Baghdad.

in the mid-1990s, and the change has been profound. Since that time, the amount of walking and biking citywide has doubled, from 15 percent to 30 percent of all trips.[24] Vancouver is not ranked number one for livability because it is so sustainable; the things that make it sustainable also make it livable.

Quality of life—which includes both health and wealth— may not be a function of our ecological footprint, but the two are deeply interrelated. To wit, if we pollute so much because we are throwing away time, money, and lives on the highway, then both problems would seem to share a single solution, and that solution is to make our cities more walkable. Doing so is not easy, but it can be done, it has been done, and indeed it is being done in more than a few places at this very moment.

PART II

THE TEN STEPS OF WALKABILITY

This may seem like an odd moment to admit this, but I love cars. As a teenager, I had twin subscriptions to *Car & Driver* and *Road & Track*. My chief skill on the school bus was the ability to name the make and model of every vehicle that passed. Until recently, I have always owned the best-handling car I could reasonably afford. I especially love high-revving Japanese sports cars like the one I drove from Miami to Washington, D.C., when I moved here in 2003. I remember the trip lasting about six hours, assisted by a tailwind and a top-of-the-line radar detector.

But an interesting thing happened when I arrived in Washington. I found myself driving less and less and paying more and more per mile. Aside from trips to Home Depot and the occasional country jaunt, I had no reason to break my car out of its garage. Between walking, biking, and our extensive Metro transit system, driving was rarely the most convenient choice. And the parking lot beneath my apartment building charged a small fortune in fees. Add to that the availability of Zipcar car sharing in my neighborhood and it soon became apparent that going car-free was the most convenient option.

Back in my Miami days, the idea of selling my car would never have occurred to me. My apartment was in the heart of

South Beach's art deco district. My job was on the mainland, in Little Havana, about a twenty-minute drive away. My gym was in Coral Gables, twenty minutes further afield. Lunch, unless I wanted Cuban food every day—a decided health risk—required another twenty minutes of driving. All told, I was spending close to ninety minutes each weekday in traffic, about normal for an American. And I was OK with that.

But, in Washington, it soon became apparent that there were other benefits to my new car-free lifestyle, besides just convenience. Six months into my autoless diet, I had lost ten pounds through walking and biking, and reduced my stress levels by avoiding traffic. I had gained thousands of dollars in transportation savings and also developed a deeper under-standing of my city by experiencing it at a walking and biking pace. Finally, in the ultimate mass-transit payoff, I met my future wife among the masses on a transit platform. It would be fair to say that I was healthier, wealthier, wiser—and happier—all due to what transportation engineers would call a simple mode shift.

This shift was caused by nothing more or less than the design of my city.

Washington, D.C., is one of a handful of American cities that can accurately be described as car-optional. New York, Boston, Chicago, San Francisco, and not many others, pro-vide an equivalent or better quality of life for the carless, thanks to a combination of pre-auto-age provenance and sub-sequent enlightened planning. In contrast, most American cit-ies have been designed or redesigned principally around the assumption of universal automotive use, resulting in obliga-tory car ownership, typically one per adult—starting at age sixteen. In these cities, and in most of our nation, the car is no longer an instrument of freedom, but rather a bulky, expen-sive, and dangerous prosthetic device, a prerequisite to viable citizenship.

I got rid of my car because my city invited me to and rewarded me in spades. Not everyone who is able to make a similar choice will benefit as I did—certainly not in the spouse department—but the benefits are clear. Independent of the global impacts of reduced tailpipe emissions and energy use, the personal financial and health advantages of losing the car are tremendous. They are not attractive to everyone, and a significant number of our fellow citizens will never trade their cul-de-sacs and SUVs for any other option. But, as we have seen, more Americans are desirous of vibrant urban living than are being offered that choice, and those cities that can satisfy that unmet demand will thrive.

This is already happening. More and more Americans are being attracted to places that offer the economy, excitement, and street life that cannot be found in the auto zone. To these people, malls are for teenagers, bicycles are cooler than cars, and a great night out includes being able to drink and *not* drive. Cities that have recently combined reinvestment in their downtown cores with the creation of transformative transit and biking facilities—like Portland and Denver—are the current relocation places of choice, for those who have a choice.

For those who don't, it could be said that every city has an obligation to free its residents from the burden of auto dependence. When a city does, everyone benefits, including the city. My wife and I again prove a useful example. When we built our new house in the District, we put an office where the garage was supposed to go, and a vegetable garden in place of the driveway—never mind that it took us nine months to void the city's parking requirement. Now I work from home and we eat (extremely) local produce in season. Without a car, we find ourselves spending most of our disposable income nearby, in neighborhood restaurants and at the farmers' market. When we need a lightbulb or an extension cord, we bike to Logan Circle Hardware rather than driving to Home Depot.

All these daily decisions, by us and our many carless neighbors, add up to more money retained within our community.

This is not an ideological discussion; we are not committed to an intentional pedestrian lifestyle. In fact, as of this writing, we are seriously considering buying a car. The birth of our second child has created a circumstance where a personal vehicle will contribute to our quality of life. Moving a pair of car seats in and out of the Zipcar is just becoming too big a chore for two parents with sore backs.

Disappointing? Perhaps, but perfectly in keeping with the idea of the car-optional city. We spent seven years productively without a car, two of them with child in tow. We will be able to live carless again in the future. In the meantime, it will be one convenient transportation choice among many, in a landscape that makes choice possible.

Walking is a simple and useful thing, and such a pleasure too. It is what brings planeloads of Americans to Europe on holiday, including even some of the traffic engineers who make our own cities so inhospitable. Somewhere, deep in their caveman traffic engineer brains, even they must understand the value of moving under one's own power at a relaxed pace through a public sphere that continuously rewards the senses. This same tourist experience is commonplace in Washington, Charleston, New Orleans, Santa Fe, Santa Barbara—and a few other places in America that have elevated walking to an art form. They are the cities that enjoy a higher standard of living because they provide a better quality of life. Unfortunately, they remain the exceptions when they should just be normal.

This situation need not continue indefinitely—indeed, we can't afford for it to. We need a new normal in America, one that welcomes walking. The ten steps listed ahead are designed to take us from where we are now to where we need to be.

THE TEN STEPS OF WALKABILITY

THE USEFUL WALK

Step 1: *Put Cars in Their Place.*
The automobile is a servant that has become a master. For sixty years, it has been the dominant factor in the shaping of our cities. Relegating the car to its proper role is essential to reclaiming our cities for pedestrians, and doing so requires an understanding of how the car and its minions have unnecessarily distorted the way that design decisions are made in American communities.

Step 2: *Mix the Uses.*
For people to choose to walk, the walk must serve some purpose. In planning terms, that goal is achieved through mixed use or, more accurately, placing the proper balance of activities within walking distance of each other. While there are exceptions, most downtowns have an imbalance of uses that can be overcome only by increasing the housing supply.

Step 3: *Get the Parking Right.*
As Andres Duany puts it, "parking is destiny." It is the not-so-hidden force determining the life or death of many a downtown. Parking requirements and pricing determine the disposition of more urban land nationwide than any other factor, yet until recently there was not even any theory on how to use parking to a city's benefit. That theory now exists, and is just beginning to affect policy nationwide.

Step 4: *Let Transit Work.*
Walkable neighborhoods can thrive in the absence of transit, but walkable cities rely on it utterly. Communities that hope to become the latter must make transit-planning decisions based upon a number of factors that are routinely neglected. These include the often surprising public support for transit investment, the role of transit in the creation of real estate value, and the importance of design in the success or failure of transit systems.

THE SAFE WALK

Step 5: *Protect the Pedestrian.*
This is perhaps the most straightforward of the ten steps, but it also has the most moving parts, including block size, lane width, turning motions, direction of flow, signalization, roadway geometry, and a number of other factors that all determine a car's speed and a pedestrian's likelihood of getting hit. Most streets in most American cities get at least half of these things wrong.

Step 6: Welcome Bikes.
Walkable cities are also bikeable cities, because bicycles thrive in environments that support pedestrians and also because bikeability makes driving less necessary. More and more American cities are making big investments in bicycling, with impressive results.

THE COMFORTABLE WALK

Step 7: Shape the Spaces.
Perhaps the most counterintuitive discussion in planning, this may be the step that is most often gotten wrong. People enjoy open spaces and the great outdoors. But people also enjoy, and need, a sense of enclosure to feel comfortable as pedestrians. Public spaces are only as good as their edges, and too much gray or green—parking or parks—can cause a would-be walker to stay home.

Step 8: Plant Trees.
Like transit, most cities know that trees are good, but few are willing to pay properly for them. This step attempts to communicate the full value of trees and justify the greater investment that they deserve in almost every American city.

THE INTERESTING WALK

Step 9: Make Friendly and Unique Faces.
If evidence is to be believed, lively streetscapes have three main enemies: parking lots, drugstores, and star architects. All three seem to favor blank walls, repetition, and a disregard for the pedestrian's need to be entertained. City design codes, focused on use, bulk, and parking, have only begun to concern themselves with creating active facades that invite walking.

Step 10: Pick Your Winners.
With the possible exception of Venice, even the most walkable cities are not universally walkable: there are only so many interesting street edges to go around. As a result, however well designed the streets, certain among them will remain principally automotive. This is as it should be, but cities must make a conscious choice about the size and location of their walkable cores, to avoid squandering walkability resources in areas that will never invite pedestrians.

THE USEFUL WALK

■

STEP 1: PUT CARS IN THEIR PLACE

STEP 2: MIX THE USES

STEP 3: GET THE PARKING RIGHT

STEP 4: LET TRANSIT WORK

STEP 1: PUT CARS IN THEIR PLACE

Highways versus cities; Because I must: induced demand;
It's not just freeways; Kill the traffic engineers first; Remove it
and they will go; A step too far: pedestrian zones; Congestion
pricing: too smart to be easy; The long view

Cars are the lifeblood of the American city. Even in our most successful walking and transit cities, they are everywhere, contributing activity and vitality to the streetscape. Past failures have taught us that banning them outright brings with it more risk than reward. Whatever technological revolutions may transform them in the years ahead, it is a safe bet that automobiles will remain a fixture of our communities for the remainder of our lifetimes. And that's OK.

But what's not OK is the current situation, in which the automobile has mostly been given free rein to distort our cities and our lives. Long gone are the days when automobiles expanded possibility and choice for the majority of Americans. Now, thanks to its ever-increasing demands for space, speed, and time, the car has reshaped our landscape and lifestyles around its own needs. It is an instrument of freedom that has enslaved us.

This outcome is not surprising, given the wandering nature of the American spirit. The first Americans were nomads, and they were displaced by a race that had found its way across the ocean. The one characteristic that all of us share is that we come from somewhere else. Imagine two brothers eating lunch alongside a dock in Dublin, Palermo, Bombay, or Formosa and looking wistfully out to sea. One of them had the balls to get on a boat and the other one didn't. Guess whose kids are the Americans?

American mobility far precedes the automobile. Before Lewis Mumford declared that "our national flower is the concrete cloverleaf,"[1] Ralph Waldo Emerson wrote that "everything good is on the highway." Soon after him, Walt Whitman waxed: "O public road, I say back I am not afraid to leave you—yet I love you. You express me better than I can express myself."[2]

But it is an easy out to say that wayfaring is an inescapable part of our DNA, and ignore the other factors that make cities in the United States different from those in Canada or Australia—two other countries that at least started the way ours did. Neither of those nations produced anything remotely like our National Interstate and Defense Highways Act of 1956 and, not coincidentally, neither was held in thrall by a lobby as powerful as our "Road Gang," the consortium of "oil, cement, rubber, automobile, insurance, trucking, chemical, and construction industries, consumer and political groups, financial institutions, and media"[3] that, along with the military, pushed successfully for new highways.

During the greatest period of American highway construction, General Motors was the largest private company in the world[4] and the secretary of defense was Charles Erwin Wilson, the former GM chief who had famously shared his belief that "what was good for the country was good for General Motors and vice versa."[*] Whether or not it was good for America, the federal highway act and its subsequent iterations began at midcentury to distinguish American cities dramatically from their counterparts in other countries.

[*]Wikipedia, "History of General Motors." This comment is interesting when one considers that GM armed the Nazis even after they had declared war on the United States (Charles Higham, *Trading with the Enemy*). Adolf Hitler awarded GM CEO James D. Mooney the Order of Merit of the Golden Eagle for his services in support of the Nazi regime.

HIGHWAYS VERSUS CITIES

The most interesting article I have read on this topic is a little-known academic paper by Patrick Condon, who chairs the landscape architecture department at the University of British Columbia. Titled "Canadian Cities American Cities: Our Differences Are the Same," this study clearly shows a compelling inverse correlation between highway investment and urban property values.

The researchers expected to find a broad range of historical and cultural causes behind the differing fates of Canadian and U.S. cities. Instead, they found that these cities appeared almost identical in 1940 and then tracked in different directions based upon relative highway investment. It didn't matter whether a city was American or Canadian: the highway-investment history was all you needed to know to accurately predict the real estate–value history.

The graphs for Portland are particularly telling, with the highway and real estate lines charting almost exactly opposite one another, like an hourglass on its side. Here's what happens: In the 1960s, highway construction inflects upward while property values lie flat. In the 1970s, highway construction inflects downward, and property values rise. In the 1980s, highway construction inflects upward and property values fall. Finally, in the 1990s, highway investment inflects downward and property values rise again.[5]

Again, correlation is not cause, but the researchers could find no other data set that consistently tracked along or against urban property values. Whether American or Canadian, the inner cities with less regional highway investment fared better than those with more. Of course, most of the latter could be found in the United States, where the federal government paid ninety cents on the dollar—versus Canada's ten cents—for road building.[6]

The jury is still out on whether, on the whole, America's highway-building blitz was a completely bad idea. It seemed to work out well enough economically—at least until our domestic oil wells started to run dry. But it was clearly very bad for the central cities and it got even worse when the big-city mayors, desperate for jobs, amended the act to include an additional six thousand miles of inner-city expressways.[7] These highways, most of which gutted minority neighborhoods, were never imagined in the original measure, which was created by people who knew better.* Even Lewis Mumford, a fan of decentralization, admitted that "the right to have access to every building in the city by private motorcar, in an age when everyone possesses such a vehicle, is actually the right to destroy the city."[8]

Ironically, the city that resisted the greatest amount of federal highway spending was probably the nation's capital. Most current residents are unaware that, at one time, the Washington area was slated to receive 450 miles of interstate highways, 38 of which would have plowed through the District itself. Thanks to an epic twenty-two-year political battle, only ten miles were ever built. Instead, much of the federal funding was diverted to the 103-mile Metrorail system,[9] now considered central to the city's recent resurgence.

Bob and Jane Freundel Levey told the story this way in *The Washington Post*:

> More than 200,000 housing units were saved from destruction. So were more than 100 square miles of parkland around the metropolitan area. The city was spared from freeways bored under the Mall, freeways punched through stable middle-class black neighborhoods, free-

---

*Norman Bel Geddes, in many ways the intellectual father of the interstate system, stated in 1939 that "motorways must not be allowed to infringe upon the city" (quoted in Duany, Plater-Zyberk, and Speck, *Suburban Nation*, 86–87).

ways tunneled under K Street, freeways that would have obliterated the Georgetown waterfront and the Maryland bank of the Potomac. . . . One would [have] run in a flattened oval around the central core of the city, about half a mile north and south of the White House.[10]

Opposition to the highways was largely grassroots, spurred on by the slogan "White Men's Roads Through Black Men's Homes." People lay down in the path of bulldozers and tied themselves to trees. The protesters make it clear that the outcome could have gone either way, since the highway proposal had been warmly supported by the D.C. power structure, including *The Washington Post, The Evening Star,* the Board of Trade, and "leading lights on Capitol Hill." This establishment support for road building was the national norm, and, ultimately, no large East Coast city got off as lightly as Washington did.[11]

It would be a mistake to think that America's pro-highway bias has diminished markedly since the rah-rah days of the mid-twentieth century, at least at the federal and state levels. You don't have to be a conspiracy theorist to believe that, if three of the world's four largest corporations are American oil companies* and those companies make millions of dollars in campaign contributions, then roads are fairly guaranteed to remain a priority. Despite all the talk about transit—and great strides made by rail advocates—the feds are still funding highways at roughly four times the rate of public transportation. This funding, about $40 billion in 2011, is supplemented by direct and hidden subsidies to the oil industry, which former California EPA czar Terry Tamminen calculates at between $65 and $113 billion annually, "more than double the amount spent on homeland security."[12]

---

*Exxon Mobil, Chevron, and ConocoPhillips (2011 Fortune 500). The largest corporation is, of course, Walmart, whose entire business model is based on cheap driving and trucking.

Significantly, most federal transportation funds are transferred directly to state departments of transportation (DOTs), which are notoriously inbred with road builders, and typically see it as their principal mission to construct highways.[13] More on them in a minute.

As a result of its unmatched historical and contemporary commitment to automobility, the United States is full of cities that have been shaped or reshaped around the car. Because there have been so many incentives for driving, cars have behaved like water, flowing into every nook and cranny where they have been allowed. Cities with more available space (Houston, Los Angeles) got more cars, while cities with less available space (Boston, New Orleans) got fewer. The first step in reclaiming our urban centers for pedestrians is simply to acknowledge that this outcome was not inevitable, is not the global norm, and need not continue. Despite all the countervailing pressures, it is fully within the capabilities of the typical American city to alter its relationship to the automobile in subtle ways that can have a tremendous impact on walkability—to welcome cars, but on its own terms. First and foremost, this means making all transportation decisions in light of the phenomenon of induced demand.

BECAUSE I MUST: INDUCED DEMAND

About once a month, I give a talk somewhere in America, typically to a chamber of commerce, a planning association, or a bunch of people in a bookstore. Topics and approaches can vary, but I have one hard-and-fast rule: every lecture, no matter what, I will talk at length about induced demand. I do this because induced demand is the great intellectual black hole in city planning, the one professional certainty that everyone thoughtful seems to acknowledge, yet almost no one is willing to act upon. It's as if, despite all of our advances, this one (unfortunately central) aspect of how we make our cities has been entrusted to the Flat Earth Society.

Traffic studies are perhaps the most inevitable activity in planning these days. If you want to add any significant use to a neighborhood, you have to complete a traffic study. If you want to change the design of a street, you have to complete a traffic study. Once, in Davenport, Iowa, I came across a street that had lost one block of its parallel parking, turning a three-lane one-way into a four-lane one-way for just three hundred feet. I recommended bringing that one block of parking back. The city's response? "We need to do a traffic study."•

This circumstance is unsurprising, since traffic congestion is the main topic of civic complaint in most American communities. Since it is the only real constraint to driving, congestion is the one place where people are made to feel the pinch in their automotive lives. Were it not for congestion, we would drive enough additional miles to make congestion. So the traffic study has become the default act of planning, and more than a few large companies can thank traffic studies for the lion's share of their income. They don't want you to read the next few paragraphs.

Traffic studies are bullshit. They are bullshit for three main reasons:

First: The computer model is only as good as its inputs, and there's nothing easier than tweaking the inputs to get the outcome you want. When we were working in Oklahoma City, the local traffic engineer's "Synchro" computer model said that our pro-pedestrian proposals would cause gridlock. So we borrowed that engineer's computer model and handed it to our engineer, who tweaked the inputs, and voila: smooth sailing. By the way, the most commonly tweaked input is anticipated background growth, which typically needs tweaking anyway: most cities' traffic models presume 1 to 2 percent annual growth, even when those cities are shrinking.

Second: Traffic studies are typically performed by firms that do traffic engineering. This makes perfect sense—who else would

•Good news: upon further deliberation, the city skipped the study and added back the parking, without incident.

do them? But guess who gets the big contract for the roadway expansion that the study deems necessary? As long as engineers are in charge of traffic studies, they will predict the need for engineering.

Finally, and most essentially: The main problem with traffic studies is that they almost never consider the phenomenon of induced demand. Induced demand is the name for what happens when increasing the supply of roadways lowers the time cost of driving, causing more people to drive and obliterating any reductions in congestion. We talked about this phenomenon at length in *Suburban Nation* in 2000, and the seminal text, *The Elephant in the Bedroom: Automobile Dependence and Denial*, was published by Hart and Spivak in 1993. For this reason, I will not take the time here to address its causes, which are multifold and fascinating. Since these books were published, however, there have been additional reports, all essentially confirming what we knew then. In 2004, a meta-analysis of dozens of previous studies found that "on average, a 10 percent increase in lane miles induces an immediate 4 percent increase in vehicle miles traveled, which climbs to 10 percent—the entire new capacity—in a few years."[14]

The most comprehensive effort remains the one completed in 1998 by the Surface Transportation Policy Project, which looked at fully seventy different metropolitan areas over fifteen years. This study, which based its findings on data from the annual reports of the conservative Texas Transportation Institute, concluded as follows:

> Metro areas that invested heavily in road capacity expansion fared no better in easing congestion than metro areas that did not. Trends in congestion show that areas that exhibited greater growth in lane capacity spent roughly $22 billion more on road construction than those that didn't, yet ended up with slightly higher congestion costs per person, wasted fuel, and travel de-

lay. . . . The metro area with the highest estimated road building cost was Nashville, Tennessee with a price tag of $3,243 per family per year.[•]

Thanks to studies like this one, induced demand is by no means a professional secret. I was delighted to read the following in a 2009 article in *Newsweek*, hardly an esoteric publication: "Demand from drivers tends to quickly overwhelm the new supply; today engineers acknowledge that building new roads usually makes traffic worse."[■]

To which I must respond: "Who are these engineers and may I please meet them?" Most of the engineers that I'm forced to work with graduated from school decades ago and apparently haven't cracked a textbook—or a *Newsweek*—since.[▲] As a result, this powerful phenomenon, for which the most and best data can be found in the United States, has had virtually no impact on road building in the United States. But there is good news: it has caused great advances in Europe! In Great Britain, where planners are no longer allowed to justify new highways on the basis of reduced congestion, road construction has dropped so drastically

[•]"Does Widening Roads Cause Congestion?" Excerpted from Donald Chen, "If You Build It, They Will Come." A 2010 study by Gilles Duranton and Matthew Turner at the University of Toronto concludes that "increased provision of interstate highways and major urban roads is unlikely to relieve congestion on these roads" ("The Fundamental Law of Road Congestion: Evidence from U.S. Cities," 2616).

[■]Nick Summers, "Where the Neon Lights Are Bright—and Drivers Are No Longer Welcome." It is important to illuminate this quote with the larger discussion that induced demand applies principally to the creation and widening of highways and arterial roads, as opposed to the creation of more intricate street networks through the insertion of small local streets.

[▲]In all fairness, my comment refers principally to the municipal and DOT engineers who must approve the projects that I plan. There are now more than a handful of professional transportation engineers who do their best to share information on induced demand. I have also had good experiences recently working with municipal engineers in Carmel, Indiana; Cedar Rapids; and Fort Lauderdale. But, for most of the profession, Upton Sinclair's famous observation still holds sway: "It is difficult to get a man to understand something when his salary depends on his not understanding it."

that Alarm UK, the main freeway protest organization, disbanded itself "on the grounds that it was no longer needed."[15]

Meanwhile, back on planet Earth, Mary Peters, a recent secretary of transportation, testified before a U.S. Senate committee that "congestion must be addressed with a long-term strategy to increase capacity."[16] It would seem that Saul Bellow's Good Intentions Paving Company is still open for business.

Nowhere is this more evident than in the propaganda put forth by the current incarnation of the Road Gang. There is an engineering firm that I work with, one of the largest in the country. I won't name it here, because I would like to work with them again. They do some really top-notch city projects, are great promoters of urbanism, and are leaders in the development of new transit systems. They also build a lot of sprawl, since they do everything and the biggest part of everything is still sprawl.

Not long ago, the firm placed a full-page ad in *Planning* magazine. It shows an old highway choking on traffic. Then it shows a sparkling new cloverleaf, with cars zipping along happily. The copy reads as follows:

> Vehicle miles travelled increased by 97 percent from 1980 to 1996. Infrastructure improvements could significantly reduce the $78 billion of fuel lost to congestion each year.

This ad is, to put it mildly, misleading. It is misleading on so many levels it is hard to know where to start pulling it apart. At the very least, it is misleading in what it says, what it implies, and what it assumes. It says that new roads can reduce congestion, when we know that new roads almost always increase congestion. It implies that the dramatic surge in vehicle miles traveled since 1980 was not explicitly caused by infrastructure improvements, when we know that it was. Finally, it assumes that congestion wastes fuel, when we know that congestion actually saves fuel—and ultimately is one of the only things that does.

All three of these statements are perhaps counterintuitive, which is why this promotion was not laughed off the copywriter's table at the ad agency. The first two refer, of course, to induced demand. The third statement, that congestion saves fuel, requires some evidence to be plausible.

It turns out that there is a strong correlation between a metropolitan area's average traffic speed and its fuel use. Cities with higher congestion use less fuel per capita, while cities with the least congestion use the most fuel.[17]

This strange circumstance exists not because driving in traffic is more efficient—it isn't—but because of the way we pay to drive. Whether we own or lease, most of the costs are fixed: the price of the vehicle (and/or financing), the driver's insurance, the registration fees, and most of the maintenance fees are largely the same whether we drive a little or a lot. The roads, bridges, and policing are largely paid by general taxes from drivers and nondrivers alike. Tolls, unless you are trying to enter Manhattan or San Francisco, are rarely significant, and even more rarely a deal killer. Parking, as will be discussed at length ahead, is typically priced below market rate and again is only prohibitively expensive in a few places. For most American drivers, the most meaningful variable cost is gas, and by global standards, our gas is dirt cheap—even at four dollars per gallon, it's about half the European rate. All told, the marginal costs are almost negligible compared to the fixed costs. According to the AAA, for a large sedan driven ten thousand miles per year, the operating costs total only one-fifth of the ownership costs.•

•AAA: "Your Driving Costs," 2010 edition, 7. The marginal operating cost of most vehicles is well below twenty cents per mile. This explains why Zipcar and the other urban car-share programs are so effective at reducing auto use. According to the company website, each "Zipcar takes at least 15 personally-owned vehicles off the road." For a Zipcar member, the fixed costs—a twenty-five-dollar application fee and a sixty-dollar annual membership fee—are negligible compared to the marginal costs of hourly rental.

This all adds up to a situation in which you are paying to drive whether you drive or not, in which the more you drive, the less each mile costs, and in which the greatest constraint to driving, then, is congestion. While the cost of the trip will rarely keep us home, the threat of being stuck in traffic often will, at least in our larger cities. Congestion saves fuel because people hate to waste their time being miserable.

That's the negative way to look at it, but there's a positive side as well. The cities with the most congestion are often the cities that provide the best alternatives to being stuck in congestion. Of the ten cities ranked worst for traffic in the 2010 Urban Mobility Report,[18] all but three—Houston, Dallas, and Atlanta—have excellent public transit and a vast collection of walkable neighborhoods. Indeed, these seven cities—Chicago, Washington, Los Angeles, San Francisco, Boston, Seattle, and New York—also appear in another list: Walk Score's ten "Most Walkable Neighborhoods" in America.•

So, with the exception of the usual Sun Belt suspects, congestion comes hand in hand with the opportunity to avoid it. And in those places like Atlanta, where congestion affects almost everyone, at least it mitigates fuel use rather than adding to it. It is certainly troubling to sit in traffic and watch the sky waver from the exhaust of a hundred tailpipes. But you can take some solace in the fact that less congestion would actually lead to more exhaust.

Nobody likes congestion, and, despite appearances, I am not arguing here for more of it. Rather, I am asking that it be better understood by those who build and rebuild our communities, so that we can stop making stupid decisions that placate angry citi-

---

•Walk Score website: "America's Most Walkable Neighborhoods." This outcome makes sense, because the best cities have often attracted the most sprawl. Footloose readers might want to relocate to one of the three cities that make it into the second list but not the first. These are Philadelphia; Long Beach, California; and Portland, Oregon.

zens while only hurting them in the long run. There is a simple answer to congestion—and it's the only answer—which is to bring the cost of driving on crowded streets closer in line with its value. That technique is the subject of the *Congestion Pricing* section ahead.

IT'S NOT JUST FREEWAYS

When I say "highway," you probably picture a limited-access six-laner with guardrails and on-ramps. But the typical American "highway" is not a freeway, but a state road running right through the middle of your town, lined by homes and businesses that are doing their best to maintain their value, often while the state DOT does its best to increase the road's volume. This is why, in the inimitable words of Andres Duany, "the Department of Transportation, in its single-minded pursuit of traffic flow, has destroyed more American towns than General Sherman."[19]

Depending on what state you live in, a few or many of your streets are the responsibility of the Department of Transportation. In Virginia, whose DOT is famous for calling street trees "FHOs"—Fixed and Hazardous Objects[20]—almost every street is state property. In most states, however, it is just the ones that carry a lot of traffic. Unfortunately, this means that many American Main Streets are not controlled by the communities that rely on them, but by state engineers. Main Streets are main streets, after all, and the state relies on them to keep traffic counts up.

This is the worst of news. Whenever I am asked to help resuscitate a city or town center, before doing anything else, I run in a panic to Google Maps to see which, if any, of the downtown streets are state property. Then, if there are many, I adjust my fee up and their expectations down. Because dealing with the

state DOT almost always means that the outcome will be a dis-
appointment.*

While all traffic engineers can be trouble, state engineers
are the toughest because they have no obligation to listen to a
local mayor or citizens. They answer to a higher authority, which
is ultimately the god Traffic Flow. They will typically claim a
concern for walkability and "context-sensitive design," but everything is still viewed through the lens of "level of service," and
level of service means smooth flow. Incidentally, state DOTs are
also a huge source of work for planning consultants, which is a
big reason why few planners are willing to stand up to them.

The same is true of county engineers in places like New York
State, where many communities are held hostage by Main Streets
that are also county highways. In both cases, fighting the DOT is
always a struggle, but there is a way to win, and it's called leadership. The communities that prevail are those whose elected officials confront the DOT head-on and publicly demand a more
walkable solution. This approach is admittedly easier for bigger
cities, but even small towns can come out on top if they make
enough noise.

This is what happened in the Village of Hamburg, New York
(population roughly ten thousand), where Mayor John Thomas
was being told by NYDOT to accept three major road widenings
that would have removed parallel parking, increased travel
speeds, and generally trashed his town center. Working with the
nationally known pedestrian advocate Dan Burden,* the mayor

---

*A few disclaimers: Some states are better than others; I have had good experiences in
Massachusetts and Michigan, and the District of Columbia (almost a state) is ahead of
most cities in its pro-pedestrian policies. Also, most state traffic engineers are very nice
people. Despite *The New York Times'* 2010 exposé about engineers' proclivities for
terror—"in the ranks of captured and confessed terrorists, engineers and engineering
students are significantly overrepresented" (David Berreby, "Engineering Terror")—I
have always found them pleasant enough to work with. Of course, they haven't seen this
book yet.

*Dan Burden is profiled nicely in Jeff Mapes, *Pedaling Revolution*.

refused the DOT "improvement" until a new design could be produced with public participation. Now Hamburg's Main Street is a delicate two-laner with bikeways and parking, and the DOT proudly showcases its award-winning design at transportation conferences.[21]

Beating the DOT is often the most important thing that a community can do to reclaim its center, and battles of this epic nature must be fought on occasion if cities are to thrive. But I would be protecting you from the truth if I were to suggest that the Boogieman always comes from out of town. In most communities, there are also daily battles to be fought within city administration, where, in the absence of mayoral leadership, traffic trumps livability.

As mentioned earlier, I spent four years working with the Mayors' Institute on City Design, a program that convenes mayors for intensive city-planning workshops. As the ranking representative of the program's main funder, I was always given a chance to speak, and my message was always the same: "Stop letting your traffic engineer design your city!"

The need for this message became all the more clear after I had attended a handful of Mayors' Institute sessions. In city after city, left to their own devices, traffic engineers were widening streets, removing trees, and generally reaming out downtowns to improve traffic flow. Much of this was happening below the mayor's radar. In the absence of any design leadership from above, the city engineer, simply by doing his job, was redesigning the city—badly.

It seems a bit unfair to blame the city engineer for this situation. Because most of the public complaints one hears in cities are about traffic, it stands to reason that any good public servant would work to reduce traffic congestion. This would be acceptable if efforts to reduce traffic congestion didn't wreck cities and perhaps also if they worked. But they don't work, because of induced demand. Most city engineers don't understand induced demand. They might say that they do, but, if so, they don't act upon that understanding.

I say this because it would seem that almost no traffic engineers in America possess the necessary combination of insight and political will that would allow them to take the induced demand discussion to its logical conclusion, which is this: Stop doing traffic studies. Stop trying to improve flow. Stop spending people's tax dollars giving them false hope that you can cure congestion, while mutilating their cities in the process.

I understand that it might be difficult to tell the public that you can't satisfy their biggest complaint. But there is a happier way to frame the message, and it goes like this: We can have the kind of city we want. We can tell the car where to go and how fast. We can be a place not just for driving through, but for arriving at. This is the story that traffic engineers should be sharing, rather than spending their careers running scared from congestion. Until they do, it will be necessary for mayors, Main Street merchants, and concerned citizens to discredit them. Toward that end, I provide the following short interlude.

KILL THE TRAFFIC ENGINEERS FIRST

Everybody likes Jane Jacobs, right? She was famous for fighting traffic engineers, and took them to task repeatedly and effectively in her masterpiece, *The Death and Life of Great American Cities*. Most planners and many public servants swear by that book, but few have read *Dark Age Ahead*, in which, forty years later, she took off the gloves. Until traffic engineers change their tune on induced demand, here is the statement from Jane Jacobs that every public official and planner needs to tape prominently above his or her desk:

It is popularly assumed that when universities give science degrees in traffic engineering, as they do, they are recognizing aboveboard expert knowledge. But they aren't. They are perpetrating a fraud upon students and upon the public when they award credentials in this supposed expertise.[22]

And a bit more:

> I thought sadly: "Here they are, another generation of nice, miseducated young men, about to waste their careers in a fake science that cares nothing about evidence; that doesn't ask a fruitful question in the first place and that, when unexpected evidence turns up anyhow, doesn't pursue it. . . . This incurious profession pulls its conclusions about the meaning of evidence out of thin air—sheer guesswork—even when it does deign to notice evidence. . . . In the meantime, each year students have poured forth from universities, a clear, harmful case of education surrendered to credentialism. One wonders at the docility of the students who evidently must be satisfied enough with the credentials to be uncaring about the lack of education.[23]

Perhaps inspired by Jane, a few brave, young, credentialed traffic engineers have recently had the nerve to come out of the closet. Foremost among them is probably Charles Marohn, who published the following piece in *Grist*. It is so powerful, and important, that it deserves quoting at length:

> CONFESSIONS OF A RECOVERING ENGINEER
> After graduating from college with a civil engineering degree, I found myself working in my home town for a local engineering firm doing mostly municipal engineering (roads, sewer pipe, water pipe, stormwater). A fair percentage of my time was spent convincing people that, when it came to their road, I knew more than they did.

And of course I should know more. First, I had a technical degree from a top university. Second, I was in a path towards getting a state license . . . which required me to pass a pretty tough test just to get started and another, more difficult, exam to conclude. Third, I was in a profession that is one of the oldest and most respected in human history, responsible for some of the greatest achievements of mankind. Fourth—and most important—I had books and books of standards to follow.

When people would tell me that they did not want a wider street, I would tell them that they had to have it for safety reasons.

When they answered that a wider street would make people drive faster and that would seem to be less safe, especially in front of their house where their kids were playing, I would confidently tell them that the wider road was more safe, especially when combined with the other safety enhancements the standards called for.

When people objected to those other "enhancements," like removing all of the trees near the road, I told them that for safety reasons we needed to improve the sight distances and ensure that the recovery zone was free of obstacles.

When they pointed out that the "recovery zone" was also their "yard" and that their kids played kickball and hopscotch there, I recommended that they put up a fence, so long as the fence was outside of the right-of-way. When they objected to the cost of the wider, faster, treeless road that would turn their peaceful front yard into the viewing area for a drag strip unless they built a concrete barricade along their front property line, I informed them that progress was sometimes expensive, but these standards have been shown to work across the state, the country, and the world, and I could not compromise with their safety.

In retrospect I understand that this was utter insanity. Wider, faster, treeless roads not only ruin our public places, they kill people. Taking highway standards and applying them to urban and suburban streets, and even county roads, costs us thousands of lives every year. There is no earthly reason why an engineer would ever design a 14-foot lane for a city block, yet we do it continually. Why?

The answer is utterly shameful: Because that is the standard.[*]

The two above selections are offered to help cities defend themselves against abuse by traffic engineers. It gives me no great pleasure to share them, and I wish it were unnecessary. But the profession of traffic planning is so desperately in need of a course correction that the most productive approach would seem to be to shame them mercilessly. That said, Marohn's essay is ultimately cause for hope. He is, after all, a traffic engineer, and he clearly gets it. He is actually only one of a growing number of traffic experts—both professional consultants and city staffers—who have been leading the charge in recent years toward a new paradigm. Because cities demand them, these engineers still do traffic studies. But these studies, like the British ones, finally take induced demand into account.

REMOVE IT AND THEY WILL GO

If more and bigger highways mean more traffic, does the same logic work in reverse? The latest twist in the induced demand

---

[*]"Confessions of a Recovering Engineer." More about Charles Marohn and his work can be found at strongtowns.org.

story might be called *reduced demand*, which seems to be what happens when "vital" arteries are removed from cities. The traffic just goes away.

The two best-known American examples remain New York's West Side Highway and San Francisco's Embarcadero Freeway, which collapsed in 1973 and in 1989, respectively. In both cases, contrary to the apocalyptic warnings of traffic engineers, most of the car trips simply disappeared. They did not pop up elsewhere, clogging surface streets; people just found other ways to get around, or felt less compelled to be mobile.* The Embarcadero was replaced by a lovely boulevard, whose cute little streetcars actually transport more riders per day than the freeway once did.

People's dawning awareness of these successes has led to a growing list of highway teardowns, both domestically and around the world. These include Harbor Drive in Portland, Milwaukee's Park East Freeway, and another elevated road in San Francisco: the Central Freeway, now replaced by the attractive Octavia Boulevard.[24] Beyond giving new life to the areas previously blighted by the highways, these road removals have actually been found to reduce overall travel times within their cities. The most celebrated, and properly so, has got to be the Cheonggyecheon (pronounced *chung-yay-chun*) Freeway in Seoul, where a traffic-choked elevated expressway was hauled down in the mid-2000s, daylighting the river that it had obscured for half a century.[25]

The Cheonggyecheon story is so intriguing that it deserves its own book. It began as a grassroots effort, with no political support whatsoever—after all, who advocates for removing a road that carries 168,000 cars per day? Since nobody in office would back it, proponents shopped the idea around to mayoral candidates, in the hope that someone would make it their platform.

---

*One British study of worldwide data found that road removals generally improve local economies, while new roads increase urban unemployment (Jill Kruse, "Remove It and They Will Disappear," 5, 7).

The one candidate who bit—ironically, the former president of the company that built the freeway—was elected on that promise. As mayor, Lee Myung-bak commenced the teardown project on inauguration day.

Mayhem ensued. Opponents mounted huge protests, including the three thousand street vendors whose livelihoods depended on hawking wares to the highway's gridlocked travelers. Some threatened suicide unless the project was stopped. Through all of that, a two-year design process was shortened to six months, and the entire effort was completed within thirty months. A sixteen-lane highway was replaced by an urban boulevard and a spectacular 3.6-mile river park.[26]

A few years later, the river's ecosystem had been significantly restored, an urban heat island had its temperature reduced by more than five degrees, and traffic congestion had dropped sharply—thanks in part to simultaneous investments in transit. As of this writing, property values surrounding the former highway have risen 300 percent. And Lee Myung-bak has been elected president of South Korea.[27]

I wish we had known about this effort in September 2004, when Seattle's Mayor Greg Nickels came to the Mayors' Institute on City Design, and brought along the Alaskan Way Viaduct as his planning challenge. Like the Embarcadero, the two-deck, six-lane viaduct had been damaged in an earthquake and needed replacement. The state DOT proposed replacing the highway with an elegant surface boulevard . . . and a $4.2 billion highway tunnel.

"That sounds perfect—just cut the tunnel!" the planners around the table shouted in unison. "But where will all the traffic go?" asked the mayor. "Not to worry!" we responded.• But we apparently weren't very convincing, as Mayor Nickels returned

---

•This exchange is obviously paraphrased from a longer and more broad-ranging discussion.

to Seattle still committed to the tunnel. Even this Democratic leader of a progressive left-coast city—and an environmentalist so devout that he didn't allow salt for snow removal—couldn't be sold on induced demand.

How did that work out for him? Well, first, Seattle's citizens voted in a referendum to reject plans to replace the Viaduct with either a tunnel or a new elevated expressway. Then, as Nickels continued to support the tunnel, Mike McGinn, a relatively unknown Sierra Clubber, announced a run for mayor centered on a no-tunnel platform. Despite raising only $80,000 to Nickels's $560,000, McGinn beat Nickels handily in the primary and is now mayor.[28]

So Lee Myung-bak is president and Greg Nickels is out of politics. . . . Is there a lesson here about induced demand? It would seem that the people are in front of the politicians as usual, except that they aren't: in a more recent referendum, the tunnel won, and now seems imminent. But that doesn't make it right.

Ultimately, this discussion is more about fiscal restraint than traffic theory. The most beautiful tree-lined boulevard can be built for a fraction of the cost of either a tunnel or a viaduct. The current (and likely permanent) cash-strapped status of our cities and states suggests that all elevated urban expressways should be replaced by surface streets when they become decrepit—although perhaps not any sooner.

But this final caveat requires more thought. Elevated expressways are a blight on cities and depress surrounding property values drastically—not only immediately adjacent, but sometimes for several blocks on both flanks. Tree-lined boulevards, of course, do the opposite. The Embarcadero boulevard project cost $171 million, but raised property values by 300 percent—the same as in Seoul—for a full 1.2-mile stretch.[29] You don't need a real estate degree to understand that a threefold increase in property taxes for 1.2 miles of downtown San Francisco has probably paid for the boulevard several times over since 2000. Some cities, if they care to do the math, might find ample economic justification for tearing down an expressway or two, even before they begin to crumble.

A STEP TOO FAR: PEDESTRIAN ZONES

Jan Gehl, the legendary Danish city planner, elegantly sums up the traffic discussion this way:

> The connections between invitations and behavior came to a head for cities in the 20th century. . . . In every case, attempts to relieve traffic pressure by building more roads and parking garages have generated more traffic and more congestion. The volume of car traffic almost everywhere is more or less arbitrary, depending on the available transportation infrastructure.[30]

This assessment, to my mind, properly conveys the noninevitable nature of the auto-dominated city, and how communities, by making concerted choices about their infrastructure, can fully dictate the quality of their landscapes and lives. In his work in Copenhagen, Gehl has presided over a gradual removal of cars from the heart of the city. From 1962 to 2005, a central zone dedicated to pedestrians and bicycles has grown sevenfold in size, from about four acres to over twenty-five acres.[31] In concert with this effort, the city has been eliminating 2 percent of its downtown parking spaces every year, for the past thirty years.[32]

Gehl has recently been consulting to the City of New York, which turned a stretch of Broadway in Times Square into a pedestrian park with great results. The city has also completed about twenty blocks of the spectacular High Line project, a former elevated railway that has been converted to a linear park, perhaps the most delightful piece of civic art to have been created since midcentury. You've probably seen the pictures, and they don't lie: these public amenities are a real boon to the livability of their neighborhoods and are well used in all but the worst weather.

These car-free successes provide a powerful lesson that unfortunately does not apply to most American cities. It is a mistake to think that similar designs will produce similar results in vastly dissimilar places. Face it: you aren't Copenhagen, where cyclists outnumber motorists.[33] You aren't New York, where pedestrian congestion can actually make it almost impossible to walk south along Seventh Avenue near Penn Station at 9:00 a.m. Unless you have similar residential and pedestrian density and stores that can thrive in the absence of car traffic—a rarity—to consign a commercial area to pedestrians only, in America, is to condemn it to death.

When I arrived at the NEA in 2003, my office was stocked with a collection of publications describing past NEA successes. One of them, in quaint 1970s lettering, celebrated dozens of Main Streets across America that had been pedestrianized using NEA funds. As I flipped through it, I was treated to page after page of failure. From Baltimore to Buffalo, from Louisville to Little Rock, from Tampa to Tulsa, from Greenville, North Carolina, to Greenville, South Carolina, almost every Main Street that was closed to car traffic in the sixties and seventies failed almost as soon as the NEA book hit the presses.

In all, of the two hundred or so pedestrian malls created in the United States, only about thirty remain.[34] Of those, most are moribund low-rent districts like Main Street in Memphis where, despite the presence of an appealing streetcar line, empty storefronts abound. The exceptions are almost all in college towns like Boulder, Colorado, and Burlington, Vermont, or in resorts like Aspen and Miami Beach. Other outliers, like Santa Monica's Third Street Promenade and Denver's 16th Street, show that successful pedestrianization is indeed possible. It's just very, very unlikely.

It would seem that only one thing is more destructive to the health of our downtowns than welcoming cars unconditionally and that is getting rid of them entirely. The proper response to obesity is not to stop eating, and most stores need car traffic to survive. With autos reintroduced, most failed pedestrian malls, like Monroe Place in Grand Rapids, have come back at least partway. The key is to welcome cars in the proper number and at the proper speed.

It is easy to catch the Broadway bug and hope to create pedestrian refuges in your city. New York could handle a lot more of them—I advised its planning commission in 2010 to add one new one every year.[35] Certain other cities with great residential densities downtown, like Boston and Chicago, could produce some successes in the years ahead and should perhaps try. But the main lesson here is to not do it the way they did last time, with the construction of expensive and expensive-to-remove streetscapes that make driving impossible. Instead, put up some temporary bollards and bring in a few potted trees and movable chairs, like they did in Times Square. Try it on a weekend and, if it works, expand the days. Don't spend a penny on gorgeous car barricades, because if a pedestrian zone is going to be successful, it will thrive due to its location, demographics, and organization—not its streetscape.

CONGESTION PRICING: TOO SMART TO BE EASY

No chapter on cars and cities would be complete without a discussion of congestion pricing, a vastly underutilized tool that communities can use to protect themselves from the automotive hordes. We have already celebrated congestion, reluctantly, as a dominant factor in limiting people's time on the road. Most cities need congestion to keep driving in check, because driving costs drivers so much less than it costs society.* But what if motorists were asked to pay something closer to the real cost of driving, so that they were once again allowed to make market-based choices about when to drive where? The result would be a solution to both excessive driving and excessive congestion. That's the idea behind congestion pricing.

In the early 2000s, London was choking on traffic, and people were desperate for a solution. Having exhausted the alternatives, Mayor Ken Livingstone proposed the only known cure, economics. Against "a massive and sustained media campaign,"[36] he introduced a roughly fifteen-dollar fee for any driver who wanted to enter the congested heart of the city on weekdays, with the revenue to be used to support a progressive transportation agenda.

Here's what happened: Congestion dropped 30 percent in the toll zone, and typical journey times went down by 14 percent. Cycling among Londoners jumped 20 percent and air pollution fell about 12 percent. The fee has already generated over a billion dollars in revenue, much of which has been invested in mass transit. London now has hundreds of new buses, providing almost thirty thousand more daily trips than before the charge. Bus reliability has jumped by 30 percent and bus delays have dropped by 60 percent.[37]

Before introduction of the congestion charge, Londoners were evenly divided on the concept. When last polled, pros beat cons by 35 percent.[38] And in the subsequent mayoral election, largely a referendum on the pricing scheme, Livingstone was reelected by a broad margin.

London is not alone in its embrace of congestion pricing. São

---

*This is a fact even ignoring externalities like pollution and time wasted. For example, general taxes in New Jersey transfer approximately $700 million from the general population to drivers every year (Charles Siegel, *Unplanning*, 29).

Paulo, Shanghai, Singapore, Stockholm, and Sydney[39] have all introduced similar measures, with varying, but all generally positive, results. San Francisco is now working on its own scheme. Not beginning with the letter *S* like all the others, New York City was apparently at a distinct disadvantage when Mayor Michael Bloomberg hatched a congestion-pricing scheme on Earth Day 2007. His proposal would have raised about half a billion dollars annually, and was additionally slated to receive $354 million off the bat from the federal government. To the surprise of many, it was killed by the State Assembly in Albany,[40] which is disproportionately composed of suburban commuters. Well, as a New Yorker would say, "Screw you, too."

Ironically, four-dollar gasoline quickly accomplished the better part of what Mayor Bloomberg hoped to do[41]—minus the revenues to the city—demonstrating the effectiveness of using price to control congestion. But gas prices are a much blunter instrument than congestion pricing, which allows cities to specifically attack problem locations, and make a lot of money in the bargain. Most cities are not beholden to their state legislatures in the same way New York is, and the more congested ones should consider pilot projects in the manner of London's. After all, Mayor Bloomberg's proposal was supported locally by 67 percent of voters.[42]

THE LONG VIEW

"Americans are in the habit of never walking if they can ride." So commented the duke of Orléans, Louis Philippe, as early as 1798 (he became king of the French in 1830).[43] This tendency, apparently established in our nation's earliest days, has had a profound impact on both our physical landscape and our physical selves. Considerably more recently, the French philosopher Bernard-Henry Lévy described our autocentric lifestyle as "a global, total obesity that spares no realm of life, public or private. An entire society that, from the top down, from one end to the other, seems prey to this obscure derangement that slowly causes an organism to swell, overflow, explode."[44] These two comments, made two centuries apart, are more connected than they at first may seem.

Lévy was not talking explicitly about our bodies, but about our society as a whole, and how we live so large on the land. To figure out what happened in the time between these two French pronouncements, we need to take a brief detour through the writings of Ivan Illich, the multinational intellectual who in 1973 wrote the smartest thing that I have yet to read about transportation: "Beyond a certain speed, motorized vehicles create remoteness which they alone can shrink. They create distances for all and shrink them for only a few."[45]

Illich was essentially making an equity argument and, if he had stopped there, his message might not have been compelling to many. Sure, it's not fair that "an elite packs unlimited distance into a lifetime of pampered travel, while the majority spend a bigger slice of their existence on unwanted trips,"[46] but since when is life fair? Statements like "extremes of privilege are created at the cost of universal enslavement"• don't win votes today the way they might have in the seventies. However, beyond discussing equity, Illich actually uncovered a vast mother lode of American waste:

> The model American male devotes more than 1600 hours a year to his car. He sits in it while it goes and while it stands idling. He parks it and searches for it. He earns the money to put down to meet the monthly installments. He works to pay for gasoline, tolls, insurance,

---

•*Toward a History of Needs*, 127, 119. It gives us little comfort to learn that Illich was no great fan of railways either: "From our limited information it appears that everywhere in the world, after some vehicle broke the speed barrier of 15 mph, time scarcity related to traffic began to grow" (ibid., 119).

taxes, and tickets. He spends four of his sixteen waking hours on the road or gathering the resources for it. . . . The model American puts in 1600 hours to get 7500 miles: less than five miles per hour. In countries deprived of transportation industry, people manage to do the same, walking wherever they want to go, and they allocate only 3 to 8 percent of their society's budget to traffic instead of 28 percent.•

This is remarkable. Compared to our colonial ancestors, we throw 25 percent more of our national and personal resources into transportation and we ultimately move no faster. But we do move farther, and Illich might as well have been speaking about contemporary Atlanta when he wrote that "everybody's daily radius expands at the expense of being able to drop in on an acquaintance or walk through the park on the way to work."▪

Illich discovered a hidden physical law: the faster a society moves, the more it spreads out and the more time it must spend moving. And he hadn't seen the half of it. Since 1983, when the American sprawl machine really kicked in, the number of miles driven has grown at eight times the population rate.[47] While almost one in ten commuters walked to work in Illich's day, fewer than one in forty do now.[48]

As disturbing as this transformation is, we must remember that it is not irreversible and—more to the point—not the current experience of every American. Walkable cities, with their

•Illich, *Toward a History of Needs*, 120. He adds: "And this figure does not take into account the time consumed by other activities dictated by transport: time spent in hospitals, traffic courts, and garages; time spent watching automobile commercials or attending consumer education meetings to improve the quality of the next buy." And let's not forget that Illich's data were from roughly 1970, when we drove considerably less and spent considerably less of our income on driving.
▪Illich, 119. For the sake of accuracy, I should note that my friend Phil Harrison walks through the park on the way to work in Atlanta. But he is the only one.

dense, vibrant, mixed-use neighborhoods, offer residents a lifestyle that combines superior economic and social opportunity with a transportation cost, in both time and money, that is not necessarily any higher than in Illich's "countries deprived of transportation industry." This is particularly true when more citizens are able to live right in the center of town, a subject for the next chapter.

STEP 2: MIX THE USES

It's usually housing; Invisible affordability; The rest of the picture

Cities were created to bring things together. The better they do this job, the more successful they become. This has always been the case, but there was a time when what was good for cities was not good for citizens. The belching fumes of the "dark satanic mills" and the rampant spread of epidemics through tenement housing shortened urban life spans dramatically. By 1900, a typical New Yorker enjoyed seven fewer years aboveground than his cousin on the farm.*

City Planning to the rescue! Before it had a name, the planning profession scored its first great victory, by reducing urban overcrowding and moving housing and factories away from each other. Life expectancies shot upward, the planners were hailed as heroes, and thus began the century of separating everything from everything else.[1] This dismantling of the city into its constituent parts became known, appropriately enough, as zoning, and zoning still rules the day in most American communities. Cities are organized not according to "planning regulations" but by "zoning codes," and different land uses still tend to be kept

---

*Edward Glaeser, comments to the Congress for the New Urbanism, June 3, 2011. For reasons already discussed, New Yorkers born in 2010 are expected to live two years longer than the national average.

apart much more than health, safety, or common sense would dictate. Most small-scale urban industry no longer pollutes and, last we checked, cholera was under control.

The zoning tendency finds its apotheosis, of course, in suburban sprawl, where an elephantine regime of separated activities enforces the bankrupting hyper-mobility that has been so destructive to our national civic life. That story has been well told. Less often discussed are the ways that zoning has undermined, and continues to damage, our inner cities. So profound was its impact that it is now not enough to just abolish zoning and let the free market run its course. Cities, if they are to become whole again, must not only reform their codes—to be discussed in Step 9—but must also earnestly labor to reestablish a proper balance of activities downtown.

IT'S USUALLY HOUSING

What is that balance? Better to ask: what do humans do? Work, shop, eat, drink, learn, recreate, convene, worship, heal, visit, celebrate, sleep: these are all activities that people should not have to leave downtown to accomplish. While there are exceptions, most large and midsized American downtowns possess a good supply of all of the above except places to sleep, lost to the twentieth-century suburban exodus. Moreover, thanks to the paucity of housing, many of the other categories are unable to thrive. Specialty shopping may remain, but food markets are rare. Restaurants do their best to survive on only a lunchtime service. Historic churches struggle to hang on to suburban parishioners who used to live nearby.

As we have discussed, the demand for downtown housing is significant and it is about to skyrocket. But supply will have a hard time meeting demand unless cities become politically committed to its provision and lend a hand. Building new housing downtown is an expensive and punishing process: unlike the suburban greenfield sites that most developers are accustomed to, city properties often come burdened with a whole range of utility issues, easements, and access challenges, not to mention pesky neighbors. Local banks, until recently all too willing to finance condo clusters on the periphery, shy away from investing in new apartments downtown.

This continues to be the situation in Davenport, Iowa, where the big local lenders have long been unwilling to support the construction of housing on the very streets surrounding their offices—this despite the fact that the three residential developments to come downtown in the last decade have all rented up or sold out almost immediately. No *It's a Wonderful Life* here: the investors have had to come in from Minneapolis, Madison, and Saint Louis. This contemporary version of redlining is a significant reason that downtown housing often cannot be built without municipal support.

What does this support look like? A great example is Lowell, Massachusetts, which is quickly transforming its downtown through a focus on new housing. I grew up not far from Lowell, and it was known as a place to avoid. Once an industrial mecca, Jack Kerouac's hometown had lost most of its vitality by the sixties, along with most of its market-rate downtown housing. As recently as 2000, the heart of the city held only about seventeen hundred housing units, of which an astounding 79 percent were subsidized and income restricted. Eleven years later, the number of units has almost doubled and, more significantly, almost 85 percent of the new housing is market rate. That means that the number of non–income-restricted homes has more than quadrupled.

According to Adam Baacke, Lowell's assistant city manager for planning and development, achieving this transformation was essentially a three-step process that could perhaps be best described as *politics, permitting*, and *pathfinding*.

Politics refers to changing attitudes (and people) on the city council, where most members shunned downtown housing because "only commercial development was considered good." Eventually, the city's new outlook motivated it to sell one of its underutilized parcels for the express purpose of creating artists' housing downtown.

Permitting refers to sidestepping the city's conventional zoning code, which, for example, caused this new artists' housing to require fourteen distinct variances just to get built. In its place, the city treated each new residential proposal as a "special permit," and then these permits were "given out like candy" to qualified applicants. Next, the city replaced its stringent requirements for parking with the new rule that developers needed only to identify one parking space per unit, anywhere nearby, that could be leased to their residents. Most of these were spaces in municipal garages that were busy from nine to five but empty at night.

Finally, *pathfinding* refers to setting up an extensive regime of hand-holding from city staff, to walk developers through the tricky process of winning every available federal and state subsidy, including historic preservation tax credits and community renewal block grants. Some of these awards are quite competitive, and the city went so far as to package all the required letters of support from the community. And, yes, this help even included cash, with the city finding ways to put money into some of the projects.[2]

To be accurate, Baacke cites one other essential step to the process of attracting downtown residents, what he describes as "a citywide commitment to creating an environment that people want to live in"—which I would call walkability. In a virtuous circle, more walkability begets more housing downtown, which begets more walkability. This chicken-and-egg relationship raises the question of which item to invest in first. The answer, of course, is both.

INVISIBLE AFFORDABILITY

Lowell raises an interesting point, which is that most American cities do not need more affordable housing in their downtowns. Most American cities have too much affordable housing downtown. Or, more accurately, too much of their downtown housing is affordable, since everyone but the poor was able to join the suburban exodus. The typical midsized American city center now contains a few market-rate apartment houses, a smattering of raw urban lofts occupied by people in black, one or two Corten-steel-walled fortress row houses of the type featured in *Dwell* magazine, and a ton of poor people, many of them in projects. These downtowns need more housing, but that housing should contribute to a more normal distribution of incomes downtown. This has been the effort in Lowell.

But not every city is like Lowell. A lucky few, larger cities—some of the heroes of this book—have already attracted so many well-off people into their downtowns and close-in neighborhoods that these places are in danger of becoming social monocultures. Despite their wealth, these can also be detrimental to street life, since yuppie overachievers tend to spend less time in the public sphere, and also because sidewalks, like communities, thrive on diversity: different types of people use the streets at different times of day, keeping them active around the clock.•

For these gentrified and gentrifying communities, two powerful remedies exist for increasing and maintaining affordability. One is well known and the other hardly so. They are *inclusionary zoning* and *granny flats.*

Inclusionary zoning—requiring a set percentage of all new

•Incidentally, monocultures also aren't very good for society. Jane Jacobs put it this way: "Does anyone suppose that, in real life, answers to any of the great questions that worry us today are going to come out of homogeneous settlements?" (Jacobs, *The Death and Life of Great American Cities*, 448).

housing developments to meet affordability criteria—hardly requires a mention, except to say that it works and it is always the right thing to do. Every city should have an inclusionary-zoning ordinance in place, and few currently do, because it has gotten the reputation of being a hidden tax on developers and an impediment to the free market. While these criticisms are technically true, they ignore the real experience of inclusionary-zoning programs in action, which is that they have never stifled development. In some cases, they have been shown to accelerate it.[3]

And while the libertarians may hate inclusionary zoning, sophisticated developers seem to be just fine with it.* This is probably because the affordable component can qualify a development for federal or state subsidies that make projects more profitable. Some of the biggest inclusionary-zoning programs are in Denver, San Francisco, San Diego, and Boston. The program in wealthy Montgomery County, Maryland, in force since 1974, has built more than ten thousand units of affordable housing. In today's moribund homebuilding climate, the "pro-business" lobby will no doubt redouble its efforts against inclusionary zoning, but it will do so with scant evidence and ultimately against its own best interests.

Granny flats, on the other hand, have yet to gain much traction in America's cities. Called "accessory dwelling units (ADUs)" by planners, and "backyard cottages" by clever marketers, these apartments are as intelligent as they are illegal. The few ADU ordinances that have been passed in the United States allow single-family houses to place a small apartment in their backyard—often atop a garage on a rear lane—that can be rented in the free market. They are typically opposed by neighbors who are worried about property values. An old college roommate of mine from

---

*I use the word *sophisticated* in order to rule out the National Association of Home-builders, who continue to advocate incessantly for sprawl despite the fact that it has bankrupted their membership.

Los Angeles put it succinctly: "We are afraid that nine illegals will move in."

Happily, there is no evidence that granny flats lower property values and it's easy to see why. First, they are almost invisible. Second, they provide the homeowners with an income stream that allows them to live in their own home more comfortably. Third, they are of course carefully regulated to avoid the tenement-style use contemplated by my Angeleno friend. (Indeed, the tenant is often a homeowner's parent or college-age child.) Fourth, they introduce affordability in a dispersed rather than a concentrated way, avoiding the pathologies that sometimes arise from the latter. Finally, they are inevitably well supervised by their landlords, who live just a few feet away.

And they are great for walkability, as they increase neighborhood density, putting more feet on the sidewalks, and making transit service and local shopping more viable. They are ideal in those older single-family neighborhoods that can often be found on the edges of downtown, where bungalows and larger homes line walkable streets. Indeed, that's where they can still be found in places like Charleston and West Hollywood. Granny flats are also big in Canada, where NIMBYs generally hold less influence over local planning matters. Vancouver decriminalized them in 2008 as part of the city's EcoDensity initiative, and hundreds have already been built and rented.•

Despite all this, even some of America's most progressive city councils have found it a struggle to make granny flats legal again. Seattle finally succeeded after a lengthy fight, with critics claiming that the cottages would double the city's density. Others suggested that neighbors would lose the privacy they required to "barbecue, entertain guests, or walk around naked if they're

---

•Incidentally, this country's densest collection of granny flats probably can be found in the new village of Rosemary Beach, Florida, which I helped DPZ design in the late 1990s. As of last count, there are 214 "carriage house" apartments there.

kinky."[4] Now about a hundred granny flats are receiving building permits in Seattle each year.[5] As of this writing, the cottages have just been legalized in Portland, Miami, Berkeley, Denver, and Burlington, Vermont.[6] If you make one of these cities home, you can build one for maybe seventy-five thousand dollars. If you live elsewhere, take heart: there are at least six working ADU ordinances that you can show to your city council.

THE REST OF THE PICTURE

This chapter about mixed use has quickly become a chapter about housing, because that is the activity most often underrepresented in American downtowns, and also because that is the activity most American downtowns have a decent shot at attracting right now. As more and more American industry is either outsourced overseas or executed by laptoppers who can live wherever they please, most city centers will struggle to maintain their current stock of dedicated work space. There will of course be exceptions, but this situation will continue for some time, until enough people have moved back downtown that the workplace follows them there, just as it followed them to the suburbs in the sixties.

For this reason, the best strategy for attracting business to your city is no longer the conventional zero-sum game of luring corporations away from other places with tax breaks, land deals, and other door prizes. Too many cities still think that economic development can occur in a vacuum of golf and giveaways, ignoring the fact that such victories are increasingly rare and don't always last. After all, the corporation that dumps Philly for Indy thanks to a 5 percent tax cut will happily run off to Cincy for 7.5—and perhaps to Tijuana soon thereafter.

Cities whose economic-development strategy is a corporate-capture strategy are typically those whose economic development director and planning director don't talk to each other. The smart cities, like Lowell, hire a director of planning and development, who is first charged with creating a city where people want to be. Rather than trying to land new office tenants in a shrinking office market, this person understands that future economic growth will take place where the creative people are, and then works to lure more residents downtown.

As Adam Baacke suggested, this strategy means building more market-rate housing while also promoting those things that residents want and need: parks and playgrounds, supermarkets and farmers' markets, cafés and restaurants—and, eventually, good schools—all embraced in a framework of top-notch walkability. Each of these items is a book in its own right, and well beyond this discussion. Suffice it to say that they are necessary, and that the first step to attracting them is to reorient economic development around creating a downtown that has them all.

STEP 3: GET THE PARKING RIGHT

What parking costs and what it costs us; Induced demand redux;
Addiction made law; The cost of required parking; Some smarter places;
The problem with cheap curbside parking; The right price; A tale of two
cities; What should we do with all this money?; A bargain at $1.2 billion

This chapter exists because of one man. He is in his mid-seventies, green-eyed, gray-bearded, and often pictured riding a bicycle. He holds four degrees from Yale in engineering and economics, and teaches at UCLA, where he was chair of the Department of Urban Planning and ran the Institute of Transportation Studies. His name is Donald Shoup and, inside an admittedly small circle, he is a rock star. He is alternately hailed as the "Jane Jacobs of parking policy" and the "prophet of parking." There is even a Facebook group called "The Shoupistas."[1]

Shoup has earned his exalted status by being perhaps the first person to really think about how parking works in cities. This effort has led him to some conclusions that have now been backed up with decades of evidence, and he is just beginning to get the attention he deserves. In the words of a former Ventura, California, mayor, Bill Fulton, "Don has been saying the exact same thing for 40 years, and finally the world is listening to him."[2] That doesn't mean that the world is yet doing what he says, but, with a little luck, that is about to change.

Parking covers more acres of urban America than any other one thing[3]—just look at an aerial photo of downtown Houston—

yet, until Shoup, nobody seems to have made any effort to figure it out; certainly not the planners, who happily institute and enforce outdated parking requirements nationwide like a barnyard of headless chickens. Shoup himself notes how the "bible" of city planning, F. Stuart Chapin's *Urban Land Use Planning*, doesn't even mention parking once.[*] We did better than that in *Suburban Nation*, but our focus was more on the *what* than the *why*, which Shoup has refined to the level of science.

What Shoup has discovered about parking—using both an economist's cold logic and the careful, sustained observation of reality—is that every city in America handles it wrong. Rather than parking working in the service of cities, cities have been working in the service of parking, almost entirely to their detriment. He has also determined, and demonstrated, that this problem can be fixed fairly easily and with great rewards for all involved. And he is just beginning to see his ideas bear fruit in places like San Francisco, which we will discuss below.

WHAT PARKING COSTS AND WHAT IT COSTS US

The first step to understanding how parking works is to get a grasp of how much it costs and who pays for it. Because it is so plentiful and often free to use, it is easy to imagine that it costs very little. But this is not the case. The cheapest urban parking space in America, an 8½-by-18-foot piece of asphalt on relatively worthless land, costs about four thousand dollars to create—and not much urban land is worthless. The most expensive parking space, in an underground parking garage, can cost forty thou-

---

[*]Donald Shoup, *The High Cost of Free Parking*, 25. Shoup's book is 751 pages long and weighs three and a quarter pounds, but after we are done, you will want to read it. Not everything in this chapter is from that book, but so much of it comes from there that I am happy if its author gets credit for the whole chapter.

sand dollars or more to build. Parking spaces under Seattle's Pacific Place Shopping Center, built by the city, cost over sixty thousand dollars each.* In between those extremes is the standard aboveground urban parking structure, which can usually be built for between twenty and thirty thousand dollars per space.

Given the size of most parking lots, these numbers add up quickly. The twelve-hundred-space Pacific Place garage cost $73 million. Shoup calculates that "the cost of all parking spaces in the U.S. exceeds the value of all cars and may even exceed the value of all roads."[4] There are also the ongoing costs of taxes, management, and maintenance. If the journal *Parking Professional* is to be believed, more than a million Americans make their living in some aspect of the "parking profession."[5] These people have to be paid. Somewhat conservatively, and based on the study of hundreds of parking lots, Shoup estimates the monthly cost of a structured parking space to be at least $125 per month,[6] or roughly $4 per day.

This amount seems reasonable, and actually quite easy to pay for. Presuming a conservative 50 percent occupancy from nine to five, that's only a dollar per hour. So, do most parking structures cover their costs? Far from it. One study of parking garages in the Mid-Atlantic region determined that annual operating revenue per space ranged between 26 and 36 percent of annual cost.[7]

I found a similar circumstance in Lowell, where I was told that the revenue from the city's six public garages was paying all the debt service on those garages. Digging a bit deeper, I learned that five of those garages, from the eighties, had already paid off their bonds—with considerable taxpayer help. So, in

---

*Shoup, *The High Cost of Free Parking*, 190. Shoup notes that the world record holders are in Japan, with one underground structure in Kawasaki costing $414,000 per space. The entire garage cost over $157 million.

actuality, the revenue from all six of the city's garages was covering only the debt service on the city's one new garage.

This circumstance exists all over the United States, principally because cities and other sponsors keep parking prices artificially low. Because there are so many parking spaces, this cumulative subsidy was calculated a decade ago at between $127 billion and $374 billion a year,[8] which puts it in the range of our national defense budget. This number seems preposterous, until you consider that the typical parking space in the United States is not in a pay-to-park garage at all, but alongside a condo cluster, inside an office park, or in front of a Walmart, where admission is free.

If parking is "free" or underpriced in so much of the United States, who is actually paying for it? The answer is: we all are, whether we use it or not. Shoup puts it this way:

> Initially, the developer pays for the required parking, but soon the tenants do, and then their customers, and so on, until the price of parking has diffused everywhere in the economy. When we shop in a store, eat in a restaurant, or see a movie, we pay for parking indirectly, because its cost is included in the price of merchandise, meals, and theater tickets. We unknowingly support our cars with almost every commercial transaction we make, because a small share of the money changing hands pays for parking.[9]

The ramifications of this situation are disturbing. Nobody can opt out of paying for parking. People who walk, bike, or take transit are bankrolling those who drive. In so doing, they are making driving cheaper and thus more prevalent, which in turn undermines the quality of walking, biking, and transit.

INDUCED DEMAND REDUX

Is this beginning to sound familiar? Like roadways in general, all this free and underpriced parking contributes to a circumstance in which a massive segment of our national economy has been disconnected from the free market, such that individuals are no longer able to act rationally. Or, more accurately, in acting rationally, individuals are acting against their own self-interest.

All in all, Shoup calculates that the subsidy for employer-paid parking amounts to twenty-two cents per mile driven to work, and thus reduces the price of automotive commuting by a remarkable 71 percent. Eliminating this subsidy would have the same impact as an additional gasoline tax of between $1.27 and $3.74 a gallon.[10] That is a price hike that would change many people's driving habits.

This subsidy could perhaps be justified if it produced some greater good for society, but it only produces one benefit: cheaper parking. How does it perform in terms of other important measures? Well, it worsens air and water quality, speeds global warming, increases energy consumption, raises the cost of housing, decreases public revenue, undermines public transportation, increases traffic congestion, damages the quality of the public realm, escalates suburban sprawl, threatens historic buildings, weakens social capital, and worsens public health, to name a few things.[*] And you wanted free parking why?

ADDICTION MADE LAW

But businesses should be allowed to provide parking to lure customers, you might protest. Fair enough. But in America, such parking is not just allowed; it's required. Some cities, like Monterey

---

[*] Shoup, 585. All these criteria except the final three are listed by Shoup.

Park, California, not only require on-site parking, but insist that it be provided to visitors free of charge.[11]

These requirements are powerfully disruptive to the way cities function. A true master of the long-form analogy, Shoup describes the situation this way:

> If cities required restaurants to offer a free dessert with each dinner, the price of every dinner would soon increase to include the cost of dessert. To ensure that restaurants didn't skimp on the size of the required desserts, cities would have to set precise "minimum calorie requirements." Some diners would pay for desserts they didn't eat, and others would eat sugary desserts they wouldn't have ordered had they paid for them separately. The consequences would undoubtedly include an epidemic of obesity, diabetes, and heart disease. A few food-conscious cities like New York and San Francisco might prohibit free desserts, but most cities would continue to require them. Many people would get angry at even the thought of paying for the desserts they had eaten free for so long.[12]

Look at any city, suburban, or rural zoning code, and you will see page after page of rules about parking. Of the six hundred or so land uses that we planners have managed to identify, each has its own minimum parking requirement.[13] Shoup documents how these requirements have often been generated from a bare minimum of data and can bear little resemblance to reality.[14] A gas station requires 1.5 spaces per nozzle. A bowling alley requires 1 space per employee, plus 5 spaces per lane. A swimming pool requires 1 space per twenty-five hundred gallons of water.* These

---

*Shoup, 80. I am particularly enamored of this requirement, which apparently supposes that a ten-foot-deep pool holds twice as many swimmers as a five-foot-deep pool, presumably stacked in two layers like a deluxe assortment of chocolates.

requirements are then passed from city to city and town to town,[15] almost always resulting in the same outcome: too much parking.

How much? In 2010, the first nationwide count determined that there are half a billion empty parking spaces in America at any given time.[16] More to our purposes, a 2002 survey of Seattle's Central Business District found that, during times of peak demand, almost four out of ten parking spaces were empty.[17] This condition of oversupply occurs most often in central cities, and is typically the result of downtowns importing zoning standards from the suburbs, where no alternatives to driving exist.

Even Washington, D.C., suffers from this phenomenon. When my wife and I built our house in the District, we were required to provide an on-site parking space, even though we didn't own a car, our property was three blocks from a subway stop, and none of our neighbors had one; ample parking was available on the street. Ironically, parking on our lot would have required removing an on-street parking space—replacing a public good with a private one—trashing a granite curb, and violating a public sidewalk with our driveway. Not owning a car, I designed a carless house, and threw our fate to the Board of Zoning Appeals. Eventually, reason prevailed, but it took nine months and a public battle that was written up in *USA Today*.[18] I think it is accurate to say that almost no other designer would have bothered. Four years later, the code has yet to be fixed.

Whenever I feel like complaining about our own Washington parking struggle, I remind myself of the story of DC USA. In the mid-2000s, construction began on what was to become the District's largest retail complex, a $145 million, 500,000-square-foot colossus anchored by Target, Best Buy, and Bed Bath & Beyond. Because the development was located at a Metro stop in the heart of Columbia Heights, with thirty-six thousand residents within a ten-minute walk,[19] the city generously modified its parking requirements. Rather than insisting on its obligatory four spaces per one thousand square feet—a truly suburban standard—the

District allowed the number to be cut in half.[20] Despite the designers' predictions that this was still way too much parking, the project went ahead with a $40 million, taxpayer-funded underground garage holding one thousand cars.

Fast-forward to 2008: DC USA has become a resounding success, having brought new life to a struggling neighborhood, thanks in part to its pedestrian-oriented design. Shops are doing even more business than expected. And the parking garage is empty—so empty that its managers routinely shut off one of its two levels completely, an unvisited $20 million underground air museum. From February through July, average peak use never rises above three hundred cars, and at no time does occupancy top 47 percent.[21]

This was an expensive lesson, a $100,000/month *I told you so* for the District and its taxpayers—now in its fifth year—as parking revenues fail to cover debt service on the garage. It was just the kick in the pants the city needed to finally rewrite its fifty-year-old regulations to eliminate parking minimums for new shops, offices, and apartments near Metro stations.[22] They have decided to leave commercial parking provision to the free market, as Donald Shoup recommends.

Even smaller suburban cities are beginning to find that their parking requirements are routinely too high. A useful experiment was conducted in progressive Palo Alto, California. Real estate developers were allowed to cheat on their parking requirements by as much as 50 percent if the land area saved was turned into a natural "landscape reserve" that could be converted to parking if the need arose. Not one such reserve has yet to make that conversion.[23]

THE COST OF REQUIRED PARKING

Even in cities with high residential densities and great transit systems, ample parking encourages driving that would not occur

without it. As Shoup likes to say, "Off-street parking requirements are a fertility drug for cars."[24] We have already discussed
most of driving's attendant woes, from global warming to obesity,
but it would be useful here to focus briefly on some of the specific social and personal costs inflicted by the on-site parking
requirement in particular.

In *Suburban Nation*, we coined the term "Pensacola Parking Syndrome" to describe the fate of so many historic cities that
had eventually managed to satisfy their parking demand. They
achieved this condition by replacing beautiful old buildings with
ugly parking lots—in such number that nobody wanted to go
downtown anymore.[25]

Certainly, the destruction of architectural masterpieces is
one of the most obvious and upsetting manifestations of modern
parking pressures. In Detroit, a parking garage even sits beneath
the rococo vaults of the reamed-out 1926 Michigan Theatre—
built, ironically, on the site where Henry Ford invented his automobile. In Buffalo, where 50 percent of the historic city center
has become parking lots, one commenter wryly observed, "if our
master plan is to demolish all of downtown, then we're only half-
way there."[26]

These days, however, with preservationists wielding greater
power, the harm perpetrated by parking demands is often more
subtle, taking the form not of destruction, but of obstruction:
things failing to happen. Most empty urban buildings—historic
or otherwise—sit on properties of limited size, with limited opportunities for increasing their parking supply. Yet many changes
in use bring with them an uptick in the parking requirement.
Shoup notes how replacing a defunct furniture store with a new
bicycle shop would typically require tripling the size of the parking lot.* Where are those spaces supposed to come from?

---

*Shoup, 153. Shoup also tells the story of an entrepreneur in South Berkeley who wanted
to replace a failed guitar shop with a restaurant, but was defeated by a twelve-space
increase in the parking requirement.

The result, of course, is that nothing gets done and old buildings stay empty. Similarly, a thriving restaurant that wants to add sidewalk dining—something every city now says it wants—can't do so without increasing its parking supply, often an impossibility.[27] The only path to providing more parking in urban areas is typically to replace surface parking lots with multistory decks, at tremendous cost. That money is increasingly difficult to come by.

This parking-induced commercial stasis is only half the story. The other half is the great burden that parking minimums place on affordability, especially for housing, and most especially in those communities that most need it. Developers in San Francisco estimate that the city's one-space-per-unit requirement adds 20 percent to the cost of affordable housing. Shoup calculates that eliminating this requirement would allow 24 percent more San Franciscans to buy homes. Even the city's chief comprehensive planner, Amit Ghosh, admits that "we're forcing people to build parking that people cannot afford."[28]

Similarly, a study in Oakland found that requiring one parking space per home "increased housing costs by 18 percent and reduced density by 30 percent."[29] Back in Palo Alto, Alma Place, a nonprofit 107-unit single-room occupancy hotel, was granted a reduced parking requirement of 0.67 spaces per unit. It was later determined that this scant requirement still increased construction costs by a whopping 38 percent.[30]

The larger question is why the future residents of Alma Place—Walk Score 95, for God's sake—should need parking at all. Does a household located three blocks from a train station in one of America's most walkable and employment-loaded communities need to own a car? Did I mention that the train station is flanked by more than three hundred commuter parking spaces that all sit empty overnight?[31]

The answer is not that future residents would come with cars, but that current residents were worried about spillover parking on their streets. Even more troubling was the city's refusal to allow the developer to charge for parking. The housing corporation was prohibited from charging a parking fee of one hundred dollars per month, which would have reduced non-drivers' rents by about 10 percent.* So, even among the city's poorest citizens, the pedestrians are subsidizing the drivers. So much for "progressive" Palo Alto.

But before we beat that city up too badly, let's turn our accusing gaze back to the Green Metropolis itself, where the New York City Housing Authority still maintains parking minimums for its publicly assisted housing stock. These minimums have caused the city to abandon plans to add much-needed street-edge buildings to several of its 1960s "tower in the park" projects. Currently, one such project, in Brownsville, Brooklyn, hangs in the balance. It would replace surface parking lots with housing, shops, schools, and gardens, but it is being held up by parking minimums—despite being directly adjacent to two stops of the 2, 3, 4, and 5 subway lines straight to Manhattan. The chairman of the housing authority admits sheepishly that "certain zoning rules may need to be reconsidered."[32]

SOME SMARTER PLACES

If you've been to the former artists' colony of Carmel-by-the-Sea, California, you've probably enjoyed strolling its picturesque main street, Ocean Avenue. This would have been due not to the smooth quality of the pavement—spike heels require a city permit, thanks to a spate of trip-and-fall lawsuits in the twenties[33]—but rather to all its other positive pedestrian qualities, including an absence of visible parking lots.

Ocean Avenue is free of off-street parking because it is

---

*Shoup, *The High Cost of Free Parking*, 150. Rent reduction was predicted at fifty dollars, with initial average rents in the five-hundred-dollar range.

illegal. Instead of providing parking lots for their customers and employees, businesses pay in-lieu fees that help finance shared city parking spaces located a few blocks away. This strategy has helped to create a unique collection of midblock courtyards and walkways, as well as ensuring a maximum amount of sidewalk activity, since nobody arrives at their destination from the rear. Carmel is now one of dozens of American cities that handle downtown parking this way, including Orlando, Chapel Hill, and Lake Forest, Illinois. In-lieu fees in these cities typically range from about seven to ten thousand dollars per space not provided, which is roughly in line with the cost of building a space in an asphalt surface lot. In Beverly Hills, where land is more valuable and most parking is structured, developers pay over $20,000 per space. In the more lefty Carmel, it's $27,520.[34]

What's most interesting—and perhaps a bit frustrating—about this solution is that it does not address the parking supply directly. Every one of these cities still has a downtown parking requirement, some quite high.[35] But instead of providing parking, businesses are only required to pay for it, which allows the parking to be located in the right place and, importantly, shared. When parking is no longer the exclusive property of an individual business, it becomes much more efficient. A space that serves an office during the day can serve a restaurant in the evening and a resident overnight. So, by simultaneously setting parking minimums and outlawing private parking lots, cities are able to indirectly reduce the amount of parking that has to be provided. Eventually, as real life determines the number of shared spaces that are actually needed, a city can adjust its in-lieu fees downward. Or it can keep them steady and pocket the difference.

For large employers, California has pioneered a second powerful strategy for managing parking, called "parking cash-out." The California Health and Safety Code requires many businesses that offer free employee parking to give their workers the option of trading that parking space for its cash equivalent. This is an ingenious law, because it is all carrot and no stick. Cities are required to reduce each business's parking requirement by the number of employees who cash out, thus placing no greater burden on the employer, while providing a great incentive for alternative transportation. On average, businesses that offered the cash-out option saw their number of driving commuters drop by 11 percent. In downtown Los Angeles, one employer saw its parking demand drop by 24 percent.[36]

These two strategies, in-lieu payments and parking cash-out, are a great start at decoupling the cost of parking from all the other activities in which it has become imbedded—that is, hidden—so that parking demand can once again behave according to the principles of the free market. This concept of decoupling makes so much sense that one would expect it to have become commonplace. Instead, it is rare, because residents of places like Palo Alto fear that costly off-street parking will cause bargain seekers to overwhelm their precious curbside parking. And they are correct in this fear, because most cities lack a comprehensive parking policy that deals with off-street and on-street parking together. Until this mandate is met, in-lieu payments and parking cash-out can serve as good transitional strategies toward a more ambitious goal, which is the elimination of off-street parking requirements entirely.

Abolishing the off-street parking requirement is one of the three cornerstones of Shoup's theory, because it would allow the market to determine how much parking is needed. He notes that "removing off-street parking requirements will not eliminate off-street parking, but will instead stimulate an active commercial market for it."[37] This would bring U.S. policy more in line with that of Western Europe. Shoup describes the situation as follows:

> American cities put a floor under the parking supply to satisfy the peak demand for free parking, and then cap development density to limit vehicle trips. European cities,

in contrast, often cap the number of parking spaces to avoid congesting the roads and combine this strategy with a floor on allowed development density to encourage walking, cycling, and public transport. That is, Americans require parking and limit density, while Europeans require density and limit parking.[38]

Such a concept seems unlikely to win many followers on this side of the pond, but it is exactly what the free market creates all by itself in America's most walkable communities. In Manhattan, developers do not feel any need to provide parking for their apartments, stores, and offices, so the outcome is more Düsseldorf than Dallas. That outcome would be unimaginable with a parking requirement in place. Eliminating parking minimums simply allows developers to give their customers what they want. But, as we will discuss ahead, it is only politically viable when combined with a safety net that protects current residents' status quo.

THE PROBLEM WITH CHEAP CURBSIDE PARKING

Cheap and plentiful off-street parking is only half the problem. The other half is what happens on the streets, and here even New York City gets it dead wrong. Because if curbside parking is not priced properly, the resulting perversity of the overall parking regime creates vast inefficiencies that are costly for drivers and nondrivers alike.

Let's take Manhattan. Off-street parking is roughly $15 for the first hour in most locations, while curbside parking costs just $3. Is it any wonder that the city's streets are choked with double-parked cars and people hunting for parking? Underpriced curb parking is no fairer than giving random discounts on other municipal services like water or electricity based upon who circles the block the longest, and just as counterproductive.

A study of six different urban sites found that roughly a third of all traffic congestion was made up of people trying to find a parking spot. In one Los Angeles neighborhood, Westwood Village, it was twice that amount—and between 1:00 and 2:00 p.m., an astounding 96 percent of cars on the road were circling for parking.[39]

Some version of this condition exists in most American cities. In downtown Chicago, curbside parking costs one-thirteenth as much as off-street parking.[40] The outcome of this market inefficiency is not just congestion and all its attendant woes—pollution, time wasted, slow emergency response—but also reduced revenue to area businesses. This counterintuitive fact can be surprising to the businesses themselves, who routinely fight bitterly against any effort to raise meter rates. These merchants forget the origin of the parking meter, in Oklahoma City, as a tool to improve business revenue. Shoup quotes an *American City* reporter from 1937:

> Merchants and shoppers are both in favor of them. When one side of the street has them, merchants on the other side demand them. When one town has them, the merchants of nearby towns demand them, showing that they draw out-of-town shoppers rather than driving them away.[41]

Why were these first meters so popular? Because they reduced overcrowding and hassle, but also because they increased turnover, ensuring more customers per hour. The result was more sales and dramatically higher downtown property values.[42] The same calculus holds true today, as underpriced curbside parking scares away potential customers who believe that there is no place to park, even as nearby parking lots sit half empty. As Shoup notes, "If it takes only five minutes to drive somewhere else, why spend fifteen cruising for parking?"[43]

I encountered just this condition in Lowell, where on-street parking became free at 6:00 p.m., while parking structures still charged admission. The result was that residents coming home from work would rush into the parking spaces on restaurant row, leaving no room for the dinner crowd.

THE RIGHT PRICE

Which leads us to Shoup's second key recommendation, that on-street parking be priced at a level that results in an 85 percent occupancy rate at all times.[44] This number may seem a bit low, but it corresponds with roughly one empty space per block face, just the right amount to ensure Daddy Warbucks a spot near the furrier. Because it is precisely the shoppers with dollars to spare who have the most to offer your Main Street merchants.

In its most sophisticated form, this approach means true variable congestion pricing, which we will discuss in a minute. But for many cities, a perfectly adequate outcome can be achieved simply by raising meter rates a notch, especially if they are currently set at zero. This was the case in both Aspen in the nineties and, more recently, Ventura, California.

Shoup reports on how, by 1990, Aspen's downtown merchants were suffering from overcrowded curbside parking. The city responded by building an expensive parking garage, but that structure sat half empty as the parking crush continued. Finally, the city proposed charging one dollar per hour on-street, and all hell broke loose.[45]

Opponents, mostly local employees, mounted a noisy "Honk if You Hate Paid Parking" campaign. This was quickly met by a rogue "Honk if You Love Dirty Air" campaign, in reference to all the cruising and double parking that had become the norm. Paid parking eventually prevailed and the new rates took effect in 1995. Almost immediately, the opponents realized that they had been wrong. Now the municipal parking structure is well used, the on-street parking and cruising are under control, the businesses are thriving, and the city receives over half a million dollars a year in new parking revenue, most of it from tourists.[46]

In Ventura, Shoupista Mayor Bill Fulton introduced on-street parking rates of one dollar per hour, aiming toward 85 percent occupancy.[47] In addition to being mayor, Fulton is a city planner, and his blog is worth following. On the momentous morning of September 14, 2010, he posted that "only 30 minutes after we instituted the parking management program, it is working." The employee vehicles that had previously crowded the curbs were happily stowed away in nearby lots.[48] Fulton went on to add:

> Some shoppers have complained over the past few months that parking at the mall is free, so why should they pay to park downtown? The answer . . . is that you're paying for access to a few hundred premium spaces. . . . After all, all the mall parking spaces are far away from the stores—farther than even the most remote free lot downtown. If it was possible to drive right inside the mall and park in front of your favorite store, don't you think the mall would charge for that space? And don't you think some people who think it's worth it would pay the price?[49]

The city plans to adjust rates as necessary: if parking use falls below 80 percent, the prices will be lowered until occupancy hits the exalted 85.[50] It's important to stress that the math works both ways. In Davenport, Iowa, the combination of free parking lots and curbside meters caused a ghost-town effect: nobody parked at the curb, the place felt dead, and drivers sped recklessly along empty streets. Our planning team convinced the city to reprice the on-street parking at zero, a regime that will remain in effect until scarcity sets in. That change immediately improved activity downtown. It also made us some friends, but perhaps for the wrong reasons. Unfortunately, we were unable to stop the mayor from decapitating a meter with the Jaws of Life, which may have sent the misleading message of *free parking forever.*

Neither Aspen, Ventura, nor Davenport has been fully studied, but the great investigation on right-priced curb parking occurred in central London in 1965. It was found that a fourfold increase in parking price shortened the average park-and-visit time by 66 percent, vastly increasing turnover for merchants. The average time spent searching for parking dropped from 6.1 minutes per trip to a mere 62 seconds.[51]

For a twenty-first-century version, we turn to San Francisco, which, thanks to Shoup, has recently introduced a true congestion-pricing regime. For seven thousand spaces in eight key neighborhoods—25 percent of the city's metered parking—prices are being adjusted block by block and hour by hour to achieve a goal of 80 percent maximum occupancy.* This means rates ranging from as little as twenty-five cents to as much as six dollars per hour. The system also includes the fourteen city-owned garages in the pilot area, as it must, since their pricing needs to be coordinated if drivers are to make wise choices. As you might expect, this being San Francisco, the project is fully supported by online real-time data, including a smartphone app that tells you how many spaces are available on any given street, and how much they cost.[52] The sfpark.org website is really quite a marvel.

Such a parking system, which includes thousands of newly embedded car sensors, does not come cheap. It was supported largely by a $20 million U.S. Department of Transportation grant[53]—one wonders what it would have cost without federal funding—and we will soon know how well it works. If it performs anywhere near as well as expected, it will earn back its huge

---

*The current SFPark on-street pricing policy (as of April 11, 2011) causes prices to rise or fall whenever occupancy rises above 80 percent or below 60 percent. Why these numbers are below Shoup's 85 percent is not explained.

price tag in short order, through increased meter receipts. This income is not the goal of the exercise, but it's nice to know it's there. Indeed, it is only because these systems pay for themselves that we can expect them to catch on.

If there are no surprises in San Francisco, full-fledged congestion-priced parking is something that many cities will want to try. But, given its novelty and significant start-up cost, smaller cities may elect not to spend millions chasing perfection, when *good enough* is close at hand. A simple repricing of downtown spaces and parking lots may solve 90 percent of most cities' parking problems. That said, since the start-up costs are easily bondable and the potential income so great, opting out of a full-fledged congestion-pricing regime could turn out to be a pound-foolish choice.

A TALE OF TWO CITIES

As if we weren't convinced, Shoup has a final morality lesson to teach, and that is the story of the two Southern California shopping districts of Old Pasadena and Westwood Village. In the late eighties, these two downtowns were fairly similar. They were roughly the same size, both were in historic sections of larger cities (Pasadena and Los Angeles), and both had the standard collection of review boards and business-improvement districts. Both had limited on-street parking and ample off-street parking. Both were challenged economically, but by no means in trouble. If anything, Westwood Village was in better shape, as it was surrounded by both a higher density of housing and a wealthier customer base. In fact, Shoup describes how residents of Pasadena used to drive twenty minutes in order to shop in Westwood Village.[54]

Then, in the early nineties, the two districts went in dramatically different directions. While both were struggling with overcrowded on-street parking, only Old Pasadena raised its parking rates, installing 690 new meters. While both maintained a conventional off-street parking requirement, only Old Pasadena allowed in-lieu fees, so that developers could pay cash in support of municipal lots rather than build additional parking themselves.[55]

What happened over the next decade was as shocking in reality as it was predictable in theory. Old Pasadena staged a brilliant revival, while Westwood Village entered a steady economic decline that continues to this day. Now residents of Westwood drive to Old Pasadena to shop. Westwood's curbs are crumbling, while the sidewalks of Old Pasadena boast new tree grates, fancy lighting, and street furniture. Not only does each parking meter in Pasadena generate an average of $1,712 in annual revenue for the city, but sales tax receipts are way up. Indeed, the city's sales-tax revenue tripled in the first six years after the meters were installed.[56]

While it is always easy to park in Old Pasadena, the average shopper in Westwood Village circles for 8.3 minutes before either finding a spot or giving up. Shoup delights in telling us how Westwood cruisers cumulatively log a total of 426 vehicle hours per day, covering more distance than a trip across the United States. Over a year, this adds up to thirty-eight trips around the globe.[57]

In the interest of telling the whole story, it is worth spending another minute describing exactly how boneheaded Westwood Village was. Faced with the perception that a parking shortage was to blame for their economic woes, community leaders responded by cutting the price of on-street parking in half. ("Adam Smith, please call your office!") Meanwhile, the city continued to enforce its draconian off-street "replacement parking" requirement, which effectively made redevelopment impossible. Even though the village's vast supply of asphalt parking lots typically held 1,250 unused spaces at peak hour, any developers who wanted to build on these lots were required to both meet their parking quota and replace half of the removed spaces.[58] This rule, still in force, effectively amounts to a requirement for expensive parking decks where there is already an oversupply of off-street parking.

Westwood's ineptitude calls attention to the fact that parking decisions are never made in a vacuum and political pressures from an uninformed public can often sway the outcome. Indeed, in Old Pasadena, things almost went the other way. When the city first proposed installing meters, it was fought vehemently by downtown merchants, who were convinced that they would lose all their business to the mall. This battle dragged on for two years before a compromise was reached.[59] Interestingly, it was this compromise that gave the new parking regime what may be its most powerful feature.

WHAT SHOULD WE DO WITH ALL THIS MONEY?

The final bone that the city threw to its reluctant merchants was this: all the net revenue from the parking meters would pay for physical improvements and new public services in Old Pasadena. And why not? This was free money, over a million dollars a year, and it was easy to identify where it was coming from. It wasn't like anybody else deserved it.

This creative leap leads us to Shoup's third cornerstone, the institution of "parking benefit districts" that put meter revenues to work locally.[60] In addition to improving sidewalks, trees, lighting, and street furniture, these districts can bury overhead wires, renovate storefronts, hire public service officers, and of course keep everything spic-and-span. They can also construct the public parking lots a block away that serve employees and shopper overflow. In Pasadena, meter revenues even paid for converting a collection of run-down rear alleys into an intricate network of pedestrian spaces.[61]

Since most of the parkers are from out of town and pricing is based on what they are willing to pay, there are few losers in this bargain, as long as employees can find parking within a reasonable walking distance. As Shoup puts it, "If nonresidents pay for curb parking, and the city spends its money to benefit the residents, charging for curb parking can become a popular policy rather than the political third rail it often is today."[62]

This is true enough for retail areas, but what about principally residential streets that have become overcrowded? What about the residents of Palo Alto who, fearing competition for on-street spaces, fought against reduced off-street parking requirements? The third rail that threatens to kill Shoup's two main proposals is not about where the money goes, but about the fact that it is just so hard to take away anybody's free anything. This is the reason that on-street parking remains free of charge in much of New York City, of all places.

Shoup is not ignorant of this fact, quoting George Costanza's famous rant: "My father didn't pay for parking, my mother, my brother, nobody. It's like going to a prostitute. Why should I pay when, if I apply myself, maybe I can get it for free."[63] It is one thing to put parking meters in front of a bunch of stores and quite another to put them on a street of houses. That is why, where theory meets reality, we may need to bend the rules a little, by using residential parking permits. These, too, can be priced at market value for maximum efficiency, but they must sometimes be deployed at a low cost to win over residents who stand in the way of a larger public benefit, like keeping affordable housing affordable. And, you didn't hear it from me, but once residents get used to the idea of paying for a coveted parking pass—even just a "processing fee" of twenty bucks a year—you would be surprised how quickly they are willing to pay considerably more.

Not having been involved in the Palo Alto fiasco, I am reluctant to suggest that there was an easy solution, but it is likely that a properly managed parking pass proposal might have turned the tide. What was certainly missing, among all the parking policy, was a parking plan, and such a comprehensive plan is ultimately what every "over-parked" place in America needs. This plan must include on-street pricing, off-street pricing, in-lieu payments supporting a collective supply, parking benefit districts, and residential permits where needed. Above all, it must be managed comprehensively with an eye toward community success, not just meter revenue. Parking is a public good, and it must be managed for the public good. Such management takes full advantage of the free market but—this is important—it is not the free market.[64] The single largest land use in every American city is very much that city's business.

A BARGAIN AT $1.2 BILLION

So, if parking is a public good, why did Mayor Richard M. Daley sell it off? This is a question many of us asked when the otherwise heroic Daley presided over the lease of Chicago's thirty-six thousand meters to Morgan Stanley for the next seventy-five years. The answer probably lies in the date—December 2008, the depths of the city's financial crisis—and the price tag— $1,200,000,000.[65]

This $1.2 billion tells us a number of things. One of them is that $20 million for a congestion-pricing regime in San Francisco is chump change. Another is that there is obviously a lot of money in privately managed parking, and, that as Chicago goes, so may go the nation. As of this writing, New Haven is one of several cash-strapped cities working toward a deal. Many have already privatized their public garages.

Unsurprisingly, Chicago's sale brought with it a dramatic hike in on-street parking rates. Neighborhood spots previously available at 25 cents an hour are on their way up to $2.00. Prices inside the Loop, already high, will more than double, to $6.50 an hour.[66]

In the short term, this strategy could perhaps be described as the wrong path to the right result. Greedy investors are pulling off what the city couldn't do, which is to bring the price of curbside parking in line with its value. As demand falls closer to supply, Shoup's 85 percent ideal may be achieved. But who's to say it will stop there? As any purveyor of private parking lots will tell you, an 85 percent–occupied lot at ten dollars a pop is less profitable than a half-empty lot at twenty dollars—and few parking-lot owners have a citywide monopoly. Morgan Stanley maximizing its return on the street does not necessarily bear any relationship to the city getting the most out of its parking in terms of all the other things that parking affects, including drivers' speed, retail profitability, and property values.

That's the scary part. The more practical frustration brought on by the Chicago sale concerns our larger discussion about neighborhood parking as a comprehensive system. Communities can only be their best if on-street parking, off-street parking, parking permits, and parking regulations are all managed collectively. In the past, this has hardly ever happened, but things are beginning to change. Places like Old Pasadena are showing us that well-managed parking is both possible and profitable. The Shoupistas are ready for their day in the sun. It would be a pity if, on the cusp of this parking revolution, cities were to sell away to the highest bidder their ability to make use of this powerful tool.

STEP 4: LET TRANSIT WORK

*Where America sits; It's the neighborhoods, stupid; Don't mess
with Dallas; The other kind of transit; What streetcars do; Transit
for drivers; Trains versus buses; Zip it if you can*

If I had to pick one word that best describes why good public transportation is a vital part of walkable cities, it would be this: dating. When I lived in Miami in my thirties, it would have been possible for me to live, work, and play all in the same neighborhood. That neighborhood could have been South Beach, Coconut Grove, downtown Coral Gables, or a few other walkable places. But I was single and looking to meet someone, and I wasn't willing to limit the gene pool to a neighborhood the size of a small town when an entire city was theoretically at my disposal. Given the sorry state of public transit in Miami, this meant buying a car.

I wasn't the only one. Put in more universal terms, it could be said that people who live in a city want to have access to everything that city has to offer. If the vast majority of those things cannot be reached conveniently via transit, then people of means buy cars and you end up with a driving city. As the city grows, it grows around the car. Its neighborhood structure dissolves and its streets widen. Walking becomes less useful or pleasant and, soon, less likely or even imaginable.

This relationship between transit and walking is borne out by the data, which clearly show that American cities with larger numbers of rail and bus commuters also have more pedestrian commuters. When more than a quarter of workers take transit, more than 10 percent go on foot. When fewer than 5 percent take transit, fewer than 3 percent go on foot.[1] It isn't just that transit users walk more, but that *non*transit users also walk more in cities that are shaped around transit. For the most part, cities support either driving or everything else.

Most American cities are driving cities and will remain so for years to come. For these cities, transit can still play an important role, by enhancing the walkability of the few walkable places and by connecting these places—more on that below. In contrast, a number of American cities, like Boston, Chicago, and San Francisco, are resolutely car-optional, and more than a few others may be on the verge of becoming so. Baltimore, Minneapolis, Denver, Seattle . . . as these cities and others invest in well-planned transit, and as younger populations make a conscious effort to drive less, it is possible to imagine a future of more comprehensive transit-based walkability.

As vastly different as these types of cities are, they all share one thing, which is that somebody in them is probably laboring feverishly to dramatically transform their transit system. From the Coalition for Alternative Transportation in Bethlehem, Pennsylvania, whose leaders steadfastly refuse to drive, to John Schneider of Protransit, who is single-handedly bringing streetcars to Cincinnati, someone out there is hunting down federal and state dollars, leading fact-finding junkets, and otherwise fighting the good fight for mass transit. And half of these people are wasting their time, because their efforts are not sufficiently informed by the relationship between transit and walking.

With rare exceptions, every transit trip begins and ends with a walk. As a result, while walkability benefits from good transit, good transit relies absolutely on walkability.

WHERE AMERICA SITS

Currently, only 1.5 percent of all trips in the United States are made on public transportation.[2] In our star cities of Washington, Chicago, and San Francisco, that number is closer to 5 percent, and the New York region, unsurprisingly, tops the list at 9 percent. But what happens when you cross the border? Toronto, with a residential density roughly a third of New York's, has a 14 percent transit share. Across the Atlantic, Barcelona and Rome hit 35 percent. Tokyo tops 60 and Hong Kong, the global leader, has reached 73 percent.[3]

The American numbers are misleading, however, as they are measured over entire metropolitan areas, and nobody in the world can match America's sprawl. Zoom in to the central cities themselves, and you find a more encouraging picture. Roughly a third of Washingtonians and San Franciscans take transit to work, and the majority of New Yorkers do. Perennial sprawl stars like Jacksonville and Nashville, on the other hand, hover below 2 percent, no matter how you measure them.[4]

These numbers are principally the result of how each city has chosen to grow, or not grow, around the automobile. European and East Asian countries, lacking America's wealth and oil reserves, chose to maintain and expand existing rail infrastructure throughout the twentieth century, while America threw most of its trains away. In 1902, every U.S. city with a population of ten thousand or more had its own streetcar system.[5] At midcentury, Los Angeles was served by more than a thousand electric trolleys a day.[6] These were torn out in a vast criminal conspiracy that is as well documented* as it was inevitable. It's

---

*This conspiracy is best summarized in Terry Tamminen's *Lives per Gallon*. As related by Tamminen, GM's Alfred Sloan, Jr., faced in 1922 with record losses, teamed up with Standard Oil, Phillips Petroleum, Firestone Tire and Rubber, and Mack Truck to create a shell company, National City Lines, "to quietly buy up the nation's mass-transit agencies and scrap the electric trains they operated. National City Lines could then replace

easy to get mad at General Motors and forget that, at the time, most cities and citizens delighted over the change from old-fashioned streetcars to streamlined buses. The real transition, of course, was from dependence on a public system to liberation via the private automobile, albeit subsidized formidably with public dollars. We trashed our trains because we wanted to and nobody said we couldn't. As David Owen comments, "There was no public force in the United States, in those days, that could have held back the death of the streetcar, even if anyone had had the will to try."[7]

Now that we have begun to understand the true costs of that choice—including watching our automotive liberation obliterated by congestion—most Americans are ready for something different. According to America's Finest News Source, *The Onion*, "98 percent of U.S. commuters favor public transportation for others." This fictional article described a campaign mounted by the American Public Transportation Association—slogan: "Take the Bus . . . I'll Be Glad You Did"—that was remarkably insightful in its recognition of the impacts of one person's transit on another's traffic, known as the "multiplier effect." In San Francisco, for example, every passenger mile traveled by rail replaces nine miles traveled by car.[8] I can also recommend *The Onion*'s video report: "Tired of traffic? A new DOT report urges drivers 'honk.'"

More seriously, a national poll funded by Transportation for America found that the average respondent would allocate 41 percent of transportation funding for public transit versus 37 percent for roads. In another poll, the devoutly nonideological Consumer Preference Survey, respondents favored public trans-

---

the trains with buses made and fueled by the conspirators. In the process, it could reduce mass-transit service and promote automobile sales as a more convenient option to millions of consumers." Also, although "the conspiracy was proven in court . . . the corporations involved were fined only $5,000 and the executives fined just $1 apiece because the judge determined that there wasn't much anyone could do about the lost mass transit" (110–11).

portation over road building as a solution to congestion by almost three to one.* The actual funding allocation currently favors roads four to one over transit,[9] so it would seem that a major correction is in order.

If only our governments were as responsive to public opinion as they seem to be in Western Australia. Emboldened by a poll that showed strong support for transferring road funds to non-automotive transportation, the state government reversed a five-to-one roads-to-transit spending ratio to one to five. This change paid for a new rail system that has increased patronage since the early nineties from 7 million to an astounding 50 million riders per year.[10] Since the shift, a pro-rail platform has led to victory in four state elections.

When American governments do give the people a choice, they tend to invest in transit. Since 2000, over 70 percent of public transportation ballot measures have passed, creating more than $100 billion in transit funding.[11] According to the National Association of Realtors, "Light rail is popular in the communities that have it and voters have shown a remarkable willingness to raise their taxes to pay for it."[12]

Perhaps the voters understand instinctively what the data are now telling us, which is that the typical household savings accrued from good public transit service clearly outpaces the cost of that service. In his study "Raise My Taxes, Please!" Todd Litman of the Victoria Transport Policy Institute compared the fifty largest U.S. cities, of which seven were deemed to have "high-quality" transit service and forty-three were found wanting. He determined that each resident of the seven high-quality cities paid roughly $370 more per year for public transportation than a resident of the other forty-three, but saved $1,040 in vehicle, parking, and road costs. These costs were measured in terms

---

*Thomas Gotschi and Kevin Mills, "Active Transportation for America," 18. Incidentally, respondents also recommended allocating 22 percent for biking and walking versus the 1 percent currently allocated.

of actual dollars spent on goods, services, and taxes, and ignored all the additional indirect savings surrounding congestion, safety, pollution, and health.[13]

The lesson from these data seems clear: big investments in comprehensive citywide transit systems pay off in spades. But it's not that simple, because the study compared cities that were different in many respects beyond transit. Its conclusions imply that building a new transit system can be expected to transform all these other factors as well. But adding trains to Miami does not make it Minneapolis.

IT'S THE NEIGHBORHOODS, STUPID

What are these other factors? Principally, they are *local density* and *neighborhood structure*. I say *local density*, because citywide density can be misleading when a city includes its suburbs or large areas of parkland; what matters is how many people live near the transit line. The transit discussion has of course included density since it began, but, until recently, it has been largely silent on neighborhood structure. This has been a huge mistake.

Neighborhood structure refers to the presence or absence of real neighborhoods, which are technically defined as being compact, diverse, and walkable. A true neighborhood has a center and an edge, and contains a wide variety of activities in close proximity within an armature of pedestrian-friendly streets and public spaces. A traditional city is composed principally of these neighborhoods, interspersed periodically with districts like universities and airports, and corridors like rivers and railways. If you live in an older city, you can probably identify its neighborhoods, like New York's West Village, Tribeca, and SoHo.*

---

*This paragraph and the next restate one of the principal arguments to be found in Andres Duany, Elizabeth Plater-Zyberk, and Jeff Speck's *Suburban Nation*, where the discussion is made in much greater detail.

Compact, diverse, walkable neighborhoods were the basic building blocks of cities from the first nonnomadic settlements over ten thousand years ago until the height of the auto age. What took shape around the measure of the human stride flourished with the advent of rail transport, since the distance between rail stops reinforced the nodal structure of the neighborhood pattern. Only the hegemony of the automobile, with its unprecedented capacity to equalize the entire landscape, allowed the abandonment of the neighborhood in favor of sprawl, which is defined as being vast, homogeneous, and unwalkable. And since it is organized around the automobile, sprawl has no use for transit. As the administrator of any suburban transit agency will tell you, running buses in sprawl is a lose-lose scenario, in which heavy subsidy yields inadequate service.

Even in areas of high density, public transportation cannot thrive in the absence of a neighborhood structure, since it is the nodal and pedestrian-friendly nature of neighborhoods that allows riders to walk to the transit stop. For this reason, the cities that are best poised to put new transit systems to good use are those that grew up around trains in the first place.

This is essentially what happened in northern Virginia, where Metro's western Orange Line extension took the new subway through an area that had originally developed around streetcars. By any measure, that investment has paid off. Indeed, over the last decade, a full 70 percent of the population growth in Arlington County occurred in less than 6 percent of the county's land area, that being the census blocks in closest proximity to the five Orange Line Metro stops. Now 40 percent of the residents in these census blocks use transit to get to work.[14]

DON'T MESS WITH DALLAS

Based on the above logic, many of the low-quality-transit cities studied in Litman's report are perfectly poised to waste transit dollars. Dallas presents an instructive example. In 1983, residents of fifteen Dallas-area cities voted to levy a 1 percent sales tax to create what has become the largest light-rail system in the United States. The multibillion-dollar system currently includes 72 miles of track, on its way to 91 miles and 63 stations by 2013.[15] Service began in 1996 with an 11-mile stretch linking the downtown to its close-in neighborhoods. Within four years, public transit ridership, formerly all on buses, had surprisingly *dropped* 8 percent below 1990 levels.[16]

Through the 2000s, the Dallas Area Rapid Transit (DART) system has continued to grow, and transit ridership has continued to drop.[17] A few billion dollars later, despite escalating gasoline costs, a greater percentage of Dallas residents are driving to work than at any time in the past quarter century.

That is not to say that DART has not produced benefits. According to a 2007 report from the University of North Texas, over $4 billion in new development has sprung up around DART stations. While this growth is currently stalled with the economy, we can expect it to continue. Additionally, the UNT study found that homes near rail stations had appreciated almost 40 percent more than homes elsewhere in the metropolitan region.[18] These figures are impressive, but they don't begin to address the original motivation for the rail system, which was to reduce highway congestion. Nor do they suggest that increased economic development will eventually pay for the system.

Were there other benefits? It is very possible that much of the new growth around DART stations would have happened elsewhere without it, which throws into question the system's economic impact. However, it is likely that this development would have occurred at lower densities, and probably at greater distance from downtown. Some Texas scrubland was saved, and some gasoline, too. But there is no getting around the fact that all this new transit-oriented development has not increased the percentage of people taking transit. Even the biggest transit fan—me, perhaps?—would have a hard time considering the DART system anything but a failure.

Which raises the question: What is Dallas doing wrong? For an answer, we turn to Yonah Freemark, the sagacious blogger behind *The Transport Politic* and probably the best-informed source on transit today. His answer, paraphrased, is "just about everything," which includes: lacking sufficient residential densities; encouraging ample parking downtown; placing the rail alignments in the least costly rights-of-way rather than in the busiest areas; locating stations next to highways and with huge parking garages; reducing frequencies to afford farther-flung service; and, finally, forgetting about neighborhoods. He suggests: "If people are going to be living in apartments anyway, have them do so in mixed-use, walkable neighborhoods within easy distance of light rail stops."[19]

All these mistakes matter—some will be addressed in detail below—but, with his final point, Freemark is nibbling around the edges of the biggest problem of all. The simple fact is that Dallas and its suburbs are almost completely lacking in neighborhood structure. As a result, you get off the train, and . . . ? The likelihood that you can then walk to any destination of utility is preposterously slim. This might be expected in the system's more exurban locations, where a park-and-ride commute is the norm. But park-and-ride only works—when it does work*—if you don't need a car at both ends. Downtown, only a few of the system's

---

*Park-and-ride thrives only in cities where driving downtown is prohibitively expensive in terms of money or time, since people who begin their commutes in a car are loath to make the dreaded *intermodal shift* unless punishment awaits (Duany, Plater-Zyberk, and Speck, *Suburban Nation*, 138–39).

stations could be said to provide anything resembling a quality pedestrian experience, and that experience doesn't last long, because very little of downtown Dallas is truly walkable. Simply too much of it consists of over-wide streets carrying high-speed traffic along treeless sidewalks flanked by blank walls and parking lots. Like so many American downtowns, Dallas's passes the Litman test of having been designed before the auto age, but it has been so transformed around the demands of the automobile that pedestrians appear to be more of a parasitic species, an appendage to the dominant creatures they inhabit.

Without much walkability on either end of the line, DART can hardly be expected to have changed people's driving habits. But, as astute readers of Step 1 have perhaps already reasoned, nothing was going to reduce the amount of driving in Dallas. Not a transit system, not walkability, not neighborhoods: Texas drivers will continue to fill the roads they have, and if America's largest light-rail system takes sixty thousand drivers off the highway—the current total—sixty thousand more will take their place. Because in Dallas, where parking is as ubiquitous as it is cheap,* the only significant constraint to driving is the very congestion that DART hopes to relieve.

This is the part of the story that the train boosters don't want you to hear: investments in transit may be investments in mobility or investments in real estate, but they are not investments in reduced traffic.* The only way to reduce traffic is to reduce roads or to increase the cost of using them, and that is a bitter pill that few pro-transit cities are ready to swallow. Civic leaders insist that driving remain as cheap and convenient as ever and new systems

---

*No quick Shoupista pricing fix here: Dallas is so overpaved that its super-cheap parking—typically a dollar per hour—is actually the free-market rate.
*This conclusion was supported by the study "The Fundamental Law of Road Congestion: Evidence from U.S. Cities," published by Gilles Duranton and Matthew Turner at the University of Toronto, which finds that "extensions to public transit are not appropriate policies with which to combat traffic congestion" (34).

like DART go hungry for riders. Why take the train when you can drive there just as quickly and park for a dollar an hour?

So how can Dallas make good on its billions of dollars in transit investment? There is a short answer and a long answer. The short answer is to congestion price the freeways for maximum efficiency—making the most of current road investment—and use the bounteous revenue to buy down transit fares to zero while shortening wait times. That will never happen, so let's look at the long answer.

We have already discussed how, to benefit from the presence of transit, a metropolis has to take shape around that transit. It is not too late for this to happen in Dallas. The city and its surrounding municipalities must make a commitment to focus development more assiduously at DART stations, including making plans for walkable neighborhoods around every one.* They must focus especially on downtown stations, creating truly pedestrian-friendly precincts with high housing densities within them. They must eliminate the on-site parking requirement near all stations, and prohibit new parking lots near stations downtown. Then they must wait . . . for gasoline to hit ten dollars per gallon.

As we have already seen in New York, oil prices can accomplish in short order what defeated congestion-pricing schemes fail to do. At some point, sooner or later, it will become much more expensive to drive around every American city, especially those like Dallas. When this happens, the cities that remain competitive will be the ones with comprehensive transit networks surrounded by high-density neighborhoods. Suddenly, a 1 percent sales tax does not seem like such a high price to pay. But without the neighborhoods—as yet lacking in Dallas—there is

---

*Yonah Freemark, "An Extensive New Addition to Dallas's Light Rail Makes It America's Longest." While some of the new station-area developments contain high density, not one of them has taken the form of a walkable neighborhood. Most are the conventional edge-city conglomerations of towers and parking lots, with nary an intimate street in sight.

no future scenario in which the city's transit investment makes sense.

THE OTHER KIND OF TRANSIT

Only big, fast transit systems have the potential to fundamentally transform cities. But that does not mean that smaller systems can't be worthwhile. When effective, these systems take one of two forms: either nodal, to connect several walkable districts together, or linear, to enhance and extend a walkable corridor.

The former, such as the gondola connecting the town of Telluride, Colorado, with Telluride Mountain Village, can be powerfully effective at both reducing car trips and improving walkability. "What, a gondola??" you ask. Yes, a gondola that carries more than 2 million riders a year[20]—roughly 10 percent of the number served by the entire Dallas system—at one-fifth the cost per passenger of local bus service. Many of these riders are tourists in jaunty moon-boots, but a significant number are low-wage workers. Small nodal systems like these are perhaps the easiest to make work: all they need is a great interface with urbanism at each stop, frequent headways, and an expedited path. They are also useful for surmounting geographical obstacles, such as Pittsburgh's famous Duquesne and Monongahela inclines, the latter of which does a pretty good job of connecting urbanism to urbanism. These systems need not be unusual machines; sometimes they are just the shuttle bus that connects a university to its downtown.

Far more common are linear corridor systems, also known as streetcars, trolleys, or trams. These distinguish themselves from conventional light-rail systems by their slower speed and frequent stops; they are not rapid transit, but "pedestrian accelerators," in the words of Portland's Charlie Hales, who helped create that city's modern streetcar. If done properly, they are also "place makers," which is another way of saying "land-appreciation tools." Hales reminds us that most old U.S. streetcar lines were short-term value-creation strategies by real estate developers with property to sell.[21] The same economics still hold sway and need to be pondered deeply by cities considering new streetcar lines.

Which, these days, seems to be everybody. I don't think I've worked for a city in the past few years which was not conducting some sort of streetcar study. These studies generally come out positive—for the same reason that roadway expansion studies by road builders generally come out positive—and they need to be supplemented, or supplanted, by a simple question: "Why do you want one?"

On the rare occasion that this question is asked, typical answers include "We want to increase walking"; "We want to enliven Main Street"; "We want to get people out of their cars"; and, my favorite, "We want to be like Portland." These are all wrong answers and here's why: Charlie Hales is careful to call streetcars pedestrian accelerators and not pedestrian creators, because they do not have any record of filling empty sidewalks. If anything, it's the other way around: it is the presence of heavy pedestrian activity that indicates a potential for streetcar success. In places like Memphis, Tampa, and Little Rock, streetcars put in place between 1993 and 2004 have done little to add pedestrian life to the sleepy Main Streets they inhabit, and their ridership is paltry at best. Memphis, the star of the bunch, attracts only 343 daily boardings per mile, which is one-eighth of what Portland logs and one-twentieth of Boston's Green Line.[22]

None of these small systems—what ArtPlace CEO Carol Coletta calls "toy transit"—connect to a larger rail network, so they don't offer the regional mobility that allows people to leave the car at home. Portland's streetcar line is roughly half the length of Memphis's seven-mile system, but it connects to fifty-three miles of MAX light rail. And, importantly, Portland's system was instituted hand in hand with a commitment to "a host of other strategies and policies, including higher density, neighborhood-based urban design, elimination of minimum parking requirements, and basically the whole list of things that add up to walkability," says Hales. "You can't just drop in a streetcar."•

WHAT STREETCARS DO

So why should a city want a streetcar? Successes like Portland teach us that streetcars make the most sense when a large area of vacant or underutilized land sits just beyond walking distance from a walkable downtown. In these cases, a streetcar may represent the best opportunity to connect that area to the downtown in a way that it has never been connected before, spurring its development. In Portland, both the city and the development community identified the Hoyt Rail Yards, north of downtown, as just such an area. They prepared a design that was both a streetcar plan and a neighborhood plan, and included an eightfold up-zoning in exchange for parks, affordable housing, and the removal of a freeway ramp. The new streetcar opened in 2001 at a total cost of $54.5 million.[23]

Since then, over $3.5 billion of new investment has sprung up around the trolley line—an astounding sixty-four times the initial investment. According to a Brookings Institution report, adjacent property values have risen by 44 to well over 400 percent, compared to the city's baseline appreciation of 34 percent. Several thousand people have moved in, and they, in turn, have caused a revolution in street life. The Brookings report notes that "pedestrian counts in front of Powell's Books, a major retailer sited along the line, went from three people per hour to over 933."[24]

•Charles Hales's presentation at Rail-Volution, October 18, 2011. The "host of strategies" included Portland's famous urban-growth boundary, which had contributed to a pent-up demand for real estate.

Portland's streetcar succeeded as a tool for increasing urban vibrancy because it was first a tool for neighborhood development. This fact is important for two reasons: first, because it is a mistake to promote a streetcar in the absence of a major real estate opportunity and, second, because such an opportunity suggests the presence of private parties who stand to benefit tremendously from the investment. And these parties should want to help pay for it.

This was precisely the case in Seattle, where landowners in the city's South Lake Union district, led by Microsoft cofounder Paul Allen, contributed fully half the cost of a new $52 million trolley line connecting their property to downtown. With another third of the money coming from federal and state sources, this left only $8.5 million unaccounted for, which the city obtained by selling surplus property along the line.[25] Only five years old, this trolley is now serving four times as many passengers as Tampa's,[26] thanks in part to the relocation of Amazon .com and the Bill & Melinda Gates Foundation. During the period of its planning and construction, property values along the line appreciated at more than twice the city average,[27] amply repaying the private investors.

The experiences of Portland and Seattle may seem a bit chastening to other cities, and rightly so—not everyone has huge housing demand or Amazon. But even the duds of Memphis, Tampa, and Little Rock produced positive outcomes, namely new development around the line averaging seventeen times the value of the rail systems.[28] The tax revenue that this construction represents is promising news in terms of finding ways to finance future streetcar lines,[29] but it still doesn't address most cities' stated goal in chasing a trolley, which is to enliven their downtown. Principally, streetcars enliven not the downtown, but the new area opened up for development. Downtown only benefits as a secondary impact, if and when thousands of people move into the previously underdeveloped area.

Indeed, more careful study of Tampa may show the opposite effect. While property values have soared where the trolley passes through former industrial land, the city's already established neighborhoods have fared less well. In Ybor City, Tampa's most walkable district, properties actually appreciated at rates from 24 to 36 percent *below* the rest of the surrounding county.[30] The lesson here is that trolleys, unless integrated into a robust citywide transit network, are first and foremost a tool for creating new urban districts, and are not necessarily the mobility-enhancing, street-enlivening walkability bomb that their promoters would have us believe. By all means build one, if you can get someone else to pay for it.

TRANSIT FOR DRIVERS

Most Americans live not in big cities with big transit systems, but in smaller places that face a dramatically different landscape when it comes to public transportation. In most American cities, everyone still drives, traffic is relatively light, and parking is cheap. What is the role of transit in these places? Or more to the point, how do you create a transit-and-walking culture in a place where driving is so easy?

It may not be possible. In some of these locations, the bus is destined to remain the "loser cruiser," the mode of choice for those who have no choice: the elderly, poor, and infirm. As such, it will always be underfunded and struggling for survival, like any social service.

If it is to become widely used, transit has to be ruthlessly reconceptualized as a convenience, not just a rescue vehicle. Or, more accurately, while certain rescue routes must remain—from the old-age home to the health center, for example—the system needs to focus on those rare opportunities where it can offer a superior experience to driving. These few lines should be earmarked for a higher level of service, and indeed only provided with service if certain conditions can be met. These conditions are what is lacking in much of transit today: *urbanity*, *clarity*, *frequency*, and *pleasure*.

Urbanity means locating all significant stops right in the heart of the action, not a block away and, God forbid, not across a parking lot. This is the *problem of the last one hundred yards* that haunts so many a bus or train station. Riders should be able to fall into the bus from a stool at a coffee shop.[31] If the dimensional requirements of your vehicle do not allow this, then you need a different vehicle. And without true walkability on both ends of the line, your system is a nonstarter.

Clarity means a route that is a simple line or loop, with as few diversions as possible. This not only expedites travel—and limits frustration—but also allows riders to form a mental image of the path, so important to their comfort. Sometimes, when I ride another city's bus for the first time, I am reminded of the one-day bus strike I encountered in Florence, Italy: the drivers showed up for work but, once the passengers boarded, they cruised wherever the heck they wanted. We got the message.

Frequency is the thing that most transit service gets wrong. People hate to look at schedules almost as much as they hate waiting, so ten-minute headways are the standard for any line that hopes to attract a crowd. If you can't fill a bus at that rate, then get a van. GPS-enabled time-to-arrival clocks at stations (and smartphone apps) are also essential, and particularly helpful after hours. What *after hours* means depends on the circumstances, but staying popular may require short headways all evening. The byword here is to provide service frequently or not at all. Limiting service due to limited ridership is a death spiral that few transit lines survive.

Pleasure is the mandate that is most often overlooked by transit officials, yet the search for its attainment is at the heart of so many human choices. As Darrin Nordahl argues convincingly in *My Kind of Transit*, public transportation is "a mobile form of public space,"[32] and can provide so many of the benefits we seek from our time spent out of the house. When I first read Nordahl's book, I was ready to dismiss this concept as so much sentimental prattle, but then I was reminded that I owe my own marriage to a train ride. What does a social, fun, *pleasurable* experience mean for transit design? Seats that face inward rather than at the back of someone's head. Big, nontinted windows that open wide—or no glass at all, as in San Diego. Wifi. And, yes, even novel vehicles, like double-decker buses, that add capacity and charm while reducing turning radii.[33]

In short, the imperative of competitive transit has a hard side and a soft side. The hard side is all about not wasting people's time and the soft side is about making them happy. If you can commit to doing both, then you can get people out of their cars.

TRAINS VERSUS BUSES

If your goals are efficiency and pleasure, rail beats bus hands down. With expedited paths, trains are almost always faster, and most trains are way cuter than your average diesel-belching bus. Even the latest zero-emissions buses are typically an intimidating presence in the streetscape compared to a delicate tram car. That's why trains cost more.

Or do they? Hartford is now building a Bus Rapid Transit (BRT) system that costs over $60 million per mile.[34] That's almost twice the cost of the average American light-rail project.* But Hartford is an exception that proves the rule, and points to the sometimes high costs of doing BRT properly, which means

---

*Light Rail Now, "Status of North American Light Rail Projects," 2002. The average cost of such projects is approximately $35 million per mile, excluding Seattle's unusual system.

giving the bus its own dedicated pathway, much like a train. I'm not sure what went wrong in Hartford, as the typical BRT costs about half as much as light rail, roughly $15 million per mile.[35]

This typically lower cost is drawing a lot of cities to BRT. If done properly, BRT is indeed a legitimate alternative to regional light rail. Just don't forget the R. True BRT systems include not only a separated path, but also signal priority at intersections, level boarding at raised pay-to-enter stations, ten-minute headways, and GPS-enabled wait-time indicators. If you can't do most of those things, don't call it Rapid. Oregon's popular Eugene-to-Springfield BRT even has its own artwork and landscaping program, not just at stations, but along the whole line.

These surface investments are often cited by BRT advocates when responding to the biggest criticism of bus systems, that they lack rail's permanence: how can you drive real estate investment around transit if the transit might leave? Well, we've already learned in America that trolleys can leave, too, but BRT infrastructure has a long way to go to match the sense of permanence that rail provides. That's half the story. The other half, rarely discussed, is that the more permanent the BRT infrastructure feels, the more ugly it usually looks. BRT buses, and the constructions that support them, just don't evoke many feelings of comfort in the fragile human bodies they serve. Sure, BRT has done great things for pedestrians in Bogotá . . . but how many Americans want to be pedestrians in Bogotá?

It would seem that everyone in this argument, except Darrin Nordahl, has forgotten just how darn adorable trolleys really are. They also last twice as long as buses and, unlike buses, the old ones often look even better than the new ones. Buses might stay in service for twenty years but, after ten, they start to make a place feel run down. Because they are not only a "form of public space," but also very often a *part* of public space, this fact deserves greater weight in the train-versus-bus calculus that many cities undertake.

That said, not all bus systems are duds—far from it. The most remarkable one nationally may be Boulder's, an inexpensive network that confounds conventional transit wisdom in a number of important ways. Thanks to its system of cleverly branded routes—including the Hop, Skip, and Jump, with each route getting its own color—the city is living up to its motto of "Breathing Required, Driving Optional." Despite gaining ten thousand new residents and twelve thousand new jobs since 1994, the city has seen zero increase in its total vehicle miles driven. Much of the system's success comes from the way that it is marketed. Households buy a $120 EcoPass that gives all members free rides all year—and also gives them special treatment at local stores, restaurants, and bars. As a result, an entire EcoPass culture has evolved, in which driving just isn't as cool.

Finally, many cities that are considering trolleys for the standard set of wrong reasons may want instead to purchase small electric shuttles like the ones that have brought increased life to places like Chattanooga and San Diego. These don't need rails, but they function as pedestrian accelerators in already-populated corridors, and each one costs less than the cheapest Ferrari.* Although technically buses, they are also cute, and can serve as an effective gateway drug to more hard-core rail transit in the future.

ZIP IT IF YOU CAN

Every city wants Zipcar. Does Zipcar want them back? Probably not. By all means, invite them to dinner, give them the key to your city, and offer them all of the concessions they usually ask, including dedicated parking spaces in the best locations—as many as they want. But understand that this superficially pro-

---

*Chattanooga's cost between $160,000 and $180,000 apiece.

driving enterprise cannot thrive in your city unless you have already moved beyond the pro-driving paradigm. Because if everybody has a car, nobody needs one. If the design of your city still makes daily driving a prerequisite to viable citizenship, then you are not yet ready for urban car-share.

Some people worry that car-share might undermine public transportation, taxis, walking, or biking, but the opposite is true. It is only in the driving-optional cities with good public transportation, taxis, walking, and biking that car-share can thrive. It is also in these same cities that car-share might push someone over the tipping point into ditching their car, as it did me. So, here's one good test: Go downtown. Stick out your hand. Does a taxi stop? If so, you might be ready for Zipcar.

And then go for it, as the benefits are tremendous. After a year of service, Zipcar Baltimore polled its members and found that they were walking 21 percent more, biking 14 percent more, and taking transit 11 percent more than before joining. Only 12 percent of members had taken more than five driving trips in the previous month, compared to 38 percent before joining Zipcar. About a fifth of members had sold their cars, and almost half claimed that Zipcar had saved them from having to buy a car.[36] There is only one challenge to Zipcar, which is that they are too smart to locate in unwalkable cities.

THE SAFE WALK

■

STEP 5: PROTECT THE PEDESTRIAN

STEP 6: WELCOME BIKES

STEP 5: PROTECT THE PEDESTRIAN

Size matters; A turn too far; Fat lanes; Keep it complicated; The safety apotheosis; The one-way epidemic; Sacred sidewalks; Senseless signals

Will the pedestrian survive? Or, more precisely: Will potential walkers feel adequately protected against being run over, enough so that they make the choice to walk?

This is clearly the central question of any discussion of walkable cities. As all the other steps make clear, pedestrian safety is not enough. But it is essential, and also so often needlessly botched by the people who build our cities. These failures stem from two principal sources: a lack of concern for the pedestrian and a fundamental misunderstanding within the professions about what makes streets safe. The first cause is political, and can be overcome through advocacy. The second cause is technical, and can be overcome by setting the record straight.

SIZE MATTERS

In his landmark book *Great Streets,* the urbanist Alan Jacobs (no relation to Jane) lays out figure-ground maps, each a mile square, of more than forty world cities. With streets in white and blocks in black, these drawings allow us to understand and compare the patterns underlying some of the planet's most walkable and unwalkable places. The lessons that emerge are unmistakable, especially as you compare cities that you have had the pleasure or misfortune to visit. The most obvious of these lessons pertains to block size.

Generally speaking, the cities with the smallest blocks are the ones best known for walkability, while those with the largest blocks are known as places without street life—if they are known at all. The preindustrial neighborhoods of downtown Boston and lower Manhattan, like their European counterparts, have blocks that average less than two hundred feet long (and the cranky medieval street patterns to match). The most walkable grids, like Philadelphia's and San Francisco's, have blocks that average less than four hundred feet in length. And then there are the pedestrian-free zones, like Irvine, California, where many blocks are one thousand feet long or longer.

There are, as always, exceptions. Much of Berlin has surprisingly large blocks. But its street maps are effectively a lie, since so many Berlin blocks are rife with interior passages and courtyards that create a hidden network of pedestrian life. The blocks of Los Angeles aren't much bigger than Barcelona's, but the latter's streets aren't engineered for high speeds. Los Angeles demonstrates that it is possible to make a small-block city unwalkable, but the larger pool of evidence confirms that it is much harder to make a big-block city walkable.

I remember the first time I visited Las Vegas, which, aside from the Strip and the old main street (Fremont Street) is a place where nobody walks. Driving into town in my rented Mustang, I checked the Hertz map for the path to my hotel. In those days, rental-car maps typically showed only a city's major roads, skipping the fine-grained network in between for simplicity. As I entered the city, I was astounded to learn that there wasn't a fine-grained network in between: the dumbed-down rental-car map *was* the city. This explained a lot.

There are two main reasons why smaller blocks make for better cities. The first has less to do with safety and more with convenience: the more blocks per square mile, the more choices a pedestrian can make and the more opportunities there are to alter your path to visit a useful address such as a coffee shop or dry cleaner. These choices also make walking more interesting, while shortening the distances between destinations.

The second, more important, reason is that bigger blocks mean fewer streets and thus bigger streets. Presuming a similar traffic volume, a city with twice the block size requires each street to hold twice as many driving lanes. The typical street in downtown Portland, with its two-hundred-foot-per-side blocks, holds two lanes of traffic.* The typical street in downtown Salt Lake City, with blocks over six hundred feet per side, holds six lanes of traffic.* And six-lane streets are much more dangerous than two-lane streets.

The definitive study on this topic was completed by Wesley Marshall and Norman Garrick at the University of Connecticut, who compared data from twenty-four medium-sized California cities. They looked at more than 130,000 car crashes that occurred over nine years, and were able to divide the subjects into twelve "safer" cities and twelve "less safe" cities. Among these two groups, they found no single variable to be more predictive of injury and death than block size. Blocks in the dozen safer cities averaged eighteen acres in size, while blocks in the dozen less safe cities averaged thirty-four acres in size. All told, a doubling of block size corresponded with a tripling of fatalities.[1]

---

*Portland's fine-grained network contains a remarkable six hundred intersections per square mile. You can fit nine typical Portland blocks in a typical Salt Lake City block. The block-size versus street-width math is not exact for a number of interesting reasons. Portland's blocks are generally taller than Salt Lake City's, but this factor is counterbalanced somewhat by the vicious circle that occurs in big-blocked cities, where an automotive environment causes many potential pedestrians to drive instead.

*Each Salt Lake City street is famously 132 feet wide, thanks to the dictate by Brigham Young that streets be wide enough to turn a wagon team around without "resorting to profanity" (Mark Haddock, "Salt Lake Streets Have Seen Many Changes over Past 150 Years"). This 132 feet now includes sidewalks, but that still leaves room for a lot of lanes.

Big-block, multilane systems result in streets that are both harder to cross and easier to speed on. Here, the most significant threshold is between one lane and two lanes in any given direction, since that second lane offers the opportunity to pass and thus allows drivers to slip into a "road racer" frame of mind. Whichever lane you are in, the other one looks faster.[2] It is possible to make an eminently walkable multilane boulevard—picture Paris—but few big-block cities have the budget or the desire to buy that many trees. And even the Champs Élysées is a nightmare to cross.

Multilane streets are much more dangerous for drivers as well, thanks to the "killed by kindness" scenario. As it typically unfolds, this story line involves a motorist signaling left and an approaching car in the adjacent lane slowing down to allow the turn. As the motorist crosses the centerline, a speeding car in the far lane, hidden by the kind driver, T-bones the turning vehicle.

The good news is that four-lane streets can be as inefficient as they are deadly, because the fast lane is also the left-hand turn lane, and maintaining speed often means jockeying from lane to lane. Thanks to this inefficiency, many cities across the country are finding it politically possible to introduce something called a "road diet." In a road diet, a standard four-lane street is replaced by a three-lane street: one lane in each direction and a center lane reserved for left turns.

What is remarkable about road diets is not that they save lives—that is to be expected. In a typical road-diet conversion, Orlando's Edgewater Drive, the number of crashes fell by 34 percent and, because the crashes were slower, the number of injuries fell by an impressive 68 percent: from one per nine days to one per month. Rather, the surprising thing is that they do not reduce a street's carrying capacity. Thanks to the inherent efficiency of maintaining a dedicated turning lane, the typical road diet does nothing to lower the traffic volume on a street. Comparison of seventeen different road diets conducted by the engineering firm AECOM found that only two streets lost capacity, while five stayed the same, and ten actually handled more cars per day after the conversion.

These numbers are important, because most road-diet opponents are fearful of increased congestion. In the 1980s, 95 percent of the residents of Lewistown, Pennsylvania, came out against a road diet proposed by some progressive engineers at PennDOT, citing concerns over increased travel times. PennDOT built the conversion anyway—as DOTs will do—and travel times remained unchanged as crashes dropped to nearly zero.[3]

This story and the dozens since then represent a great opportunity for almost every American city. There is hardly a downtown in the United States that does not have a four-laner that would benefit from a road diet tomorrow. A happy by-product of the road diet is the additional ten to twelve feet of roadway freed up by the eliminated lane. This space can be used to expand sidewalks, plant trees, create a missing parking lane, or replace parallel parking with angled parking in a business district. Since most urban four-laners already have sidewalks, trees, and parking, this pavement is often redeployed as two ample bicycle lanes, further humanizing the street. This solution presents the additional benefit of avoiding the expense of rebuilding any curbs.•

A TURN TOO FAR

Now that I've fully sung the praises of turn lanes, let me attack them. Road diets aside, left-hand turn lanes have done more

---

•San Francisco is also no stranger to road diets of this type, having converted five important streets from four lanes to three: Dolores, Guerrero, Valencia, Mission, and South Van Ness. On all five streets, driving times remained unchanged, while bike volumes soared. On Valencia Street, for example, the number of commute-time cyclists rose from 88 to 215 per hour (Michael Rankin, presentation at New Partners for Smart Growth, February 10, 2007).

than their share to wreck a good number of American down-towns. Why? Because, by inserting them where they are not needed, or making them much longer than needed, engineering departments have caused many Main Streets to become a lane too wide.

This wouldn't be as big a problem if it were only a matter of ten feet. Unfortunately, the big problem is where those ten feet are found, in what used to be a parking lane. This is the situation in Bethlehem, Pennsylvania, where the once-bustling Wyan-dotte Street has the misfortune of also being State Route 378. Here, the same enlightened DOT engineers who brought us Lewistown's road diet decided that a two-laner needed a center turn lane, and they scraped an entire block face of its parallel parking to get it. Without convenience parking for their customers, the stores that line Wyandotte Street are all dead or dying; those that remain will not last long. And here's the kicker: the DOT's turn lane—four hundred feet long, enough for a stack of two dozen cars—serves a minor side street containing a mere eleven houses.

This is highway engineering perversity at its most wasteful . . . were it only an isolated incident! Most American downtowns suf-fer from unnecessary and overlong left-hand turn lanes that eliminate parking, broaden streets, speed up traffic, and other-wise detract from the pedestrian experience. While most can't be eliminated without a negative impact on traffic flow, most can be shortened. A three-car-long turn lane that eliminates three parking spaces at a corner is a vast improvement over the block-long monsters that most cities install without a second thought.

FAT LANES

Contrary to perceptions, the greatest threat to pedestrian safety is not crime, but the very real danger of automobiles moving quickly. Yet most traffic engineers, often in the name of safety, continually redesign city streets to support higher-speed driving. This approach is so counterintuitive that it strains credulity: engineers design streets for speeds well above the posted limit, so that speeding drivers will be safe—a practice that, of course, causes the very speeding it hopes to protect against.

Even my old South Beach neighborhood, known for its walkability, was not immune to this sort of thinking. If you have seen the remake of *La Cage aux Folles,* you might remember the lively streetscape of Espanola Way, where Robin Williams buys a birthday cake for his partner. Follow that street two blocks west and you will find that already-narrow sidewalks have been cut in half in order to widen a roadway that functioned perfectly well before. Why? Because *the standards had changed*—from walkable to not.

I have never heard a proper explanation for the creeping expansion of America's street standards. All I know is that it is very real and that it has a profound impact on the work that city planners do every day. In the late nineties, I was helping to design Mount Laurel, a new town outside of Birmingham, Alabama, that was modeled on that city's most successful prewar neighborhoods. We had measured the streets of Homewood, Mountain Brook, and the city's other best addresses, and planned our thoroughfares with the same dimensions. We were then told that our streets did not meet the standard, and our engineering firm was unwilling to stamp the drawings for fear of legal liability.

I remember one particular afternoon, when we convinced the county engineer to tour these great neighborhoods with us in our van. Perhaps anticipating our consternation, he gripped the door handle with white knuckles and shouted "We're gonna die!" as we motored calmly around the narrow, leafy streets of Mountain Brook. I'm pretty sure he was joking, but his ultimate pronouncement was clear: we had to reengineer our streets with a higher design speed.

This logic—that higher design speeds make for safer

streets—coupled with the typical city engineer's desire for un-
impeded traffic—has caused many American cities to rebuild
their streets with lanes that are twelve, thirteen, and sometimes
even fourteen feet wide. Now cars are only six feet wide—a Ford
Excursion is 6'6"—and most Main Streets were historically made
of ten-foot lanes. That dimension persists on many of the best,
such as ritzy Worth Avenue in Palm Beach, Florida. Yet many
cities I visit have their fair share of twelve-footers, and that is
where much of the speeding occurs.

For me writing this and you reading it, it is undoubtedly
clear that building wider lanes would cause drivers to speed.
After all, if highways have twelve-foot lanes, and we are comfortable negotiating them at seventy miles per hour, wouldn't we feel
the same way on a city street of the same dimension? Yet in the
bizarre parallel universe of the traffic engineer, no such relationship exists: motorists will drive at the speed limit, or slightly
above, no matter what sort of drag strip we lay in their path.

As with induced demand, the engineers have once again
failed to comprehend that the way they design streets will have
any impact on the way that people use them. By their logic, just
as more lanes can't cause more driving, high-speed lanes can't
cause high speeds. Ladies and gentlemen, allow me to introduce
you to the second great misunderstanding that lies at the root of
most urban degradation today: widening a city's streets in the
name of safety is like distributing handguns to deter crime.

Just in case you think I am making this up, let's turn to the
calm analysis of Reid Ewing and Eric Dumbaugh, professors at
the University of Maryland and Texas A&M, respectively. In
their 2009 study, "The Built Environment and Traffic Safety: A
Review of Empirical Evidence," they assess the situation this way:

> Considered broadly, the fundamental shortcoming of
> conventional traffic safety theory is that it fails to ac-
> count for the moderating role of human behavior on

crash incidence. Decisions to ... widen specific roadways to make them more forgiving are based on the assumption that in so doing, human behavior will remain unchanged. And it is precisely this assumption—that human behavior can be treated as a constant, regardless of design—that accounts for the failure of conventional safety practice.[4]

How costly is this failure? In another study, presented at the eightieth annual meeting of the Transportation Research Board, Rutgers professor Robert Noland calculated that increased lane widths could be blamed for approximately nine hundred additional traffic fatalities per year.[5]

We can only hope that these studies eventually have an impact on thoroughfare engineering as it is practiced in the typical American city. Currently, engineers still deny their stamp of approval to streets configured without "adequately" high design speeds. "We're afraid of being sued," they say. Someday, I might get up the nerve to respond as follows: "Afraid? You should be. Now that we've publicly presented to you that narrower roads save lives, we are going to sue you when people die on your fat streets."

There is some good news. Thanks to the labors of the Congress for the New Urbanism, a nonprofit focused on making more livable cities,* we have made a start in changing the standards. The CNU teamed up with the Institute of Traffic Engineers to create a new manual, *Designing Walkable Urban Thoroughfares*, that recommends street lanes of ten and eleven feet wide.[6] With the imprimatur of the ITE, this book can now be waved at planning meetings in support of more reasonable standards. I just wish that "eleven" wasn't in there.

---

*Full disclosure: I am a charter member of this organization, which over the past two decades has been laboring arduously in support of the ideals presented in this book. You can join us at cnu.org.

Another cause for hope is the growing "20's Plenty for Us" movement that, having taken the United Kingdom by storm, is just beginning to win followers in the United States. Recognizing that only 5 percent of pedestrian collisions at twenty miles per hour result in death, versus 85 percent at forty mph,[7] the British have introduced twenty-mph speed limits in many of their cities. There are currently more than eighty "20's Plenty" campaigns in the UK, and about twenty-five British jurisdictions, with a combined population of over 6 million, have committed to a twenty-mph speed limit in residential areas. In June 2011, the European Union Transport Committee recommended such a rule for the entire continent.[8] It is easy to imagine twenty mph becoming a standard throughout Europe in the near future.

On this side of the pond, Hoboken, New Jersey, may be the first city to have instituted a "20's Plenty" campaign. Unfortunately, in true Jersey fashion, the twenty is just a suggestion, while higher official speed limits remain in place. As I write this, New York City is pioneering some legitimate twenty-mph zones. These developments are important—but not as an end in themselves. As any London pedestrian will tell you, a twenty-mph sign does not a twenty-mph driver make. Most motorists drive the speed at which they feel comfortable, which is the speed to which the road has been engineered. "20's Plenty" is most useful as a first step to slower design speeds. Once twenty-mph zones proliferate, we may finally be able to convince the engineers to design twenty-mph streets.•

KEEP IT COMPLICATED

Narrower lanes are not the only way to slow traffic down. Each and every aspect of the built environment sends its own cue to

---

•As you might expect, this is far from likely, for the reasons already discussed. Most engineers would insist that streets posted with a twenty-mph speed limit be laid out according to a design speed of twenty-five or thirty mph so that speeders are "safe."

drivers and too many of those cues say "speed up." Most of them, unfortunately, are the law. Two more that deserve our attention are intersection geometry and sight triangles.

Recently, my wife and I took a road trip to Philadelphia. It was our first weekend alone without the two kids, and we were determined to make it count. The first stop, about a mile south of the Liberty Bell, was the intersection of Ninth Street and Passyunk Avenue. Fast-food aficionados will recognize this address as the location of Geno's Steaks and Pat's King of Steaks, the two oversized food stands that have been duking it out for decades over the title of Best Philly Cheesesteak.

I had heard about the cheesesteak duel, but I was not aware of the odd urban condition that surrounds it. As befits their embattled circumstances, the two restaurants sit nose-to-nose on opposing flatiron lots, like two skinny slices of pie, framed by two streets that cross in a sharp thirty-degree X. Pat's points north, directly at Geno's pointing south. With all their flashy signage, they look like two casino yachts playing a game of chicken.

For me, the question wasn't which sandwich was better (my vote goes to Pat's*). Rather, the question was: After all the cheese-steaks these two establishments had undoubtedly served to traffic engineers throughout the years, why is it still illegal in most of America to intersect two streets at a thirty-degree angle?

Observing the intersection at work, it would be hard to imagine a safer scene. First, there were the snaking lines of customers that made their way right into the street. We planners call this "human traffic calming"—as opposed to "human speed bumps," another common phenomenon—and the traffic was further slowed by all the cars pulling in for curbside pickups. But even without this confusion—we returned when the crowds had abated—the simple fact was that nobody drove dangerously through this intersection, precisely because the intersection felt dangerous.

*Thanks mostly to Geno's xenophobic political displays.

Welcome to the world of *risk homeostasis*, a very real place that exists well outside the blinkered gaze of the traffic engineering profession. Risk homeostasis describes how people automatically adjust their behavior to maintain a comfortable level of risk. It explains why poisoning deaths went up after childproof caps were introduced—people stopped hiding their medicines—and why the deadliest intersections in America are typically the ones you can navigate with one finger on the steering wheel and a cellphone at your ear.[9]

The best risk-homeostasis story comes from Sweden, a nation that is obsessed with traffic safety. If you look at the bar chart of Swedish traffic fatalities through the years, most of what you see is not surprising. There is the rise in deaths into the sixties, the decline as seatbelts are introduced, the leveling off in the eighties, and then a further decline as airbags become standard equipment. But, wait a minute, what happened in 1967? In a single year, fatalities dropped from more than thirteen hundred to fewer than eleven hundred, a decline of 17 percent. It turns out that, on March 9, 1967, Sweden switched from driving on the left-hand side of the road to driving on the right-hand side of the road.[10]

As might be expected, everyone was quite worried about this transition. The steering wheels were on the wrong side of the cars, a ton of signals and signs all had to be moved at once, and the government feared a bloodbath. But, precisely because people were scared, car crashes dropped precipitously, and didn't return to the prior level until 1970.

The lesson from this experience is clear: if you value the lives of your countrymen, you should switch sides of the road every three years. Since that is unlikely to win popular support, let's turn to the larger lesson: the safest roads are those that feel the least safe, demanding more attention from drivers.

This lesson has yet to crack through the ossified shell of the mainstream traffic engineering profession. In most cities, intersections are required to meet at ninety degrees or close to it.

Staggered intersections, great for slowing speeds, are strictly for-bidden. Five-ways, common in older places, are also off the ta-ble. My house sits on just such a crazy intersection, and in three years we have yet to witness a crash. Actually, we have: about once a season, on the perfect ninety-degree intersection a block away.

The shape of the intersection is half the story. The other half is the visibility at that intersection, and the second rule that foils the best attempts of city planners to make memorable places: the sight-triangle requirement. This standard mandates that all ver-tical objects such as buildings and trees maintain a minimum distance from street corners, so that drivers can see around them. Such a requirement makes perfect sense in a world in which de-sign can't affect behavior. But on planet Earth, it causes speed-ing at intersections.

Many of the best places in America, with leafy, well-shaped public spaces, violate the sight-triangle requirement.* Many of these places are located in those very cities that enforce sight triangles on all new construction. Luckily, each jurisdiction has the right to enforce its own sight-triangle rules. While they are hard to throw out entirely, they can often be rejiggered to the point where they do no harm. Hint: it all comes down to how you measure the triangle.

THE SAFETY APOTHEOSIS

If greater perceived danger leads to safer driving, how do you make the safest streets in the world? That question was probably best answered by Hans Monderman (1945–2008), the Dutch traffic engineer who pioneered two wonderful and interrelated

*See *The Boulevard Book* by Alan Jacobs for a thorough discussion of how sight-triangle requirements make great streets illegal. In one trenchant drawing, Jacobs demonstrates how applying the American standard would wipe out one-third of the trees on Barcelona's gorgeous Passeig de Gràcia (118–19).

concepts: *naked streets* and *shared space*. While not appropriate everywhere, these techniques have a lot to teach us as we work to improve our cities.

Naked streets refers to the concept of stripping a roadway of its signage—all of it, including stop signs, signals, and even stripes. Far from creating mayhem, this approach appears to have lowered crash rates wherever it has been tried. Following Monderman's advice, the Danish town of Christiansfeld removed all signs and signals from its main intersection, and watched the number of serious accidents each year fall from three to zero. The British county of Wiltshire, home to Stonehenge, pulled the centerline off a narrow street, and witnessed a 35 percent drop in the number of collisions.[11] Drivers passed oncoming cars at a 40 percent greater distance than on a striped street, even though the striped roadway was wider.[12]

Monderman described his approach this way: "The trouble with traffic engineers is that when there's a problem with a road, they always try to add something. To my mind, it's much better to remove things."[13] This makes particular sense in the Netherlands, where there is a tradition of reticent roadways—you are unlikely to see a stop sign there[14]—but the idea has also spread to Austria, France, Germany, Spain, and Sweden.[15]

Naked streets are also beginning to appear in the United States, typically in conjunction with Monderman's other big idea, *shared space*. In some ways, shared space is simply the extension of the naked streets concept to include the elimination of physical cues and barriers as well, such as curbs and distinct materials for streets and sidewalks. The goal is to create an environment of such utter ambiguity that cars, bicyclists, and pedestrians all come together in one big mixing bowl of humanity.

As David Owen notes, "This sounds to many people like a formula for disaster." Not so: "The clear experience in the (mainly) European cities that have tried it has been that increasing the ambiguity of urban road spaces actually lowers car speeds, reduces accident rates, and improves the lives of pedestrians."[16] In Monderman's terms, "Chaos equals cooperation."[17]

Monderman was a man with the courage of his convictions. One of his favorite tricks with television reporters was to speak to them while standing in front of a shared-space intersection he had built in the Dutch village of Oosterwolde. Without missing a beat, he would blindly walk backward into the flow of traffic, parting it like the Red Sea.[18]

America has no shared-space examples as pure as Monderman's, but one of the first attempts can be found on Espanola Way in Miami Beach—just two blocks from the street that was unnecessarily widened a few pages ago. In good political fashion, the city asked the street's neighbors to participate in the redesign of one of its key intersections, unaware that the neighborhood was infested with urban designers just back from Europe. "No curbs," we said. "Just pave it with bricks from building face to building face." Completed around 2000, Espanola Plaza works just fine, albeit with fairly low car counts. When the traffic engineers come to their senses, we will see Shared Streets begin to proliferate in the United States.

THE ONE-WAY EPIDEMIC

In 1918, a flu pandemic killed more than 75 million people worldwide. Almost exactly fifty years later, the United States was hit by another epidemic that, while less harmful to humans, laid waste to city after city from coast to coast. I am talking, of course, about the wholesale replacement in downtowns of two-way traffic with one-way traffic, a plight that few American cities escaped. Its impacts were profound, and haunt us to this day.

The logic was simple enough: to stay competitive in the face of suburban out-migration, cities needed to retool themselves around the goal of moving suburbanites in and out of the downtown quickly. One part of this effort—the obvious part—involved building elevated interstates, with the near-suicidal outcomes that have been well documented. The other part, less discussed, involved the remaking of downtown street networks around free-flowing systems of one-way pairs. By replacing two-ways with one-ways, cities were able to introduce synchronized signals and eliminate the slowdowns caused by left turns across traffic.

Like the interstates, these retrofitted streets were indeed effective at speeding commuters, enough so that there was no longer any reason to live downtown. They also turned what had once been a great urban asset—the public realm—into little more than a collection of surface freeways. Thoroughfares that once held cars, pedestrians, businesses, and street trees became toxic to all but the first. Freed of other uses, they effectively turned into automotive sewers.[19]

We have already discussed how multilane streets contribute to antipedestrian driving. Add to that the elimination of all friction from cars headed in the opposite direction and the sheer momentum represented by two to four columns of unopposed traffic, and you can see why these streets quickly depopulated. It is difficult to name a midsized or larger American city that was not damaged by this technique, whether it takes the form of a largely one-way network—Saint Louis, San Diego—or just a single one-way pair—Alexandria, Virginia; Cornelius, Oregon. Indeed, driving west from Portland to the Oregon coast, I witnessed how a single DOT had managed to send a good number of a state's Main Streets onto life support with this one trick.

One-ways wreck downtown retail districts for reasons beyond noxious driving, principally because they distribute vitality unevenly, and often in unexpected ways. They have been known to kill stores consigned to the morning path to work, since people do most of their shopping on the evening path home.* They also

---

*Just such a numbskull move devastated Calle Ocho, the main drag of Miami's Little Havana, in the seventies (Andres Duany, Elizabeth Plater-Zyberk, and Jeff Speck, *Suburban Nation*, 161n).

create a situation in which half the stores on cross-streets lose their retail visibility, being located over the shoulders of passing drivers. They intimidate out-of-towners, who are afraid of becoming lost, and they frustrate locals, who are annoyed by all the circular motions and additional traffic lights they must pass through to reach their destinations.

Indeed, these looping motions call deeply into question the presumed greater efficiency of one-way systems. Sure, they move vehicles faster, but does that greater speed make up for the additional distances that motorists have to travel . . . especially lost motorists? While there are plenty of studies documenting the congestion-busting efficacy of one-ways, I have yet to see one that factors in the marginal congestion caused by circling.

I was reminded of this fact on my first visit to Lowell, Massachusetts, on the day I was hired to work on their downtown. After twenty minutes spent lost—despite Google Maps—I finally had to call the deputy city manager, who talked me in for a landing. For a city planner with what I thought was a well-calibrated internal compass, this was a profound embarrassment. Later, as I got to know the city, I began to feel a bit better. The superimposition of a one-way network on Lowell's cranky preindustrial grid, interrupted by canals and rivers, had created one of the most discombobulating street networks in America. In my eventual report, I took great pleasure in documenting how the drive from the Memorial Auditorium to its designated parking lot, a mere two hundred yards away, required a looping five-turn odyssey of more than a mile.

At this point, some astute readers will be asking about Portland: it has a one-way grid and it's doing great. What gives? Portland adds a major caveat to this discussion: if the grids are simple and the blocks small, corresponding to a dense network of fairly tiny streets, then one-way systems can function quite well—picture most of the residential cross-streets in Manhattan. But Portland has a number of one-ways that are simply too big to invite walking, and so does Seattle, another small-block gem.

When the streets get more than two lanes wide, it takes some pretty tall buildings to make them feel comfortable, buildings that most American cities don't have.

Take Savannah. In 1969, a one-way system was applied to many of the north-south streets in Oglethorpe's delicate grid. Most still remain, and create perhaps the only significant impediment to pleasurably strolling this otherwise eminently walkable city. Recognizing this problem, the city government commissioned the architect Christian Sottile to study what happened to just one thoroughfare, East Broad Street, when it became a speedway. He dug into the tax rolls and counted the number of active (taxpaying) addresses located along the street in 1968 and then a few years later. He learned that, as a result of its conversion, the street lost almost two-thirds of these addresses.[20]

Happily, there's a flip side to that story. Worried about speeding as it built a new elementary school, the city returned East Broad Street to two-way. In short order, the number of active addresses shot up by 50 percent.[21]

Savannah's experience is not alone. Based on a few well-publicized successes, dozens of American cities are beginning to revert their one-way systems back to two-way traffic. These include Oklahoma City, Miami, Dallas, Minneapolis, Charleston, Berkeley[22] . . . and, soon, Lowell. Perhaps the best documented of recent reversions was accomplished in Vancouver, Washington. As told by Alan Ehrenhalt in *Governing* magazine, Vancouver had "spent millions of dollars trying to revitalize its downtown," but these investments "did nothing for Main Street itself. Through most of this decade the street remained as dreary as ever."[23] He continues:

> Then, a year ago, the city council tried a new strategy. Rather than wait for the $14 million more in state and federal money it was planning to spend on projects on and around Main Street, it opted for something much simpler. It painted yellow lines in the middle of the road,

took down some signs and put up others, and installed some new traffic lights. In other words, it took a one-way street and opened it up to two-way traffic. The merchants on Main Street had high hopes for this change. But none of them were prepared for what actually happened following the changeover on November 16, 2008. In the midst of a severe recession, Main Street in Vancouver seemed to come back to life almost overnight.[24]

The success has continued, and business owners remain ecstatic. Twice as many cars drive past their businesses each day and the once-feared traffic congestion has never occurred. Now the head of Vancouver's Downtown Association, Rebecca Ocken, has some planning advice for other cities: "One-way streets should not be allowed in prime downtown retail areas. We've proven that."[25]

For small and midsized cities like Vancouver (population 162,000), she is almost certainly right. For larger cities, it depends. I, for one, am not about to revert Manhattan's Columbus and Amsterdam Avenues back to two-way traffic, but it's fair to say that New York would be an even more walkable place if that change were made. Bottom line: if your downtown lacks vitality and it's got one-ways, it's probably time for a change.

SACRED SIDEWALKS

Now that we are almost done talking about pedestrian safety, maybe it is time to actually discuss where pedestrians spend most of their time. I have avoided the subject until now, because sidewalk design has almost nothing to do with pedestrian safety. Pedestrian advocates always fight for wider sidewalks, but that's largely irrelevant. Some of America's most walkable cities have some of the narrowest sidewalks—picture Charleston, Cambridge, or Georgetown. In New Orleans's French Quarter, sidewalks are seven feet across.

What makes a sidewalk safe is not its width, but whether it is protected by a line of parked cars that form a barrier of steel between the pedestrian and the roadway. Have you ever tried sidewalk dining on a sidewalk without curbside parking? Those sorry little table installations rarely last long. Whether they are two feet away or ten feet away, nobody wants to sit—or walk—directly against a line of cars traveling at sixty feet per second. On-street parking also slows traffic down, since drivers are wary of other cars potentially pulling into the roadway.[26]

Few sidewalks without parking entice walking, yet cities routinely eliminate it in the name of traffic flow, beautification, and, more recently, security. Many curbs in Oklahoma City have lost their parking spaces based on the assumption that terrorist bombers are afraid of getting a parking ticket. This line of reasoning is so patently ridiculous that it has been embraced by the federal government.* Fortunately, at least local leadership has shown a capacity for reform: our new plan for OKC's central business district more than doubles the number of on-street parking spaces—from fewer than eight hundred to more than sixteen hundred. According to the National Trust's Main Street Center program, each eliminated on-street parking space costs an adjacent business ten thousand dollars each year in sales. If the inverse is true, we've just made Oklahoma City merchants $9 million richer every year.

The latest enemies of on-street parking to make the scene are two erstwhile friends: bikeways and transit lines. Stripping a sidewalk of its protection in order to add bike lanes is just sacrificing one form of nonmotorized transportation for another. And since transit depends on walkability for its success, any trolley system that undermines pedestrian comfort is shooting itself in the foot. If they are truly to offer an alternative to the automobile, bikes and trolleys must displace moving cars, not parked ones.

---

*As in many American cities, it is the curbs in front of federally owned buildings that have seen the greatest application of antiterrorist parking bans.

Can trees and landscape make up for an absence of curb parking? Not completely, unless you are willing to build big, chunky planter boxes like those found on Chicago's State Street—and, even then, cars are likely to drive too fast. Trees are typically essential, however, for pedestrian comfort, as I will cover in Step 8, and they do slow drivers down a bit. They can also stop a car that has hopped the curb. For that reason, the safest sidewalks are lined by both parked cars *and* trees.•

The other great threat to pedestrians on sidewalks, beyond cars that jump the curb, is cars that are welcomed across it by drop-offs and drive-thrus. In the interest of driver convenience, most American cities handed out curb cuts in the seventies like candy at Halloween, to banks, restaurants, dry cleaners, hotels . . . anyone who asked. These now send a very clear message to pedestrians that the sidewalk does not belong to them.

Many of these can now be eliminated. If a city has rear alleys, there is no justification for providing businesses additional access at the curb. Without alleys, there are still remedies. Most bank drive-thrus—often three and four lanes wide—can be necked down at the sidewalk, to widen beyond it. Indeed, with

---

•One fun battle that has been raging lately is the dispute between head-in and back-in angled parking. Many cities include business districts where the width of pavement is appropriate for angled parking. The recent tradition has been for this parking to be nose-to-the-curb although, historically, many Main Streets did it the other way around. Enter the traffic engineers, and somebody's discovery that back-in parking is actually safer than head-in, and a new movement is born. Now dozens of Main Streets nationwide have reintroduced back-in parking—including Charlotte, Honolulu, Indianapolis, New York, Seattle, Tucson, and Washington—and accidents are down, especially those involving bikes. Tucson, for example, averaged about one bicycle-car crash per week before converting from head-in to rear-in parking. Now, more than four years into implementation, no such crashes have been reported (see brunswickme.org/backinparking.pdf).

It is easy to see why. With back-in parking, the reverse motion is into the curb, while head-in parking requires drivers to back into moving traffic. Back-in parking is also more convenient for loading and unloading. The only major problem with back-in parking is that almost everybody hates it, mostly because they are not used to it. This was the case in Cedar Rapids, Iowa, where the typical public reaction was summed up in the online comment of one Brent B.: "Amazing, it only took the dum-dums on the city council three years to realize what an idiotic idea while those of us with common sense

the rise of online banking, many drive-thru lanes can just be eliminated. Whether or not businesses can be made to give up their current curb cuts, the best strategy now is to simply not allow any new ones. Even hotels, unless they are quite large, should be able to handle drop-offs easily at the curb, in the parking lane. In Philadelphia, we stayed at the 230-room Hotel Palomar, which welcomes all its cars this way. To be stingy with curb cuts, cities must be generous with small no-parking zones at places like hotels, where drop-offs occur continuously.

SENSELESS SIGNALS

In the last step, I mentioned the visible presence of taxis as one indicator of a city's walkability. Another reliable bellwether is the visible absence of push-button traffic signals. In my travels, it is almost always the cities with push-button crossings that need the most help. I remember when these were introduced during my

---

knew it was stupid to begin with" (comment to Rick Smith, "Cedar Rapids Phasing Out Back-In Angle Parking," *The Gazette*, June 9, 2011). To his credit, one council member, Jerry McGrane, said that he had voted in support of back-in parking "for the entertainment value if nothing else" (ibid.).

Back-in parking has also been implemented in some communities that are simply not ready for it. I mean this not intellectually, but urbanistically. If residents are not accustomed to parallel parking—which is more difficult than back-in—and if almost all local parking is head-in at strip malls, then reverse parking may just be too big a stretch. That was the case in Fremont, California, where back-in parking was discontinued after one year when 70 percent of poll respondents said they would be "less likely to stop" at retail shops with back-in parking (City of Fremont, City Council Agenda and Report, May 3, 2011). But take a look at Fremont: it's pure sprawl—217,000 residents without a single block of urban walkability.

The best argument I have heard against back-in parking is that the exhaust fumes can be noxious to sidewalk dining. This point makes sense and needs to be taken into account when back-in parking districts are located. As suggested by Tucson, bike routes need to be considered as well, as cycle lanes behind head-in parking are basically suicidal. With those two cautions, I am happy leaving it up to the citizens. When asked, I usually put it this way: "Back-in parking works just fine in Washington. Are you better or worse drivers than we are?"

childhood, and they seemed at the time like a gift. Wow, I can actually control the traffic light. What power! But the truth is quite the opposite. Push-buttons almost always mean that the automobile dominates, as they are typically installed in conjunction with a new signal timing in which crossing times are shorter and less frequent. Far from empowering walkers, the push button turns them into second-class citizens; pedestrians should never have to ask for a light.

It is fascinating to talk to blind people about push-button walk signals. They push the button and wait for a lull in the noise. But then they can't tell if what they hear is a red light, or just a gap in the speedy traffic. The alternative are those annoying chirping signals that now mark the pace of daily life in crunchy towns like Northampton, Massachusetts. These are unnecessary in a standard (non–push-button) crosswalk, where the visually impaired can hear and predict the direction of traffic.

Another recent favorite among traffic planners is the "Barnes Dance" intersection, popularized in the United States by Denver's Henry Barnes, in which all pedestrians wait a full cycle for all cars to stop and then are briefly given free rein over the entire intersection—including diagonally. The Barnes Dance is a sexier version of the generic "dedicated-cycle" intersection, which lacks the diagonal paint job, but functions the same way. This system was introduced to avoid conflicts between turning vehicles and pedestrians in crosswalks, another example of "pedestrian safety" being used as an excuse to limit pedestrian convenience in the service of traffic flow. There are more than three hundred of these intersections in Japan, and they do make sense in places with pedestrian crowding, like Manhattan's Union Square. But there is no pedestrian crowding in Bethlehem, Pennsylvania, which is why I have an impressive photo collection of dedicated-cycle jaywalkers. Smaller cities need to be aware that some big-city best practices just aren't made for them.

What makes dedicated-cycle intersections so frustrating to

pedestrians is the likelihood that they will have to stand still at almost every street they cross. Experienced Manhattan walkers will confirm that, in a true grid with standard signals, it is possible to cover huge swaths of a city without stopping once. Most pedestrian routes are not due north-south or east-west, but diagonal, and every intersection provides the opportunity to cross in one direction at all times. Walkers like to keep walking and dedicated signals kill the momentum.

Denver has recently eliminated its diagonal Barnes Dances due to the introduction of streetcars, but it has kept its dedicated-crossing cycles and—in a horrible move—increased the length of each cycle from an already-too-long seventy-five seconds to ninety seconds.* The city claims that this change is partly due to a federal recalibration of pedestrian speed downwards from 4 feet per second to 3.5 feet per second (as Americans become fatter and slower targets). But do the math: it takes 9 seconds to cross three driving lanes at the old, fast speed, and 10.3 seconds at the new, slow one. And you need 15 more seconds why? The clear winners, as usual, are the automobiles, which the city is afraid of inconveniencing with trolleys. Let's hope that the high altitude bestows superhuman patience on Denver's pedestrians.

The other way that cities increase traffic flow at the expense of pedestrians is with the "right on red" rule. God knows, I love this as a driver, but, as Jan Gehl puts it, "the widespread American practice of allowing cars to 'turn right on red' at intersections is unthinkable in cities that want to invite people to walk and bicycle."[27] It is banned in the Netherlands.[28]

Of course, the obligatory right-on-green is even more dangerous to pedestrians—and left-on-green worse than that[29]—

---

*The ideal signal cycle timing is almost always sixty seconds or less. Longer signal cycles have long been favored by traffic engineers, who calculate that these contribute to system throughput. However, their calculations ignore the associated negative impacts of the speeding and road rage that result from drivers having to wait inordinately long times at stoplights, not to mention the jaywalking accidents.

since the driver is being told to go. One recent safety innovation, just implemented in Washington, D.C., is the leading pedestrian interval, or LPI, better known as the "pedestrian head start." With the LPI, the "walk" signal appears about three seconds prior to the green light, allowing pedestrians to claim the intersection before cars do. This is the ideal form of walkability enhancer, since it improves both pedestrian safety and pedestrian convenience, rather than pitting the two against each other. Meanwhile, in Los Angeles, the city's bright idea for improving pedestrian safety is to remove crosswalks.[30]

Finally, though, with signals as with road design, the safest approach may turn out to be "less is more," as embodied in the four-way stop sign. What if, instead of simply telling drivers when to go, we asked them to think for themselves? Four-way stop signs, which require motorists to approach each intersection as a negotiation, turn out to be much safer than signals.[31] Drivers slow down, but never have to wait for more than a few seconds, and pedestrians and bicyclists are generally waved through first.* Clearly, these are not possible on the busiest streets, but most cities have many intersections that would benefit from the removal of their signals in favor of stop signs.

If stop signs are so much better than signals, why do signals still proliferate on local low-traffic streets? Indeed, why does the typical corner include not just a signal in each direction, but a distinct signal in each direction over every single lane of traffic, such that the typical urban four-lane intersection now bristles with a good dozen lights? In the sixties, one signal hanging over the middle of the crossing was enough.

The answer may lie in who makes the rules. As director of the Davenport, Iowa, Design Center, Darrin Nordahl did a little

---

*Indeed, four-way stops are in most cases a biker's dream, as they generally allow confident bikers to blow through intersection after intersection without even having to slow down.

digging, and found out that the firm the city hired to design its signalization regime was the same firm who then sold the city its signals. Enough said.

Would most intersections be safer with one traffic signal rather than twelve? Maybe, maybe not. But many streets would be safer with four-way stop signs. And we could sure use the savings.

STEP 6: WELCOME BIKES

A better way to go; Amsterdam, Copenhagen, Portland, and other foreign cities; Hey! I'm bikin' here!; How safe is safe?; I run afoul of the vehicular cyclists; Bike lanes, separated paths, and shared routes; Advanced cycling; Don't get greedy

Perhaps the greatest revolution currently under way in—only some—American cities is the dramatic rise in biking. This has not happened by accident. New York City recently saw a 35 percent jump in ridership in one year alone, thanks specifically to its strong commitment to an ever-improving bicycle network. Almost every American city is currently well stocked with would-be bike riders who are only waiting for an invitation to hop on the saddle, and it is likely that those cities that invest now in (relatively inexpensive) biking infrastructure will have a meaningful advantage in attracting the next generation of new residents. Millennials routinely cite biking as an important motivator in location choice, and today's seventeen-year-old is a third less likely to have a driver's license than a baby boomer was at that age.

To anyone who lived in New York during the eighties, it might seem a bit odd to advocate for bicycles in a discussion of pedestrian safety. The only cyclists at that time were reckless messengers who broke every traffic law and took out pedestrians with alarming frequency. But visit the city now and it's hard to spot the messengers among the throngs of civilians, most of whom do a pretty good job of sticking to their newly minted bike lanes.

Not that there aren't exceptions.* In a heart-stopping aerial video, "3-Way Street," by Ron Gabriel,[1] one can witness some more adventurous Manhattan cyclists weaving through multiple lanes of oncoming traffic to surprise hapless pedestrians in crosswalks. Clearly, some people have yet to get with the program. After a few minutes of the video, it becomes apparent that these bikers probably pose the greatest danger to themselves, so we can only assume that Darwinism will cull the herd. Every evolution involves growing pains, and these daredevils hide a deeper truth, which is that cities with more bicyclists are considerably safer for both bicyclists and pedestrians.

Take a step back and it's easy to see why. A street with bikes, once the drivers get used to them, is a place where cars proceed more cautiously. And a city with bikes everywhere is a different kind of city. As bike lanes have been added along New York's avenues, injuries to pedestrians have dropped by about a third. Indeed, on Broadway and on Ninth Avenue, reported accidents and injuries to all users were cut in half,[2] outpacing even the advocates' expectations.

A BETTER WAY TO GO

Safety is but one of many reasons why our cities need more bicycles. As anyone who has taken advantage of a good biking city will tell you, cycling has got to be the most efficient, healthful, empowering, and sustainable form of transportation there is. Using the same amount of energy as walking, a bicycle will take you three times farther.[3] Bicycle commuters enjoy about double the

---

*Indeed, it is in some of the most advanced biking cities, like Amsterdam and Berlin, where I have had my closest calls with speeding bicyclists. In both cases, though, I was firmly at fault, strolling mindlessly in well-marked bike lanes, just off the plane and not yet adjusted to the eminently logical and well-marked street divisions. And one close brush was all it took to correct my course for the remainder of my visit.

amount of daily physical activity of drivers.[4] Bikes are cheap, and the fuel is free. And it's fun. As one happy biker put it, "It's like being able to golf to work."[5]

I have friends who bike to and from their offices instead of joining a gym, saving time and money and generally having a great time of it. (Yes, they have showers at work.) As Robert Hurst says in *The Cyclist's Manifesto*, "If you need to exercise, and you need to get around, why not do both at the same time?"[6]

Compared to the car, the bicycle's spatial demands are minimal. Ten bikes can park in the space of a single car, and the typical bike lane handles five to ten times the traffic volume of a car lane twice its width.[7] As already mentioned, money spent on bike lanes generates more than twice the jobs of money spent on car lanes. And if every American biked an hour per day instead of driving, the United States would cut its gasoline consumption by 38 percent and its greenhouse gas emissions by 12 percent, meeting the Kyoto Accords instantly.[8]

In Washington, I have found that there is simply no faster, easier, or more convenient way to get around. If I have an appointment almost anywhere in the city, I just set my alarm for fifteen minutes prior and I will be there on time. Were I to take transit or drive and park, that would require twice as long. Just the other morning, I biked the two miles to my doctor's office, had a checkup, and biked home, all in half an hour. Two caveats: I have America's only on-time doctor and I had to take a shower when I got home—it's August.

As one compares different biking and nonbiking places, it is interesting to see that climate plays a surprisingly small role. Canada's Yukon Territory—up there next to Alaska—has twice the rate of bicycle commuters as California.[9] In October 2011, icy Minneapolis was named "America's #1 Bike City" by *Bicycling* magazine, with 4 percent of all work trips being made by bike.[10] Nor is topography a significant factor: San Francisco has three times the ridership of relatively flat Denver.[11]

Rather than environmental or cultural, it seems that the biggest factors in establishing a biking city are strictly physical, and of two different types. First, there needs to be urbanism. As John Pucher and Ralph Buehler suggest in their report to the Institute of Transport and Logistic Studies, the main reasons that Canadians "cycle about three times more than Americans" are "Canada's higher urban densities and mixed-use development, shorter trip distances . . . [and] higher costs of owning, driving and parking a car"[12]—all conditions associated with city living. Second, and also cited by the authors, are "safer cycling conditions and more extensive cycling infrastructure"•—in other words, streets that have been designed to welcome bikes.

Of these two categories, the former equates with walkability. The conditions that support pedestrians are also needed to entice bikers. Once they are in place, the further provision of a truly useful biking network should be enough to allow a cycling culture to grow. Build it and they will come.

AMSTERDAM, COPENHAGEN, PORTLAND, AND OTHER FOREIGN CITIES

Since Americans are not constitutionally prohibited from embracing cycling in the same way that so many other nations do, it might be useful to look at some of the societies in which biking is a mainstay to see what is possible. Any such investigation probably has to begin with the Netherlands, which has the planet's highest percentage of people cycling. The Dutch statistics are staggering. Fully 27 percent of all trips are made on bicycle. School buses are uncommon, as the vast majority of high schoolers

---

•"Why Canadians Cycle More Than Americans," 265. The authors conclude that "most of these factors result from differences between Canada and the United States in their transport and land-use policies, and not from intrinsic differences in history, culture or resource availability."

bike to class.[13] Indeed, 95 percent of ten-to-twelve-year-olds bicycle to school at least some of the time.[14] Women take more bike trips than men, and roughly a fourth of all trips made by the elderly are on a bicycle.[15] In Amsterdam, a city of 783,000, about 400,000 people are out riding their bikes on any given day.[16] In a telling detail, spandex sightings are exceedingly rare; nobody wears anything special to bicycle, certainly not a helmet.

Bike safety, etiquette, and respect for bikers are taught from an early age. Drivers learn to reach for the door handle with their opposite hand, so that they cannot exit the car without checking for bikes. Food shopping is more likely to occur daily than weekly, to fit it in the bike basket. As Russell Shorto notes in *The New York Times*, biking means that the Dutch eat fresher bread.[17]

Biking in the Netherlands is a virtuous circle, in which more bike paths—the most in the world—has led to more biking, which has led to more bike paths. It is empowering to know that things were not always this way. Amsterdam's chief planner, Zef Hemel, told Shorto that "back in the 1960s, we were doing the same thing as America, making cities car-friendly." He credits Jane Jacobs, of all people, with the transformation of Dutch thinking.[18] It's nice to know that *somebody* was listening to her back then.

Like the Netherlands, Denmark has also seen a revolution in cycling, much of it recent, and most of it spearheaded by government investment in bike infrastructure. In Copenhagen, most of the city's major four-lane streets have been converted to two lanes plus two bike paths. As a sign of the city's priorities, these bike lanes are always cleared of snow before the driving lanes are. The minimum recommended bike path width is over eight feet,[19] which makes America's five-footers look pretty dinky.

The impact of this investment has been profound. Forty years ago, peak-hour motorists in Copenhagen outnumbered bicyclists by three to one. In 2003, the two modes reached parity, and now cycling is the most popular way around town.[20] Forty percent more people bike to work than drive.[21]

Closer to home, and supposedly part of America, the most bike friendly of our sizeable cities has got to be Portland. Although no match for Europe, Portland has accomplished something remarkable. A mere fifteen years ago, only 1 percent of Portlanders biked to work; today, that number tops 8 percent.[22] Between 1993 and 2008, peak-season bike traffic across the Willamette River climbed from about 3,600 trips per day to more than 16,700.[23]

This change is palpable. I was recently e-mailed some photos of the city's morning commute and I had to ask the sender: "What was this, Bike to Work Day?" No, he said, it was just Tuesday.

As in Europe, this change was led by an investment in bicycle infrastructure, but at a limited cost. According to Mia Birk, the city's bicycle coordinator at the time, "For less than one percent of Portland's transportation budget, we've increased bicycling from negligible to significant. For the cost of one mile of freeway—about $50 million—we've built 275 of bikeways."[24] Spending 1 percent of transportation funds on a network serving 8 percent of commuters sounds like a good deal, even better when you consider the indirect economic benefits. In contrast to widened roads and other highway "improvements," new bikeways actually increase the value of nearby real estate.

It's not for nothing that Portland even has a woman called "the Bike Realtor," Kirsten Kaufman, who specializes in selling overpriced homes next to bike routes. Her website, bikerealtor.com, lays it out simply enough: "I get it. I specialize in helping people who want to drive less and enjoy life more. I know from personal experience that the less time my family spends in the car, the happier and healthier we are."[25]

If bikeways make houses more valuable, some of that value accrues back to the city in higher property taxes—undoubtedly enough to pay for the bikeways. Of course, these dollars are only a fraction of the savings that result from time and money not spent in traffic, as Joe Cortright says (see page 29).

And then there are the noneconomic benefits to a community that has reshaped itself around bicycles. In *Pedaling Revolution*—the seminal book on urban cycling—Jeff Mapes describes one popular local activity, "bike moving," in which people literally help each other change homes through the exclusive use of pedal power. It sounds like a great way to meet people, although perhaps not as effective as North America's largest annual naked bike ride, also claimed by Portland.[26] (Don't forget the baby wipes.)

Before turning to New York's recent transformation, it is worth mentioning one other American city, Boulder, Colorado. In a mere three years, from 2000 to 2003, the percentage of residents' commute trips by bike tripled, from an already hefty 7 percent to an epic 21 percent, thanks to investment in biking and transit.[27] Ninety-five percent of Boulder's arterial streets—the type usually most dangerous to cyclists—have been made bike friendly, with what can now be described as the expected results. Similar things are happening in Seattle, Chicago, Madison, Minneapolis, and elsewhere.• It can now be said with some confidence that any urban road investment that ignores bicyclists is money that could be better spent.

HEY! I'M BIKIN' HERE!

Street space in New York has always been contested, so you can imagine the furor that erupted when Janette Sadik-Khan, Mayor

---

•"America's Top-50 Bike Friendly Cities," bicycling.com. For example, Chicago's Rahm Emanuel has committed to adding twenty-five miles of bike lanes during each year of his first term. Seattle is executing a ten-year, $240 million bike plan that will add 450 miles of bike paths.

Michael Bloomberg's transportation chief, started taking lanes away from cars and giving them to bicycles. Manhattan was one thing, but Brooklyn? That's looking for trouble.

Here's what happened: The city converted one lane of Prospect Park West from driving to biking. As a result, the number of weekday cyclists tripled, and the percentage of speeders dropped from about 75 percent of all cars to less than 17 percent. Injury crashes went down by 63 percent from prior years. Interestingly, car volume and travel times stayed almost exactly the same—the typical southbound trip became five seconds faster—and there were no negative impacts on streets nearby.[28]

Sounds pretty good, right? Well, as of this writing, Sadik-Khan has personally been subpoenaed by the ironically named Neighbors for Better Bike Lanes (just replace "Better" with "No," and you'll get the picture) for trying to turn this successful and popular trial project into a permanent installation. Other opponents include Borough President Marty Markowitz, who calls bike lanes "discrimination to those who prefer to own or need their cars for their livelihood or convenience."[29] Not without a sense of humor, Mr. Markowitz put a cartoon of the bike lane on his annual Christmas card, flanked by additional crowded lanes for sitting, walking, holiday revelry, and, yes, driving—the narrowest lane of all. The cartoon was accompanied by a song, to the tune of "My Favorite Things":

> Strollers and schleppers and skaters and joggers
> Holiday lanes just for egg-noggers
> But let's not forget cars—it's getting insane
> Welcome to Brooklyn, "The Borough of Lanes."[30]

If this opposition fails, which is likely given its lack of supporting data, Prospect Park West will continue to serve close to 10 percent more commuters than it did before, with greatly reduced risk to life and limb. One can only hope that Markowitz, undeterred by the facts, will be swayed by the constituents he suppos-edly serves, who support more bike lanes at a ratio of almost two to one.[31]

The Prospect Park West controversy is just one part of a much larger and happier picture of New York City that includes 225 miles of bike lanes added since 2006, with more to come. These lane miles have contributed to a massive rise in com-muter cycling, from 8,650 riders recorded in 2006 to 18,800 today. In the past year alone, biking has risen by 14 percent.[32] According to a Quinnipiac University poll, support for bike lanes across the city has also been growing every year, hitting 59 per-cent in 2011.* The remaining New Yorkers, of course, are still pissed off.

HOW SAFE IS SAFE?

We know that biking cities are safer cities. But is biking really worth the risk? The numbers could be more encouraging. The safety expert Ken Kifer found that "bicycling was nineteen to thirty-three times more likely to result in injury than driving a car the same distance." Shortly after publishing his research, Kifer was killed by an automobile while biking.[33]

I try to stay mindful of Kifer's story as I bike around Wash-ington, as there is always a temptation to cut corners to avoid slowing down. Like many cyclists, I treat red lights as yield signs and blow through stop signs when I can. Using this method, my only close call in nine years has been at a four-way stop, with another bicyclist of similar bent. This experience made me won-der whether the much-advertised salubrious benefits of "active

---

*Andrea Bernstein, "NYC Biking Is Up 14% from 2010; Overall Support Rises," trans-portationnation.org, July 28, 2011. This 59 percent is up from 56 percent in 2010, which matched the percentage of New Yorkers who don't own cars (U.S. Census, 2010).

transportation" get canceled out by the occasional tumble. Did I really want to be ten pounds slimmer with a broken wrist?

I am aware of only one study that addresses this, by the British researcher Mayer Hillman. From his study of British factory workers, he concluded that the health benefits of biking outweigh the risks by twenty to one. In Hillman's estimation, the regular cyclists were as fit as the noncyclists ten years younger[34] and enjoyed such better health that their few biking injuries were almost statistically insignificant. This conclusion is comforting, but one does have to remember that it is British, from a town that is likely to have developed a prominent biking culture.

This presence of an established cycling population, as it makes for more aware drivers, seems to be the biggest factor in bike safety. From city to city, the "strength in numbers" theory holds sway. In New York, with bicycling up 262 percent since 2000, injury risk has declined by 72 percent.[35] In Portland, a fourfold increase in cycling has brought with it a 69 percent reduction in the crash rate.[36] Davis, California, "America's Bicycle Capital"— where one trip out of seven is by bike—has the lowest bicycle fatality rates of sixteen similarly sized California cities.*

Of course, we have a long way to go to equal the Netherlands, whose fatality rate is less than a third of ours, despite the lack of helmets.[37] This evidence has prompted some American cyclists to stop wearing helmets, as if the wind blowing through your hair somehow magically turns your city into Amsterdam. This is a bad idea, even though it is bolstered by the recent discovery that passing cars give more elbow room to bikers without helmets—and, incidentally, even more space to bikers wearing blond wigs.[38] This latest episode of risk homeostasis threatens to

---

*Jeff Mapes, *Pedaling Revolution*, 23, 128. Referred to as "ten square miles surrounded by reality" (135), Davis also has the lowest rates of pedestrian and vehicular deaths of the sixteen cities studied.

camouflage the larger fact that 63 percent of bicycle fatalities are the result of head injuries.[39]

Bottom line: it would seem that we are presented with two statistics that could potentially cancel each other out. If biking is nineteen to thirty-three times more dangerous than driving, but the health benefits of biking (in bikeable cities) are twenty times greater than the risks, then maybe we can call it a wash. Most important to this discussion is the fact that bicycle safety seems to depend largely on how many people are biking, and that the resulting mandate—to create as many cyclists as possible— needs to drive the design of our urban bicycle networks. As we shall see ahead, this mandate leads to some counterintuitive conclusions.

I RUN AFOUL OF THE VEHICULAR CYCLISTS

Not very long ago, I was against bike lanes in downtown areas, mostly because they can widen streets that are already too wide, encouraging cars to speed. More recently, for reasons that will become evident, I changed my mind. I hardly ever change my mind about anything, and I had every reason to expect that my revised position might win me some friends in the cycling community. Imagine my surprise, then, when I released my proposals for Davenport, Iowa, and was soon directed to the following (excerpted) e-mail message: "This is the same 'solution' he's trashing downtown Oklahoma City with. . . . He defines the problem without seeing it. Because he's only looking in his own lane. . . . Snake oil!" Yikes, what gives? I thought you people *liked* bike lanes! Utterly confused, I forwarded the exchange to Mike Lydon, a consultant who specializes in urban biking. It was then that I learned about the fascinating technique called *vehicular cycling* and the waning but still significant influence of its ardent practitioners.

In many cities, if you take a lesson in bicycle safety, there is a good chance it will be taught by a vehicular cyclist. You will be instructed essentially to drive your bike as if it were a car, albeit a slow one. This includes "claiming your lane," staying near its center and only allowing cars to pass when there is ample room. In the words of the movement's founder, John Forester: "The vehicular-style cyclist not only acts outwardly like a driver, he knows inwardly that he is one. Instead of feeling like a trespasser on roads owned by cars he feels like just another driver with a slightly different vehicle."[40]

Forester is motivated principally by rider safety and by what he earnestly believes is the best way to stay safe: visibly claiming the proper amount of roadway at all times. But he is also driven, as it were, by a conviction that cyclists should not be assigned second-class status to motorists. For this reason, as Robert Hurst puts it, "Forester's crusade has always been directed primarily at bike lanes and the idea that bicyclists should be 'shoved over to the side' [as he puts it] to make way for motor traffic."[41] For Forester and his disciples, bike lanes are worse than "separate but equal," and must be eradicated from the landscape. As a result, he has become a darling of the libertarian American Dream Coalition, where he sits on the Speakers' Bureau with the rest of the Road Gang, making sure that not a single transportation dollar gets diverted from highways.

The biggest problem with vehicular cycling is neither its politics nor its relative safety—which has not been discredited—but whom it serves. John Pucher and Ralph Buehler summed up the predicament in their important paper, "Cycling for Few or for Everyone":

In the vehicular cycling model, cyclists must constantly evaluate traffic, looking back, signaling, adjusting lateral position and speed, sometimes blocking a lane and sometimes yielding, always trying to fit into the "dance" that is traffic. Research shows that most people feel very unsafe engaging in this kind of dance, in which a single mistake could be fatal. Children as well as many women and elders are excluded. While some people, especially young men, may find the challenge stimulating, it is stressful and unpleasant for the vast majority. It is no wonder that the model of vehicular cycling, which the USA has followed de facto for the past forty years, has led to extremely low levels of bicycling use.[42]

And there's the rub. Vehicular cycling may indeed be the safest way to bike, but it is also the most exclusive. Perhaps the ideal candidate for vehicular cycling was the fellow I met in Davenport, who was so aggressive a cyclist that he had dispensed with his bike saddle. I suspect that the next step in this evolution is to wear a thong and to tattoo "Hard Core" on your buttocks.

If bike safety is largely a factor of the number of cyclists, as the numbers insist, then any technique that works against their proliferation can hardly be considered safe. Jeff Mapes notes that Forester "didn't think that cycling would ever become a mass form of transportation in America, and that was fine with him."[43] Now, as that outcome is already happening, it's time to show the vehicular cyclists the bike path out of town. More important, it's time to create bicycle facilities that not only allow for cyclists, but actively and boisterously invite them to share the road.

BIKE LANES, SEPARATED PATHS, AND SHARED ROUTES

That said, there is a good argument against bike lanes. Because narrower streets are safer streets, and because the perception of potential conflict is what makes all road users act with caution, it is likely that adding bike lanes to a street makes it less safe. This conjecture is supported by several studies in different countries, cited in Tom Vanderbilt's book *Traffic*, that found that "drivers tend to give cyclists more space as they pass when they are on a street without a bicycle lane. The white marking seems to work as a subliminal signal to drivers that they need to act less cautiously—that it's the edge of the lane, and not the cyclist, that they need to worry about."[44]

This experience suggests that most bike routes should be unmarked. However, unmarked bike routes do not attract bikers and most cities do not have enough bikers to make biking safe. For that reason, I believe that it often is wiser to include bike lanes anyway—not everywhere, but in locations where they make sense.

And where is that? That tricky question can be answered by working through a series of simpler questions. The first is whether bike lanes can be used to take up excess street space. As seen in Brooklyn, trading driving lanes for biking lanes need not make a street less efficient for automobiles. The same goes for the "road diets" of the previous chapter: trading four lanes for three lanes plus cycling rarely reduces car capacity when it introduces a center turn lane.

However, in some cases, turning driving lanes into bike lanes will indeed slow down drivers. That trade-off may well be worthwhile, especially if a street sits along an important cycling trajectory. It is important to remember that, in a robust street network, traffic redistributes itself intelligently, with parallel roads able to pick up the slack. For that reason, any analysis of likely impacts needs to look not just at the street in question, but at the larger system. Of course, you already know that reducing capacity reduces traffic, so the real challenge here is not technical, but political.

Another good way—and good reason—to add bike lanes is to right-size existing lanes that are too fat. We did that in Lowell, where a street misdesigned as a highway, with (four) twelve-foot driving lanes and eight-foot parking lanes, will be remade with ten-foot and seven-foot lanes, yielding ten extra feet for biking. Since a standard bike lane is five feet wide, we were able to add a bike lane in each direction. This change will have no impact on the road's car capacity, but it will encourage safer speeds.

But five-foot bike lanes up against car doors are nobody's favorite, so the next question is whether there is enough room to build a *separated path*. These typically claim at least eleven feet of roadway, to allow for two adjacent four-foot paths protected by a three-foot buffer. If you haven't seen them, these paths—the type employed in Brooklyn—take some getting used to. They are located between one curb and that curb's parallel parking aisle, which gets pushed out into the street. The buffer is marked with striping and often holds vertical posts. Once you get the hang of these paths, however, it's hard to go back to a plain old bike lane. My wife will go three blocks out of her way to take the new separated path in our neighborhood. It goes down one side of a formerly four-lane one-way street, a street that now operates perfectly well with one fewer eleven-foot lane. D.C. planning czar Harriet Tregoning, a master communicator, shrewdly refers to streets with this much pavement as having "extra lanes."

The final question to ask is whether a bike lane is in keeping with the nature of the street. While carving bike lanes out of existing retail Main Streets can sometimes make sense, they should not be allowed to replace curbside parking, nor can they be allowed to create an impediment between cars and shops. For this reason, separated paths rarely belong in a retail environment. All those stripes and posts may send a message of sustainable transportation, but it is still a message of motion, not of the stasis appropriate to a Main Street. The design objective for this type of street should be to create an environment of such slow driving that bikes and cars can mix comfortably at biking speeds. The technical term for this sort of facility is a *shared route*, and the vast majority of bikeways must remain unmarked streets that belong to everyone. To use an extreme example, a residential cul-de-sac is no place for a bike lane. Only when car speeds get well into the thirties does the need for lanes kick in.

ADVANCED CYCLING

As long as we're getting technical, let's mention some of the more sophisticated bikeways that have recently hit the streets. If you are not a cycling nut, feel free to skip this bit.

One technique that's been getting a lot of play lately is the *sharrow*, which is a wide lane shared by cars and bicyclists, indicated by a prominent biker decal in the right-center of the pavement. In *The Cyclist's Manifesto*, Robert Hurst comes out strongly in favor of sharrows over bike lanes, noting that "the sharrow doesn't really tell the bicyclist or the driver to do anything specifically, and therein lies much of its beauty. It's art that conjures awareness, and that, as we've seen, is what traffic safety is all about."[45]

He is, of course, right, but the problem is that all things fade, and those sharrow markings seem to disappear faster than almost any other type of road decal. In many northern cities, where they effectively sandblast the streets every winter, a townful of sharrows can disappear in two seasons. And then all you're left with is a super-fat lane. For this reason, sharrows are best used to encourage and announce the presence of bikes in streets that are a bit too wide, but not wide enough to hold a dedicated lane instead. In my experience, if a driving lane is approaching fifteen feet wide, a bike lane is far better than a sharrow.

Another interesting development is something called the *bi-*

cycle boulevard, which has taken Portland by storm and can also be found in Madison, Tucson, Minneapolis, Albuquerque, and a handful of California cities. To create a bicycle boulevard, you take a street that is long enough to be of regional significance and hobble its intersections so that only bicycles can flow quickly from block to block. Residents can enter with their cars, but diverters at the cross-streets quickly free the street of cut-through traffic. Then, if you're really serious, you time the signals at each intersection to match the twelve-mph speed of the average cyclist,* and you end up with what is called a *green wave*. Green waves on bicycle boulevards contribute mightily to Portland's bike commute and cycling culture. Clearly, they are best limited to residential areas where, indeed, they contribute to property values, as the Bike Realtor will tell you.

Finally, investment in a different kind of cycling infrastructure, pioneered in Europe, has begun to take root in American soil: urban bike share. After some small and mostly failed attempts in prior decades, this concept is finally catching on, thanks largely to new technologies that remove some earlier inconveniences. The best-known bike share is the twenty-thousand-bike Vélib system in France, which is considered a resounding success despite the fact that more than 80 percent of its bikes have been damaged, dumped in the Seine, or shipped off to Africa.[46] The French program is actually dwarfed by one in Hangzhou, China, where bike stations are located only 330 feet apart, and where not one of the system's 60,600 bikes has yet to be stolen.[47]

Recently, Washington, D.C., pioneered large-scale bike sharing in the United States, and our bright red Capital Bikeshare cycles have become a fixture of urban life in the District. Here's how it works: you check your smartphone for the location of a

---

*Mapes, *Pedaling Revolution*, 81. Since the timing only enhances travel in one direction, these are paced to ease the inbound and outbound rush-hour commutes.

bike docking station near you, and make sure that there are bikes available. The city currently has 1,100 bikes distributed among 114 stations. Show up, stick in your key, take a bike, and go. The first half hour is free—that's enough time to get almost anywhere in the District—and then you start paying a nickel a minute. This price escalates to discourage all-day rentals, to the point that each hour after ninety minutes costs twelve dollars. Near your destination, you locate another docking station—again, you can check your phone for open docks—and you're done.

Given the system's convenience, and the continually improving bikeability of the District, public buy-in has been huge.* After one year, the program had amassed fourteen thousand annual riders, as well as over forty thousand day memberships.[48] In August 2010, Capital Bikeshare members logged almost 150,000 trips, and that was during the most sweltering four weeks in D.C. history.* In response to the program's success, its sponsors hope to create a regional system of more than five thousand bikes within a few years.[49] Across the Potomac, Arlington, Virginia, already has fourteen docking stations, with sixteen more on the way.[50]

Washington was first out of the gate, but similar programs are now in place—or will be soon—in a dozen other American cities, including the usual sustainable suspects (New York, San Francisco, etc.) as well as some surprises (San Antonio, Des Moines).[51] These bike-sharing programs are not cheap. Washington's took about $5 million to start, and costs a couple million to operate each year. This means that the District has paid more than six thousand dollars so far for each bicycle in service, which seems awfully steep, even though almost all of it has been other

---

*While some local bike shops initially feared the competition, they are now celebrating a major uptick in sales, fueled by Capital Bikeshare renters who decide that they want to own.

*One can only assume that they were principally downhill—the bike-share staff use vans to redistribute the bikes, which tend to settle at lower altitudes.

people's money. Some of that cash has been recouped by selling advertising space, but the system will never break even—nor should it be asked to. Just like highways and transit, bicycle transportation will require public investment to succeed. Given the environmental and health benefits of turning drivers and riders into bikers—and the very real public savings associated with those benefits—that six thousand dollars is a better deal than it looks. All the more so when you consider the free publicity these systems bring.

DON'T GET GREEDY

There is no doubt in my mind that many bicycle advocates will find this chapter's prescriptions woefully inadequate. What, five feet for a bike lane? They will remind me of Copenhagen's eight-footers, and quote Bogotá's Enrique Peñalosa, "If a bike lane isn't safe for an eight-year-old child, it isn't really a bike lane."[52] Some will bemoan my suggestion that separated paths and bike boulevards are best kept out of commercial areas. These complaints are certainly valid, and also correct—from the perspective of a bicycle advocate.

But bicycle advocates are specialists. Like the highway specialists who reamed out our cities with freeways, they are often focused myopically on the one aspect of the public realm that concerns them, sometimes at the expense of all the others. It is for this reason that specialists are the enemy of the city, which is by definition a general enterprise. Let's consider for a minute what would happen to the typical American Main Street if we were to redesign it to keep all of the specialists happy.

First, we would need at least four travel lanes and a center turn lane, to keep the transportation engineers happy. These would need to be eleven feet wide—no, wait, make that twelve feet, because the fire chief might want to pass a bus without slowing down. To satisfy the business owners, we would need angle parking on both sides (another forty feet), and eight-foot separated bike paths against each curb for you-know-who. Then we would have to add two ten-foot continuous tree trenches to satisfy the urban forester, and two twenty-foot-minimum sidewalks for the pedestrian advocates. Have you been doing the math? We now have a Main Street over 175 feet wide. This is more than twice the normal width and about as efficacious an urban environment as a large-jet runway—and just as conducive to shopping.

The moral of this story is that everyone has to compromise if our cities are going to be any good and also if they are going to be affordable. Greediness costs too much, and can also cause you to end up shortchanging yourself. In New York City, they have built a stunning "cycle track" along Sands Street in Brooklyn. This massive center-road facility cost taxpayers $13 million per mile. That's almost ten times the cost of a signal-protected bike path, and *one hundred times* the cost of a standard separated path.[53] Presuming that budgets have limits, could it possibly be worth losing one hundred miles of separated path to build one mile of cycle track?

The goal of an intelligent cycling plan should be to allow bikes access to every address in the city. Some of those trips will be on separated paths, others on bike lanes, and most will be mixing with traffic on slower streets. Some may even be on sidewalks, which surprisingly is still legal in many places. The dream is to get bicyclists where they need to go, not to apportion them a slice of every road, tied up with a bow.

That said, there is reason to go a bit overboard, especially when it comes to lane markings. If the evidence is to be believed, bike lanes—especially separated lanes—basically mint cyclists. But, beyond that, they also send a message. A bold green stripe down the side of a street—or many streets—tells residents and potential residents that a city supports alternative transportation, healthy lifestyles, and cycling culture, and that it welcomes the sort of people who get around on bikes. For the most part, those people are the millennials and creatives who will help a city thrive. For that reason, even if nobody in town even owns a bike, a few snazzy new lanes are probably a good idea. Or you can just skip right to the Naked Ride and see how that goes.

THE COMFORTABLE WALK

■

STEP 7: SHAPE THE SPACES

Embrace me; Object fetishism; Tiny is tastier; Weather or not

Do snakes disturb you? Don't be embarrassed, it's not your fault. Thousands of years of your ancestors' being bitten by snakes have planted that fear in your unconscious mind. Without it, your bloodline may never have lasted long enough to create the crowning achievement that is you.

The same sort of process explains why, contrary to common perception, people need to be spatially contained by the walls of buildings. Most of us enjoy open spaces, long views, and the great outdoors. But we also enjoy—and need—a sense of enclosure to feel comfortable as pedestrians. Evolutionary psychologists tell us how all animals seek two things: prospect and refuge. The first allows you to see your prey and predators. The second allows you to know that your flanks are protected from attack. Prospect and refuge explain why, when I first moved into my new apartment in Washington, my cats ended up on top of the refrigerator in the corner of the (open) kitchen.

For Homo sapiens, the need for prospect and refuge may have an even more specific source. The ecologist E. P. Odum argued that it was not grassland or forest that provided the ideal early habitat for humans, but rather the boundary between the two, the "forest edge," where both distant views and physical enclosure were present. Thomas Campanella of the University of

North Carolina notes that the "recollection of the forest edge may explain why architectural and urbanistic elements evocative of this space—colonnades, loggias, arcades, verandas, even porches—are so appealing and comfortable."[1]

EMBRACE ME

From an ecological perspective, then, most U.S. cities offer too much grassland and too little forest. The need for refuge, deep in our DNA from millennia of survival, has led us to feel most comfortable in spaces with well-defined edges, and those edges have gone missing. Forget that emblematic image of Madison Avenue, where the craggy towers turn the streets into canyons. The typical American urban experience is a profound lack of spatial enclosure. I am not talking just about the parking lot at the mall, but also about the centers of our cities, where once-substantial buildings have been torn down and replaced, almost always, by surface parking.

I remember in 1998, when I was helping Andres Duany redesign downtown Baton Rouge and we were taken to the top floor of the tallest banking tower for a bird's-eye view, that a tremendous amount of development was on display—the city had abolished its downtown height limits—but every block of construction was surrounded by at least three blocks of parking. The result was a checkerboard city, almost completely devoid of two-sided streets in which a pedestrian could feel comfortable.

In towns and cities of every size, with buildings of every height, otherwise promising pedestrian environments have been rendered uninviting by these empty lots—what planners call "missing teeth." It takes only one of them to wreck a place for walking. Akron, for example, has spent millions improving its Main Street area, building a minor-league baseball stadium and a canal park along it, in what by all rights should be the walkable heart of the city. They paid extra money for a Camden Yards–style stadium, complete with storefronts facing brick sidewalks and historic streetlamps. But someone forgot about the piece of property directly across the street, where almost a full mile of continuous building fronts is interrupted by a single, three-hundred-foot-long stretch of parking. This one relatively tiny tear in the downtown's urban fabric, which could be repaired with a single building, provides remarkably convenient game-day parking for sixty lucky baseball fans . . . at the expense of a Main Street that people would want to use.•

Most city-planning offices are aware of these missing teeth and know that they are a problem. But what are they doing about them? In Akron, the city clearly has not made a priority of getting something built there, when a mere half-acre of construction would transform what, for many, is the central experience of visiting downtown. This oversight is sadly typical, as most cities undervalue the role of spatial definition in urban vitality.

Indeed, many cities actively work against spatial definition with the requirement for shadow studies, which are often used to chop the tops off tall buildings in urban centers. These make sense against public greens and in dark, northern cities like Boston, where light and air are at a premium, but what are they doing in Miami Beach, where shadows are what make summer walking possible? Where they are necessary, shadow studies need to be supplemented by "shaping studies" that show how well buildings make streets into spaces. When the two are combined properly, you get Vancouver: elegant point towers sitting atop lower sidewalk-hugging bases . . . and another great city to move to.

•What is so heartbreaking about Akron's Main Street neighborhood is how far it has come—with great adaptive reuse of historic properties, a sexy new art museum, and some delightful restaurants and cafés—and how easily it could be brought to the next level if energy were only directed at a few problem sites that nobody seems to care about.

OBJECT FETISHISM

The success of "Vancouver urbanism" shows us one path toward the happy resolution of a great war that has been raging in city planning for decades: figural space versus figural object. Traditional, walkable urbanism is grounded in figural space. It believes that the shape of the spaces between buildings is what matters, because this is the public realm—the place where civic life plays out. In traditional urbanism, buildings often take on odd, unsatisfying shapes in order to surround extremely satisfying streets and squares, what can be called outdoor living rooms. Figural space is one of the things that allows traditional cities to so generously support pedestrian life. Look at an aerial photo of Paris and you will be astounded by how contorted some of the buildings become in order to shape the delightful spaces they frame.

In contrast, modern urbanism was founded on the cult of the figural object. It became the role of the hero architect to create buildings as three-dimensional sculptures akin to a Brancusi or a Calder, floating freely in space. The shape of this space became residual and meaningless—and inhospitable to pedestrians. Most urban designers now consider this evolution to have been a horrible mistake. Most architects also agree with this assessment publicly, even as they hope against hope for their chance to design the figural object building that will land them on the cover of a hero architect magazine. And then there are the starchitects, most of whom don't care about figural space at all.

A fairly typical battle in this war was fought at the Mayors' Institute on City Design, when Mayor Frank Cownie presented a plan for a piece of Des Moines that was based on the Vancouver model. A collection of quirky, expressionistic towers were shown in red, sitting atop a series of block-filling bases, shown in blue, that shaped the streets beautifully. "That's a really interesting plan," said the one starchitect at the table. "Just get rid of the blue bits and you'll have something special."

Wow. First of all, when a designer says something is "interesting," it's time to get your guard up. Now that both beauty and truth are considered subjective among the intellectual class, "interesting" has become the new term of highest praise, which can lead to all manner of architectural mischief in the hands of aging *enfants terribles* like Rem Koolhaas. Second, and more to the point, I was surprised to learn that, despite all that I had read about the utter failure of the modernist spatial program (code name: Pruitt Igoe•), there were still ardent advocates for object urbanism on the loose among us.

This was the 2000s, and I was tempted to take a plaster cast of the offending architect for my fossil collection. But fast-forward a decade and, at least in the academy, tower-in-the-park city planning is once again ascendant. This time it has taken the guise of "landscape urbanism," the dominant ideology at Harvard and elsewhere, where the ostensibly overriding objective of enhancing each site's natural ecology has led to a newfound disregard for creating well-shaped public spaces. We are being banished to the grasslands once again—but at least this time the grasslands are made of grass. Starchitects of course adore landscape urbanism, as the vast distances between buildings allow each sculptural object to be seen to best effect.

We can give the last word on this topic to Jan Gehl: "If a team of planners was asked to radically reduce the life between buildings, they could not find a more effective method than using modernist planning principles."[2] Gehl obviously has not seen Monty Python's hilarious abattoir-designer-as-architect sketch,• but his point is hard to discredit. The evidence suggests that any environmental benefits that accrue from landscape urbanism

---

•For the uninitiated, Pruitt Igoe was Minoru Yamasaki's award-winning tower-in-the-park housing project in Saint Louis that had to be abandoned and demolished due to its complete social collapse. Most people agree that this failure, while caused in part by improper management, was also the result of an urban design that failed to provide physical spaces for which tenants could feel a sense of ownership.
•Just Google "Monty Python Architect."

will quickly be outweighed by the increased car trips of residents who refuse to walk.

TINY IS TASTIER

Jan Gehl may be the world's leading observer of how people use places. In *Cities for People*, he notes how we walk just under 3 miles per hour in warm weather, and just over 3.5 miles per hour in cold weather; how we bow our heads ten degrees while walking; how we can see a person's movement at one hundred yards and recognize and hear them at about fifty.[3] These sorts of observations have powerful implications for how we should design public streets and squares and, more often than not, the lesson is to make them smaller. He shares the aphorism "When in doubt, leave some meters [yards] out," and reminds us that "if a dinner party is held at narrow tables, a festive mood quickly catches on because everyone can talk in several directions across the table."[4]

This analogy is apt. It is often surprising to measure some of America's favorite and most successful public spaces—New York's Rockefeller Center, San Antonio's Riverwalk, San Francisco's Ghirardelli Square—and discover how small they actually are. Few are much broader than sixty yards across.* And let's not forget Disney's Main Street, famously built at three-quarters scale. Large public spaces, increasingly demanded of developers by citizens' committees and planning boards, can often end up offering less of an amenity than smaller ones, especially if the buildings surrounding them are not very tall. Since the key measure of a place's spatial definition is its height-to-width ratio, wide spaces only feel enclosed when flanked by buildings of considerable height.■

*Times Square? Sixty yards across. Rome's Piazza Navona? Sixty yards across.
■As discussed in Andres Duany, Elizabeth Plater-Zyberk, and Jeff Speck's *Suburban Nation* (78), a width-to-height ratio above 6:1 is generally agreed to exceed the limits of spatial definition, with a 1:1 ratio historically considered the ideal.

Yet Gehl's well-earned distaste for large things extends to building heights as well. This stance puts him in the company of some of our most prominent urban thinkers while alienating him from others. In A *Pattern Language*, the bestselling design book of all time, Christopher Alexander drew the limit at four stories, noting that "there is abundant evidence to show that high buildings make people crazy."[5] The fertile-minded Leon Krier, Luxembourger godfather of the New Urbanist movement, is likewise adamant in his dismissal of skyscrapers, which he terms "vertical cul-de-sacs," arguing instead for cities limited to four stories, the convenient height for a walk-up. This position is embraced by peak-oilers like Jim Kunstler, who worry—or celebrate—that escalating energy costs will eventually put all our elevators out of service.

Gehl's beef with tall buildings comes from his concern for the public realm, and the fact that only people in the lower stories of a building can interact with people on the street. He wryly comments that "above the fifth floor, offices and housing should logically be the province of the air-traffic authorities."[6] He also notes that tall buildings capture the air currents that circulate around the ten-story level, which "can cause wind speed at the foot of tall buildings to be up to four times greater than in the surrounding open landscape." He observes that, in Amsterdam, umbrellas protect people, while in (high-rise) Rotterdam, people protect umbrellas.[7]

Gehl and Krier are probably right that the most pleasant and livable cities are those like Amsterdam and Paris that were principally built before elevators. This outcome is, of course, more dependent on the fact that they were also built before cars, but the human scale of the buildings contributes as well. The more important discussion, however, concerns whether taller buildings degrade walkability by their presence as much as they improve it with their capacity. The more people a building can hold, the more people on the street, and the superlative pedestrianism of Manhattan and Hong Kong suggests that inhumane, vortex-generating skyscrapers have little negative effect on street life. Indeed, it is essential to recognize that, in Manhattan, it is precisely the continuous presence of tall buildings along the avenues that allows them to support a continuous array of shopfronts for block after block after block.

It is for this reason, among others, that while some urban designers rail against tall buildings, most economists clamor for more. Ed Glaeser, today's noisiest advocate for skyscrapers, insists that they are necessary for preserving affordability in our blossoming urban cores, and Chris Leinberger has notoriously dared to question Washington, D.C.'s century-old height limit. This position is right in theory, but the economists don't seem to have fully processed one thing the designers know, which is how tremendously dense a city can become at moderate heights. Boston's North End, in Jane Jacobs's day, achieved 275 dwelling units per acre with hardly an elevator in sight.[8] A ten-story city like Washington simply does not need towers to achieve great walking density. Indeed, outside of Midtown and the Financial District, most of Manhattan's lively avenues are lined by buildings closer to ten stories tall.

Ultimately, since most cities are not New York, there is a much more important argument to be made for height limits than Gehl's call for sociability and calm winds. The typical American downtown is not faced with the volume of development, even in good times, that needs tall buildings to contain it. In most places, the challenge is the exact opposite: a preponderance of vacant properties and parking lots, the missing teeth that make walking so unpleasant. Raising or abolishing the height limit, as occurred in Baton Rouge, creates the outcome of Baton Rouge, where a single skyscraper lands on an empty block and sucks up an entire year's worth of development activity, while all the surrounding blocks stay empty—or fill up with skyscraper parking.

Meanwhile, witnessing the success of the skyscraper developer, the surrounding landowners begin to speculate. They won't build a midrise on their lot, because that's not the most the lot can hold. And they won't sell it for a reasonable price, because it's "worth" building a skyscraper on.[9] The next thing you know, all the would-be urban developers have fled to the beltway.

In this context, it is tempting to do a bit of our own speculation, on how tremendous the District of Columbia's height limit has been for the city and its walkability. That limit, set at twenty feet taller than the width of each building's enfronting street, has caused new development to fill many more blocks than it would have otherwise. This strategy has created street after street of excellent urbanism, even in places where the architecture could be better. (The running joke is that Washington is the place where the best architects go to do their worst work.) A case in point would be the K Street neighborhood, northeast of the Watergate, where hardly a single building is worth a second look, but where every boring glass-and-steel-lined sidewalk is perfectly hospitable to its promenading lobbyists.

Does this experience suggest that skyscrapers are always a bad idea in typical American cities? Not necessarily, as long as they follow the Vancouver model of a skinny tower atop a broad base. While a bit more expensive than fat slabs, narrow towers create a skyline instead of blocking out the sky, and don't cause the same wind problems. They can also satisfy the developers who, far from chasing Leinberger's density or Glaeser's affordability, are most often hoping to sell luxury condos.

WEATHER OR NOT

Talking to audiences across the United States, I am always surprised to hear that—no matter where I am—their city's weather makes it somehow less capable of supporting pedestrian life than the rest of planet Earth. Never mind the crowds of happy visitors who flock to New Orleans in the summer, Quebec City in the winter, Seattle in the rain, and Chicago in the wind . . . "people won't walk here because it's just too hot/cold/wet/blustery!"

There is no doubt that climate exerts some influence on walking, but the evidence suggests that this factor is not half as impactful as street design. In that regard, I have always found these three questions to be especially useful: What North American city has the most linear feet of successful retail-fronted sidewalks? Toronto. What developed country has the highest share of urban trips going to walking instead of driving? Sweden.• How many months out of the year do sidewalk cafés stay open in Copenhagen? Twelve.[10]

The lesson we learn from these places is that walking down a narrow, shop-lined street in icy Boston or sweltering Savannah is a vastly superior experience to walking down an arterial between parking lots and car dealerships on San Diego's best day. Get the design right and people will walk in almost any climate.

•29 percent versus 6 percent in the United States (Pucher and Dijkstra, "Making Walking and Cycling Safer," 27).

STEP 8: PLANT TREES

Trees for life; The greenest of green products; Trees pay;
What tree where?

I used to work in Little Havana, the heart of Cuban Miami, where the main drag, Calle Ocho, is flanked by literally hundreds of blocks of one-story houses. As I would drive from street to street, I developed first impressions about which places were richer or poorer, safer or more dangerous. One day, the landscape architect Douglas Duany suggested that I take the same tour while thinking about trees. Not sure what he was getting at, I tried it . . . and found that all my "rich" and "safe" streets had good tree cover, and all my "poor" and "dangerous" streets did not.

It's best not to pick favorites in the walkability discussion—every individual point counts—but the humble American street tree might win my vote. Often the first item in the budget to be cut, street trees are key to pedestrian comfort and urban livability in so many ways. In addition to offering shade, they reduce ambient temperatures in hot weather, absorb rainwater and tailpipe emissions, provide UV protection, and limit the effects of wind. Trees also slow cars and improve the sense of enclosure by "necking down" the street space with their canopies. A consistent cover of trees can go a long way toward making up for an otherwise nasty walk.

Because they have such a powerful impact on walkability, street trees have been associated with significant improvements in both property values and retail viability. Since this enhancement translates directly into increased local tax revenue, it could be considered financially irresponsible for a community to *not* invest heavily in trees.

TREES FOR LIFE

We already know that trees are good for us. This is something most of us understand intuitively, but it doesn't hurt to have studies. The most famous such investigation, conducted in a suburban Pennsylvania hospital between 1972 and 1981, tracked the recovery patterns of surgical patients in a single wing of rooms. Half of these rooms faced (at some distance) a brick wall, while the other half faced a row of trees. All other factors were held constant. Under these conditions, those patients with tree views had fewer negative evaluations, required many fewer doses of potent narcotics, had a lower likelihood of postsurgical complications, and were discharged from the hospital, on average, a day earlier.[1]

This evidence aligns with the work of Dr. Roger Ulrich at Texas A&M University, who has found that "in laboratory research, visual exposure to settings with trees has produced significant recovery from stress within five minutes, as indicated by changes in blood pressure and muscle tension."[2] Given the stress that so many commuters complain of, this phenomenon might help explain the engineer Walter Kulash's finding that a drive on a treeless street is perceived to be significantly longer than an equal-length drive on a street lined with trees.[3]

If trees are so good for us, and indeed make driving less stressful, it would stand to reason that they are encouraged along our roadways. But of course, they are not, because the traffic engineers are quite reasonably worried about people smashing into them. The Georgia DOT outlaws placing trees within eight feet of a state-owned street because, in the words of one reporter, "sidewalks are auto recovery zones where drivers have space to correct course if they've veered off."[4] And only recently did the Virginia regulations stop referring to street trees as "Fixed and Hazardous Objects."

Clearly, this approach bodes ill for walkability, as it presumes that only drivers' lives are at risk. This makes good enough sense along truly rural highways, but not along streets with sidewalks, where it has also been indiscriminately applied. As a result, soft pedestrians have proved a much lesser threat to moving vehicles than hard trees.

In the face of this challenge, there are two complementary tactics for convincing transportation engineers to advocate for street trees. The first is to shame them into placing pedestrian safety on par with driver safety. But since this approach is not always effective, the larger strategy would be to convince them that street trees make roadways safer for drivers as well as pedestrians. This counterintuitive supposition has one important argument on its side, which is that it appears to be true. Thanks to risk homeostasis, drivers respond to the presence of broad "recovery zones" by speeding, and crashes become both more frequent and more deadly.

This was the case in an investigation of arterial streets in Toronto, which found that the presence of street trees and other vertical objects along the road edge correlated with a 5 to 20 percent decline in midblock crashes. (Accidents at intersections were relatively unaffected.) A University of Connecticut study of two-lane roadways found that although broad shoulders "were associated with reductions in single-vehicle, fixed-object crashes, they were also associated with a statistically significant increase in total crashes." Most recently, the researcher Eric Dumbaugh compared four years of crash statistics from two different sections of Colonial Drive in Orlando and found that the section without trees or other vertical features experienced 12 percent more midblock crashes, 45 percent more injurious crashes, and a dramatically higher number of fatal crashes: six versus zero.[5]

THE GREENEST OF GREEN PRODUCTS

As always, car crashes remain the greatest individual threat to our physical health, but we shouldn't underestimate the additional nuisance of heat waves, which are unsurprisingly on the rise and kill dozens of Americans annually. Before long, many of our cities could begin to experience scorchers like the one that hit Moscow in 2010, killing more than seven hundred people every day. When this happens, we will wish we had planted more street trees. Measurements of ambient temperatures taken on exposed versus canopied streets around the United States document temperature differentials ranging from five to fifteen degrees (Fahrenheit) between the two,[6] which can make a big difference when temperatures hit the triple digits. The relevant term here is "urban heat island," a downside of city living that can largely be eliminated by proper tree cover. According to the U.S. Department of Agriculture, the cooling impact of a single healthy tree "is equivalent to ten room-size air conditioners operating 24 hours a day."[7]

Our reliance on air conditioners means that the ambient temperature of our treeless cities exerts a global warming double whammy, complete with feedback loop. Not only do shade-deprived neighborhoods make the world hotter, but they require much more electricity to cool, most of which is still sourced from coal. A properly shaded neighborhood is said to require 15 to 35 percent less air conditioning than a treeless one.[8] Climate change begets air conditioning begets carbon pollution begets climate change. Denser urban canopies could help short-circuit this vicious circle.

But even this factor pales next to the astoundingly large role that trees perform simply as a carbon sink. In what economists call an "ecosystem service," trees are unsurpassed in the landscape at gobbling up CO_2. And urban trees, located as they are in close proximity to roadways, are ten times more effective than more distant vegetation at hijacking car exhaust before it hits the stratosphere.[9] All greenery absorbs CO_2, but trees are by far the most effective. A study in Leicester, England, found that aboveground vegetation stores more than 200,000 tons of the city's carbon, of which over 97 percent is stored by trees rather than in groundcover—even counting those ample British gardens.[10]

That's just the air. What about water? One of the biggest and costliest problems facing many cities is the pollution caused by combined sewage overflows (CSOs). More than nine hundred American communities, many of them large cities like mine, have old collection systems that combine stormwater with sanitary sewage. When it rains hard—something that has been happening with increasing frequency—the commingled waste surges into local waterways. A rainstorm in the summer of 2010 caused the city of Milwaukee to dump more than a billion gallons of raw sewage into Lake Michigan. All told, the EPA estimates such overflows to surpass more than 1.2 trillion gallons annually— "enough to keep Niagara Falls roaring for eighteen days."[11]

Here in Washington, where CSOs are a regular occurrence, we are seeing some unnerving impacts. Male smallmouth bass in the Potomac River are growing eggs in their sex organs. These involuntarily transgendered fish are being blamed in part on pharmaceuticals, including birth control pills, that have been dumped down toilets (or transported through urine) and then discharged due to CSOs. We get our drinking water from the Potomac, so this concerns us. In Maryland, cancer rates of the people who drink this water are markedly above the state average.[12]

What does this have to do with street trees? Well, here's what happens when an inch of rain falls on a tree: the first 30 percent of the precipitation is typically absorbed directly by the leaves and never even touches the ground.[13] Once the leaves are saturated, up to 30 percent more of the rain seeps into the soil, made more porous by the tree's root structure. This root structure then slurps the water back up into the tree, from which it is eventually transpired back into the air. This process allows a mature tree to absorb about half an inch of water from every rainfall.[14] As a result, communities that add 25 percent additional tree cover will reduce their stormwater by 10 percent.[15] In many American cities, this 10 percent would be enough to eliminate most CSOs.

Lacking these trees, and the public will to plant them, we are faced with a huge financial challenge. New York State anticipates a bill of $36 billion over the next twenty years to solve this problem. Philadelphia alone is currently collecting $1.6 billion to prevent CSOs.[16] In Wheeling, West Virginia, where median income is eighteen thousand dollars, residents are anticipating a sewer repair bill that could top fifteen thousand dollars per household.[17] How much better things would be if, in the 1990s, each household had planted a $150 tree!

The several-decade time lag between planting and maturity is the obvious hitch here. Our water systems are in crisis now, and you want to plant trees? Obviously, there are a lot of sewer repairs and upgrades that need to be made immediately, but many more are simply anticipated. A twenty-year window, for water systems planning, is not a long stretch of time. Any sensible analysis of present and future costs would conclude that we should plant trees now.* But since asking a sewer specialist to plant trees is like asking a pig to fly, we need to make the case to the generalists who are hopefully in charge, like mayors, to make

---

*On a recent visit to the Kentlands—a new community in Gaithersburg, Maryland, designed by DPZ in 1989—I was thrilled to discover that the trees we planted twenty years ago are already forming a complete canopy over many of the streets.

trees a priority. Fortunately, there are even greater financial rewards that can be reaped by doing so.

TREES PAY

"The first duty of the inhabitant of forlorn neighborhoods is to use all possible influence to have the *streets planted with trees*."[18] So intoned the dominant landscape architect of the antebellum period, Andrew Jackson Downing. In *Republic of Shade*, Thomas Campanella's masterful history of the elm tree, an editorial taken from the 1835 *New England Farmer* shares that sentiment:

> Would it not be a regulation well deserving of the attention of the General Court to require every town to plant the sides of the public roads with forest trees? . . . The value of most farms would be raised ten or fifteen per cent by the addition of shade trees about the buildings and along the public road. [Moreover, trees] give the country an appearance of wealth, that nothing else can supply. . . . The most spacious and princely establishments without them appear covered with the most prison-like gloom. . . . A bald head is not comely, neither is a street seemly which is not well set with trees.[19]

It is hard to know whether the editorialist's calculation regarding real estate value was supported by economic studies, but we have them now and he wasn't too far off. According to a study conducted by the University of Pennsylvania's Wharton School of Business, trees planted within fifty feet of houses in one Philadelphia neighborhood caused home prices to increase by 9 percent.[20]

A more comprehensive study, this time of Portland's east side, reached conclusions that were less dramatic but, taken as a whole, no less compelling. Comparing houses with and without nearby street trees, it found that an adjacent tree added 3 percent to the median sale price of a house, an uptick of $8,870—the equivalent of an additional small bedroom. Interestingly, since there are more houses than street trees, each individual tree was deemed responsible for almost $20,000 in increased real estate value. Taken across the entire east side, the benefit from street trees was calculated at a whopping $1.12 billion.[21]

How does that increased value affect the city's bottom line? Extrapolating to Portland as a whole, the study's authors found that the presence of healthy street trees likely adds $15.3 million to annual property tax revenues. Meanwhile, the city pays $1.28 million each year for tree planting and maintenance, resulting in a payoff of almost exactly twelve to one.[22]

That powerful ratio should become the mantra of urban foresters everywhere, but it is probably an underestimation. Focused strictly on housing, it ignores the benefits that accrue to cities when their businesses are more profitable: one recent study shows 12 percent higher income streams accruing to shops on tree-lined streets.* I am a bit suspicious of this study, because its outcomes depend on so many other factors that are difficult to hold constant, but few would argue that a healthy tree canopy doesn't contribute mightily to establishing both the cachet and the comfort of a walkable shopping district.

In any case, the residential numbers should be enough. Absent a sophisticated carbon tax, it is difficult to monetize the environmental benefits of planting more street trees; even the stormwater savings can be a tough sell, given the time lag. But a clear outcome in which city revenues dramatically outpace city investment seems a steady foundation on which to build policy.

---

*Dan Burden, "22 Benefits of Urban Street Trees." In another six-city study conducted by the University of Washington, polled consumers interestingly rated products 30 percent higher for quality when those products were purchased on streets with good tree cover ("Trees and Commercial Business," coloradotrees.org).

For this reason, it would be wise for other cities to pursue their own Portland-style investigations in order to help justify the multimillion-dollar investment in street trees that they invariably need.[*] I call such an investment a Continuous Canopy Campaign and, while I have yet to convince a city to commit to such a lofty goal, this means that the catchy moniker is yours for the taking.

It is astounding to me, given the vast and multifarious advantages of a continuous urban canopy, that most American cities care so little about their trees. This philistine disregard is not a universal condition; in Melbourne, for example, five hundred new street trees have been planted every year for the past seventeen years.[23] New York City, where one can walk entire neighborhoods without a single tree sighting, has recently set a goal of planting a million trees over the next decade, including 220,000 street trees.[24] But this campaign is the exception. Most progressive American cities only go so far as to become a "Tree City USA," a status achieved through the faint-hearted commitment to spend two dollars per capita on trees. Apparently, every citizen gets a handful of acorns to scatter.

Here in Washington, the District plants trees and abandons them for the residents to tend, a common strategy in the United States, and one that would be more effective if it were actually known to the residents. It took me three years to learn that I was my street tree's keeper, and that was by accident. Now I water my tree when I water my garden, but I'm the rare tree hugger who cares. Clearly, letting trees loose in the world without designated caregivers is a pound-foolish strategy. Particularly in distressed neighborhoods, where trees can mean so much but residents are not conditioned to take charge, a commitment to planting trees

[*]To assist in this effort, the USDA's Forest Service has created a software package called i-Tree Streets, which can be downloaded at www.itreetools.org/streets/index .php.

has to be matched with a commitment to keeping them alive. This takes more than two dollars per capita, which is why mayors need to both embrace and celebrate the fact that trees may be the best investment a city can make.

WHAT TREE WHERE?

Now that you're committed to a continuous canopy, there are a few things you should know. The first, for my southern friends, is to stop planting palm trees. Correction: only three cities in America should be planting palm trees: Palm Beach, Palm Springs, and Hollywood—and there, only along Sunset Boulevard. The point is: if you've got great, palm-lined avenues, by all means, keep them. But understand that palm trees are merely decorative, and don't begin to offer the same environmental benefits as deciduous trees. The last time I checked, most Florida cities had not learned this lesson.* The same goes for crepe myrtles, spruce pines, and those other bushes masquerading as trees that somehow grace many a city's tree list.

My second suggestion is to abolish the current practice of refusing to plant more than a few of the same tree in a row. Too many American cities are held hostage by urban foresters who, fearing the next Dutch elm disease, require that every street be planted with a tutti-frutti species mélange, so that no single blight can denude a whole street. While based on sound logic, this proscription typically prevents cities from doing what they once did, which was to create streets of distinct character based upon their consistent use of a single tree species. Many of us grew up in towns with an Elm Street, a Maple Street, a Beech Street, and a Walnut Street. In contrast to the current tradition of streets named after the developer's daughters, these streets

*Incidentally, we had another term for palms in Miami: hurricane missiles.

were actually planted according to their name, and each had its own unique landscape. Residents of Philadelphia will find this discussion familiar.

The tutti-frutti rule makes most of America's best streets illegal. As many observers have commented, a street with consistent, mature trees is like a cathedral, with the trunks serving as columns and the branches forming the vaults. This happy outcome is only truly possible when a single species of tree is planted at a consistent spacing distance.•

Moreover, when the next blight comes, better that it wipe out one street out of ten than one-tenth of every street, because, in most cities, nobody gets a phone call unless the die-off is pronounced and localized. A mandate for replanting often only arises when a street is impacted dramatically. When this happens, that street can be reforested with trees that will once again reach skyward in unison.

•One compromise position is worth mentioning here: in the hands of a truly skilled forester, streets can be planted with two or three species that appear almost identical yet have a distinct genetic makeup.

THE INTERESTING WALK

∎

STEP 9: MAKE FRIENDLY AND UNIQUE FACES

STEP 10: PICK YOUR WINNERS

STEP 9: MAKE FRIENDLY AND UNIQUE FACES

Invisible parking; Sticky versus slippery edges; Attack of the starchitects;
Too much of a thing; Boring nature

If only safety and comfort were enough. More Americans would stay in their marriages, we would eat the same dinner every night, and we could limit ourselves to Eight Steps of Walkability. But we are humans, after all, and our motivations are more complex. Among other things, we demand almost constant stimulation. Pedestrians need to feel safe and comfortable, but they also need to be entertained, or else those with a choice will choose to drive.

And what could be more boring than a parking lot? Whether the windblown tarmac of a surface lot or the incommunicative blank walls of a parking garage, there is little appeal to walking when faced with such an unrewarding view.

But it is not only parking that contributes to a blight of boredom in many American downtowns. Almost every city that has witnessed construction since 1950 has its share of cold, uninviting buildings fronting the sidewalk with rough concrete, tinted glass, or other such nastiness. Most architects have moved on from this style of building, but that is not to say that they are any more motivated to engage the pedestrian. Evidence would suggest that, among the leading starchitects, *creating street life* still ranks low on the list of priorities, somewhere down there with *staying on budget* and *keeping the rain out*.

In most cities, however, the culprit is less likely to be a starchitect than a Rite Aid, as pharmacies and other national chains refuse to put windows where shelves can go. These standards can be overcome, but only by cities that throw off the beggar mentality and outlaw the practice.

Finally, in their quest to become more sustainable, cities need to remember that, for the typical pedestrian, the most mundane storefront is still more interesting than the most luxuriant landscape. A determination to increase walking means not allowing the greening impulse to undermine the core qualities of urbanity that draw people downtown in the first place.

INVISIBLE PARKING

Mayor Joe Riley of Charleston, South Carolina, now in his tenth term, tells the story of when he tried to convince a local architect to make a new parking garage look instead like a traditional Charleston building. "We learned in school that form follows function," the architect said, "so this building needs to look like a garage." "Yes, I learned that too," replied the mayor. "We're just not going to do that in Charleston."

That building now graces East Bay Street, where it does three important things right. First, it places high-ceilinged commercial space on the ground floor directly against the sidewalk, giving it windows, doors, and human activity. Second, it hides its tilted car ramps away from the edges of the building, so that it doesn't shout "I am a garage." Placing the flat parking areas at the building's perimeter also allows for its eventual transformation to nonautomotive use.* Third, it details its upper floors as if they were inhabited, with window-sized openings equipped with

---

*Most parking structures, with ramping perimeter floors, can never serve any use other than parking. When the ramps are instead placed at the center of the garage, they can eventually be removed to create a light court surrounded by flat floors that can become offices or housing. Garages served by lateral spiral ramps, while a bit more expensive, are even more easily converted to nonautomotive uses.

Charleston-style shutters. The shutters are closed, which limits the building's gregariousness but also hides the cars behind them. Upon closer inspection, this building clearly serves cars more than humans, but you have to look hard to see it.

Five blocks west of this garage can be found another essay in urban parking. This newer, bigger structure sits twenty-five feet back from Market Street. At its corners, this setback is occupied by two mixed-use buildings that hide the parking lot from view. At the ground floor, these attractive structures—one of them historic—contain a beauty salon and a pet-oriented gift store. Between them, the setback is occupied by a shallow urban plaza that holds outdoor dining for Chucktown Tavern, located at grade under four stories of parking.

The main lesson from this garage is that it only takes 25 feet of occupied building edge to hide 250 feet of parking lot. Indeed, thanks to sight angles from the sidewalk, three stories of building can hide four or five stories of garage. On Market Street, three hundred cars have effectively disappeared into thin air. The same technique can be practiced even more cheaply with surface parking lots, where a thin crust of wood-frame structures can conceal acres of tarmac. At Mashpee Commons, a strip mall on Cape Cod that was retrofitted into a new downtown, this feat is accomplished by tiny one-story shops, each about the size of a two-car garage.

Enlightened developers like the ones at Mashpee know that hidden parking boosts retail sales and property values. Enlightened mayors like Joe Riley know that hidden parking boosts downtown appeal and livability. The rest of us need to be kept in check by building codes, the everyday city ordinances that determine what can be built where. It is fairly easy to gauge the intelligence of a city's planning department by asking a simple question: in downtowns and other areas of potential pedestrian life, do your rules require that all parking lots be hidden behind a habitable building edge?

STICKY VERSUS SLIPPERY EDGES

In America, most advanced city codes go that far when it comes to attracting street life. Few go much farther. This fact can be demonstrated by a walk down almost any Main Street, where drugstores, banks, and other businesses either place blank walls to the sidewalk or fill up their windows with signs designed to obscure the shelving and other *stuff* located behind them. This common activity runs exactly counter to what we know about making pedestrians happy. Jan Gehl puts it this way: "No single topic has greater impact on the life and attractiveness of city space than active, open, and lively edges."[1]

In *Cities for People*, Gehl talks about the "edge effect": how "wherever people stay for a while, they seek out places along the edges of the space."[2] He photographs Siena's famous Piazza del Campo, where the main pavement is surrounded by chunky man-size bollards, each one having accumulated the appendage of a standing or sitting man. These simple stone posts serve as anchors in a sea of activity, inviting people to tether themselves and stay a while. Most often, this job is performed by the fronts of buildings which, if adequately porous and deep, attract both walkers and lingerers. By *porous*, I refer to windows and doors, proper interior lighting, and any other measure that better connects the interior of the store to the sidewalk. By *deep*, I mean the degree to which the facade provides opportunities for shelter, leaning, sitting, and other physical engagement, and also how effective the design is at blurring the distinction between public and private while drawing out the experience of entering and exiting.

Outdoor dining and sidewalk displays are perhaps the most common and impactful contributions to a deep facade. Awnings also help, as they can give a potential shopper the feeling of already being inside the store. In the early 1990s, Andres Duany and I had lunch with a fellow who was the retail expert for one of Canada's largest real estate developers. His employers had spent untold thousands of dollars sending him around the globe for a full year, visiting dozens of successful shopping districts. We asked him: "Is there anything that all of the best places shared in common?" His immediate reply: "Awnings you can touch."

Deep facades are also thick facades. Do columns stick out beyond the front wall? Is the front door recessed? Are the windowsills substantial enough to sit on? Or maybe there's a bench built in? All of these things help. As an art history student, I was always impressed that the Palazzo Medici in Florence was constructed with a stone bench surrounding its entire perimeter. In Renaissance Florence, there were knife fights in the streets—and bars on the windows—but still the Medici saw fit to invite passers-by to rest their *posteriori*. When we built our house, I put a sitting-height wall on both sides, and a prominent sidewalk-hugging bench by the front door. You would be surprised how often someone sits there. Never mind that on occasion that person is a homeless crack-smoking schizophrenic . . . it was the right thing to do.

Jan Gehl's observations of successful downtowns even extend to facade geometries, noting that a more vertical orientation, such as that provided by columns, makes for a seemingly shorter walk. "In contrast," he says, "facades designed with long horizontal lines make distances seem longer and more tiring." He adds: "It is interesting to note that shops and booths in active, thriving commercial streets all over the world often have a façade length of 16–20 feet, which . . . means that there are new activities and sights to see about every five seconds."[3]

Unfortunately, most cities' building codes, while maddeningly specific on certain statistical measures like *floor area ratio*, say little to nothing about those things that matter to pedestrians, like the window-to-wall ratio and the presence of awnings. This is fairly easy to change, but cities need to ask. A bit ahead of the curve, both Melbourne and Stockholm have adopted active facade policies. Melbourne's code, for example, requires that "60 percent of street facades in new buildings along major streets must be open and inviting."[4] While many new communities have recently been designed with such rules in place, few older cities have adopted equally prescriptive guidelines requiring friendly building fronts on new buildings.

A dozen years ago in *Suburban Nation*, Andres Duany, Elizabeth Plater-Zyberk, and I advocated for the replacement of conventional city zoning codes with a new type of instrument that we called the Traditional Neighborhood Development Ordinance.[5] First created by my coauthors in the 1980s, this ordinance was notable for how it supplanted the land-use and statistical orientation of conventional coding with a focus on the physical form of buildings: how they met the ground, the street, and the sky; how they handled the transition from public to private realms; and how they hid their parking.

Since that writing, this type of ordinance has come to be known as a "form-based" code and hundreds of cities and towns have enacted them, most notably the City of Miami in 2009. The most prominent version of this ordinance, called the SmartCode, is a piece of open-source shareware available for free download.•
This document is a comprehensive tool for making better places, and almost every growing city would benefit from throwing out its current zoning in favor of the SmartCode or something similar. However, replacing an entire code is a big job. In the short term, a few simple rules, like Melbourne's open-facade law, can make a big difference.

In most cases, fixing a code is a two-part process: adding a few new rules and deleting a few old ones. In 1993, I was working with Andres Duany on the resuscitation of 5th Avenue South, the main street of Naples, Florida. One of the things we noticed

•The SmartCode can be downloaded from the Center for Advanced Transect Studies at www.transect.org/codes.html.

was that most of the shops had awnings no bigger than umbrellas, little semicircular zits that didn't begin to shade the street's parched sidewalks. We looked into the building code, and found that, unbelievably, any awning larger than a certain tiny size had to be sprinkled for fire suppression. We got rid of that rule first.

ATTACK OF THE STARCHITECTS

We've come a long way since the seventies, when every city endeavored to build its own version of Boston's fortress-like City Hall, a structure that only architects love (yes, I love it). This style of architecture was called brutalism, supposedly after Le Corbusier's *béton brut*—rough concrete—but the name stuck for other reasons. It was characterized by walls so abrasive they could rip your arm open. Happily, this technique is no longer in vogue, but many architects, especially the starchitects, still build blank walls where they least belong. The Spaniard Rafael Moneo, my old professor, is probably the leading blank wall composer, a veritable Copland of Concrete. In his studios, like all my architecture-school studios, nobody ever talked about how buildings need to give life to the sidewalk. We did discuss such things as a facade's thickness and depth—"sickness and death," in Moneo's formidable accent—but these were architectonic qualities, not practical ones. Most architecture schools still promote an intellectual and artistic sensibility that has little patience for such mundane questions as whether a building will sustain pedestrian activity.

This issue was the subject of a now famous exchange that took place at the 2009 Aspen Ideas Festival between Frank Gehry and a prominent audience member, Fred Kent. Kent, who runs the Project for Public Spaces, pointedly asked Gehry why so many "iconic" buildings by star architects fail to give life to the streets and sidewalks around them. Gehry, who was once quoted as saying "I don't do context,"[6] claimed to be above this criticism, but Kent didn't buy it. I wasn't there, so we'll let *The Atlantic*'s James Fallows tell the rest:

> But the questioner asked one more time, and Gehry did something I found simply incredible and unforgettable. "You are a pompous man," he said—and waved his hand in a dismissive gesture, much as Louis XIV might have used to wave away some offending underling. He was unmistakably shooing or waving the questioner away from the microphone, as an inferior—again, in a gesture hardly ever seen in post-feudal times.[7]

Gehry was clearly having a bad day, but his imperiousness is worth recounting as a metaphor for some of his work—not all, but some. Kent was no doubt recalling his son Ethan's visit to Gehry's masterpiece, the Guggenheim Bilbao, an experience he describes in the Project for Public Spaces website's "Hall of Shame." After failing to find the front door and taking note of the treeless, depopulated plaza, Ethan observed a mugging, something he later learned was common there. He adds, "In the span of 10 minutes that we spent around the museum, I witnessed the first mugging of my life—and I've lived my entire life in New York City."[8]

Robberies are no longer very common in New York, but the same goes for Bilbao—except for certain problem places. That one of these places enfronts the Guggenheim is partly Gehry's fault, the outcome of a landscape (more of a *landscrape*) conceived as a tabula rasa to show off the building to its best effect.* Gehry is actually perfectly capable of contributing to attractive, engaging landscapes—as he has done in Chicago's Millennium

---

*Equally at fault are the city planners who worked with Gehry to so completely disengage the museum from the adjacent neighborhood.

Park—but he rarely does so with his buildings, most of which do not reward proximity. His Disney Hall, in Los Angeles, has about fifteen hundred feet of perimeter, perhaps one thousand feet of which is blank wall of the most slippery sort.

But it's a concert hall, you say . . . it needs to have blank walls. Well, take a stroll around the Paris Opera, or even Boston's Symphony Hall, and let's talk again. These older buildings' facades are awash in engaging detail, so that even their blank walls don't feel blank. Walking next to them is a pleasure.

This discussion reminds me of a wonderful set of drawings by Leon Krier in which he shows two buildings side by side from three different distances. From far away, we can see that one is a classical palace, the other a modernist glass cube. The palace has its base, middle, and top, while the glass cube is articulated with the horizontal and vertical lines of its large, reflective windows. As we get closer, the palace reveals its doors, windows, and cornice, while the glass cube remains the same as before: horizontal and vertical lines. Zooming in to just a few paces away, we now observe the palace's decorative string course, the window frames, and the rafter tails supporting the eaves. Our view of the glass cube is unchanged and mute. We have walked a great distance to its front door but received no reward.[9]

Krier presents these drawings as a powerful argument against modernism. But this is not merely a question of style. Any architectural style—except minimalism, I suppose—is capable of providing those medium- and small-scale details that engage people as they approach and walk by. The high-tech Pompidou Center, by celebrating its mechanical systems on its exterior, gives life to one of the most successful public spaces in Paris. What matters is not whether the details were crafted by a stone carver or a cold extruder, but whether they exist at all. Too many contemporary architects fail to understand this point, or understand it but don't care.

TOO MUCH OF A THING

But a preponderance of human-scaled detail is still not enough if a streetscape lacks variety. However delicate and lovely a building facade, there is little to entice a walker past five hundred feet of it. As Jane Jacobs noted, "Almost nobody travels willingly from sameness to sameness and repetition to repetition, even if the physical effort required is trivial."* Getting the scale of the detail right is only half the battle; what matters even more is getting the scale of the buildings right, so that each block contains as many different buildings as reasonably possible. Only in this way will the pedestrian be rewarded with the continuously unfolding panorama that comes from many hands at work.

This fact seems to be lost on the vast majority of architects, especially the big names, whose unspoken goal is to claim as much territory as possible for their trademarked signature, even if it means a numbingly repetitive streetscape. It is rarely taught in architecture schools, where there persists a deep misunderstanding of the difference between city planning and architecture, such that most urban-design projects are seen as an opportunity to create a single humongous building. Design superstars like Rem Koolhaas, in their giddy celebration of "bigness," have adopted this confusion as doctrine.■

---

*The Death and Life of Great American Cities, 129. She adds: "No special form of city blight is nearly so devastating as the Great Blight of Dullness" (234), and "in architecture as in literature and drama, it is the richness of human variation that gives vitality and color to the human setting" (229).

■Koolhaas, who is a commanding presence and writes beautifully, has by now mesmerized two full generations of architecture students with his compelling dogma. In the essay "What Ever Happened to Urbanism?" he sums up his larger agenda this way: "The seeming failure of the urban offers an exceptional opportunity, a pretext for Nietzschean frivolity. We have to imagine 1,001 other concepts of city; we have to take insane risks; we have to dare to be utterly uncritical; we have to swallow deeply and bestow forgiveness left and right. The certainty of failure has to be our laughing gas/oxygen; modernization our most potent drug. Since we are not responsible, we have to become irresponsible" (Koolhaas, Werlemann, and Mau, S,M,L,XL, 959–71). Surely this quote is something to keep in mind before giving him the key to your city.

To be fair, egotism and the desire for celebrity are only partly responsible for this orientation. It also comes from an insistence on intellectual honesty. Just as a building supposedly bears the obligation to be "of its time," it must also be "of its author." For the designer of a large structure to pretend to be many different designers is to falsify the historical record, especially since the modern myth of the genius architect insists that every designer's personal style is as unique as his fingerprint. I still remember (how could I not) the critic at my architectural-school-thesis final review who said, "I don't understand: your two buildings seem to have been designed by two different architects." My fantasy-world response, twenty years after the fact: "Why, thank you, sir."

There is of course an easier way to solve this problem: give some of the project away. When presented with a "building" that is rightly the size of a bunch of buildings, call up your friends and share the wealth. . . . And exactly how many architects, particularly in these slim times, do you expect are willing to take that leap? Only those rare few that consider city planning as important as architecture itself.

That's exactly what happened in early 2000, when DPZ entered an international competition to redesign the Piazza dei Navigatori, a prominent site on the main southern road out of Rome. The program brief called for half a million square feet of building on roughly a dozen acres. The other invited architects were Rem Koolhaas, Rafael Moneo, Rafael Viñoly, and three leading Italian firms. Each designer came forward with a single megabuilding in his inimitable style. Our strategy was a bit different. We proposed dividing the large site into seven distinct building blocks, and assigning each block to one of the competitors, ourselves included. We wrote a one-page form-based code that controlled the volume and placement of each building, and admonished the judges that, rather than sponsoring a single monument, they could build a diverse neighborhood.

The next part was the most fun. I went to the Harvard design library and got pictures of each of our competitors' most famous building. I handed these to our renderer, with the instruction to reshape them into their assigned locations in our plan, and brought the resulting artwork to Rome for the final judging. We did not win, but the look on our competitors' faces when they saw their buildings in our renderings was well worth the trip. When they learned that we wanted to beat them in order to share the job with them, they seemed equal parts angry, grateful, and embarrassed.•

Since so few architects are willing to give away design to others, or to pretend, Sybil-like, to possess multiple design personalities, the responsibility lies with cities to force them into it. Most of the design codes that I write for governments include a paragraph that goes something like this: "While even smaller units of design are encouraged, no more than 200 feet of continuous street frontage may appear to have been designed by a single architect." Along with an active facade policy, such a rule can help save a street from succumbing to Jane Jacobs's "Great Blight of Dullness."

Ultimately, however, this is as much a business discussion as a design discussion. Too much of real estate practice in this era has been about faking variety, about creating the impression of multiple actors when control has unwisely been concentrated in the hands of too few powerful players. As in the new suburbs, individual developers are invited into cities and given control over huge swaths of land, such that the future of those parcels ends up depending entirely on the skill and magnanimousness of those developers.

This common approach is certainly expeditious, and may be the only way to get something built quickly in blighted neighbor-

---

•We came in second to the one Roman architect in the bunch, an outcome that, given local politics, felt like a victory. His winning proposal, a gravity-defying megabuilding, has yet to be built. (Of those invited, Moneo and Koolhaas ultimately decided not to submit.)

hoods. But that redevelopment comes at a price, which typically includes the sense of character and variety engendered by the outcome. It also presents a greater risk, which is that the whole deal falls apart, leaving you nowhere or—sometimes worse—that construction produces such drastic change that a place loses all of its original character, not to mention its population. This is what Jacobs referred to as "cataclysmic money" versus "gradual money."[10]

On large projects, the path to avoiding this sort of outcome is straightforward and involves naming a master developer who oversees the project but who is not the developer of the individual buildings. That role can be played by the city, by a public authority, or even by a private developer in certain cases.* What matters is that different buildings are built by different people. The result, in true *Small Is Beautiful* practice, is the city of chipmunks, not of gorillas. Happily, while gorillas usually come in from out of town, chipmunks are mostly homegrown and have a greater vested interest in the outcome.

BORING NATURE

In *Green Metropolis,* David Owen tells the story of how he used to take long walks around Manhattan, running errands with his baby daughter in a Snugli. She would never complain and, planning a move to Vermont, Owen was anticipating how much more she would enjoy walks in the country. Here's what happened instead: "The first time we walked to the village green to buy the

---

*Probably the best-known example of such an approach is Manhattan's Battery Park City, which was developed and remains owned by a public-benefit corporation. As described by Witold Rybczynski, "It was designed to grow piecemeal, building by building, with individual projects financed and built by different developers, in response to changing market demands, but following the architectural guidelines of the master plan" (Rybczynski, *Makeshift Metropolis,* 151).

morning newspaper, on a spectacular autumn morning, she fussed and squirmed in her backpack almost the whole way. As far as she was concerned there was nothing to look at."[11]

Green spaces in cities are a lovely, salubrious, necessary thing. But they are also dull, at least in comparison to shopfronts and street vendors. Our kids may be suffering from nature deficit disorder, but they also know instinctively what we have been taught to ignore, which is that verdant landscapes do not entertain. As Owen further notes, large open areas "can encourage some people to *take walks*. But if the goal is to get people to embrace walking as a form of practical transportation, oversized greenways can actually be counterproductive."[12]

This critical outlook toward open space puts Owen in the company of Jane Jacobs, who had this to say fifty years prior:

> The first necessity in understanding how cities and their parks influence each other is to jettison confusion between real uses and mythical uses—for example, the science-fiction nonsense that parks are "the lungs of the city." It takes about three acres of woods to absorb as much carbon dioxide as four people exude in breathing, cooking, and heating. The oceans of air circulating about us, not our parks, keep cities from suffocating.[13]

Like Owen, Jacobs was fighting a dominant ethos that more green space makes cities more healthy, when in truth their microcosmic appearance belies their macrocosmic impact. By separating useful things from each other, they can contribute to an automotive culture that exacerbates pollution. Jacobs's case in point was Los Angeles, with the most open space and the most smog of any contemporary American city.[14]

This doesn't mean that we should stop building parks—Chicago and Seattle are two cities with new, big, expensive waterfront parks that nobody regrets—but rather that we shouldn't allow open space to rip apart the urban fabric of our walkable city centers. Every city, particularly if it is to attract millennials, needs to provide easy access to nature, including regionally scaled trails for hiking and biking. Likewise, frequent small pocket parks and playgrounds are key for retaining citizens into their parenting years. But meeting these needs is a very different brief from turning the city into a garden. Current impulses to make our downtowns more sustainable by filling them with pervious surfaces, prairie grass, and the latest craze—"rain gardens"[*]— threaten to erase one of the key characteristics that distinguishes cities from the suburbs that remain their principal competition.

Indeed, it was desire to somehow magically merge city with country that created the environmental, social, and economic disaster that is sprawl. Still, it is common to come across architecture-school proposals and design-competition entries that have us questing for "a new and unprecedented relationship between man and nature,"[■] as if there is some undiscovered way to improve the city by diluting its best qualities. We know better. And we know that central among these qualities is the street life that is only possible in a truly urban environment, where there are more buildings than bushes.

[*]Rain gardens, which allow streets in certain climates to drain naturally, are a worthy alternative to conventional stormwater systems. They can be provided in ways that do not enlarge the street space or impede pedestrian access.
[■]This quote is paraphrased from the winning entry in a 2000 competition to remake the site of the Fornebu Airport in Oslo. (We lost that one, too.)

STEP 10: PICK YOUR WINNERS

Urban triage; Anchors and paths; The lesson of LoDo; Downtowns first

The previous nine steps embody a comprehensive strategy for creating walkable places. As I have stressed throughout, following all these steps, rather than just a few of them, is essential if we are to convert a large segment of drivers into walkers. But following these steps everywhere would bankrupt most cities. Moreover, the universal application of walkability criteria is simply not in keeping with the way that cities actually work: great swaths of any significant metropolis are necessarily dedicated to activities that don't and shouldn't attract street life. To give an obvious example, a container depot is not a place to encourage sidewalk dining.

URBAN TRIAGE

But it is the less obvious examples of this phenomenon that require our attention, or rather, our concerted disregard. A shockingly large amount of money is currently being spent adding walkability enhancements to streets that will never attract more than the occasional stranded motorist hiking for gasoline. In half the cities I visit, I am given a tour of some newly rebuilt street, often the main corridor out of downtown, that has been dolled up with the latest streetlights, tree grates, and multicolored pavers, as if these modifications will create walking in a place where there is almost nothing to walk to. The corridor has been made more attractive for driving, certainly, but at a much greater cost than if that had been the goal.

This error points the way to the first question to ask before investing in walkability: where can spending the least money make the most difference? The answer, as obvious as it is ignored, is on streets that are already framed by buildings that have the potential to attract and sustain street life. In other words, places where an accommodating private realm already exists to give comfort and interest to an improved public realm. Most cities have their fair share of streets like this, where historic shopfronts and other attractive buildings line sidewalks that are blighted only by a high-speed, treeless roadway. Fix the street, and you've got the whole package, or close to it.

In contrast, there is little to be gained in livability by improving the design of a street that is lined by muffler shops and fastfood drive-thrus. When you're done, it's still the auto zone and not worthy of our attention. Let it go.

This more mercenary approach to urban revitalization is what we have come to call *urban triage*, an apt moniker for a technique initiated in the battlefields of World War I.* In pedestrian crises, as in combat, the worst off must sometimes be sacrificed for the greater good. Here, the categories of patient are slightly different: first to receive care are the "A" streets that are best poised to benefit from it. Second are the "B" streets that might present a bit of a tougher win, but are needed to tie the best streets together into a proper network—more on that in a minute.

---

*Andres Duany, Elizabeth Plater-Zyberk, and Jeff Speck, *Suburban Nation*, 162. The phrase was coined, like so many, by Andres. Battlefield triage involves withholding care from those patients very likely to either live or die and focusing resources principally on those whose fate could go either way.

Third, and off the table, is what remains: the automotive city. These "C" streets should not be allowed to go to seed; by all means, fill the potholes and pick up the trash. But don't worry about sidewalk widths, street trees, or bike lanes—at least, not in this decade.

ANCHORS AND PATHS

The second category above, streets that connect, requires the greatest amount of thought, along with—dare I say it—some design. Because, in any city's downtown, there is a network of walkability, sometimes hidden, that is waiting to emerge. Coaxing it to the surface requires some careful observation and then a decisive design effort. At its heart is the concept of anchors and paths.

Say what you will about shopping malls, you have to admit that in their heyday they did certain things very well. One of these was the almost scientifically determined placement of stores in relationship to each other to encourage maximum spending, which included separating the anchor tenants by a certain distance in order to get people walking past the smaller shops in between. Creating pedestrians in front of the in-line stores was so important to the design of the mall that the anchor tenants were often welcomed rent-free.[1]

In a downtown, the anchors are few and fairly easy to identify: major retailers, large parking structures, movie theaters, and any other use that generates significant foot traffic on a regular basis, such as a performance hall or a baseball stadium.* An already-walkable street network is also a type of anchor, as it creates pedestrians who are willing to stroll farther afield if that walk is rewarded. Sometimes these anchors are quite close to

---

*Baseball needs to be distinguished from football, in which games happen so rarely that a stadium is much less effective at spurring revitalization.

each other, but almost nobody walks between them because of the poor quality of the connection. Beyond the conditions of the roadway itself, this street may suffer from a lack of well-defined, active edges that puts it firmly in "B" or even "C" territory. If this stretch is short enough and opportunities exist for its development, it might make sense for the city to spend money to fix it quickly.

Let's say we are faced with a situation in which two walkable neighborhoods are located a few blocks away from each other. One holds a convention center, hotels, and an arena. It is full of people but few walk very far. The other neighborhood contains restaurants, bars, galleries, and is surrounded by working-class housing. It has tremendous character but needs a bit of a lift. Conventioneers and arena visitors would love to visit it, but few ever do, because the short distance between the two neighborhoods is utterly uninviting. What's a city to do?

This was precisely the scenario in Columbus, Ohio, where the city's convention center and arena were cut off from the gritty Short North neighborhood by a below-grade interstate highway, reamed through in the sixties. Getting from one side to the other meant crossing a barren, windswept bridge, complete with chainlink suicide screen. When it became necessary in 2003 to reconstruct this bridge, the city and state did an unusually smart thing: instead of building a one-hundred-foot-wide bridge, they built a two-hundred-foot-wide bridge, creating two retail pads on its flanks. They gave these pads to an enlightened developer, who built a modern-day Ponte Vecchio, lining the sidewalks with shops and restaurants.

For an additional public cost of $1.9 million, this novel bridge performed an act of magic: it made a highway disappear. Now conventioneers regularly visit the Short North, and the difference to businesses there is described as "night and day."[2] Two walkable districts have been unified into one, and an entire sector of the city has changed its character.

Many cities contain depressed highways and railways, and some of these places are contemplating caps like the one in Columbus. But these are an obvious example of what can be a much subtler situation, in which a few parking lots or lube joints sever what would otherwise be a walkable connection between anchors. Stitching this fabric back together can be even less expensive than the Columbus effort, and just as impactful, but doing so requires an explicit act of identification.

For this reason, when I do a walkability plan, it is a multistep process. First, I study every street that has a chance of being walkable and I grade it in terms of its urban qualities. I ignore the street's traffic characteristics, since they are simple to fix, and look only at comfort and interest: spatial definition and the presence of friendly faces. This effort produces a map in which the streets are colored from green through yellow to red based on their potential to attract pedestrian life. From this map, a pattern emerges, in which certain streets that are good enough come together to form a clear network of walkability. I then supplement this network with the additional streets that are necessary to connect it to the key anchors that it almost reaches, including other pieces of itself.

The result is an urban triage plan: streets are either in or out. This plan mandates the pattern for both public and private investment over the next decade. Only the "in" streets are to receive walkability improvements like safer traffic patterns, street trees, and better sidewalks. Only the "in" street properties are to receive city redevelopment support, whether that means money or just expedited permitting. And the "missing teeth" within this network—especially along the key severed connections—get the full front-burner treatment. Ideally, the entirety of the city leadership, both public sector and private sector, comes together around a simple understanding: Build These Sites First.

THE LESSON OF LoDo

The plans that emerge from this process can have some surprising features. For example, a neighborhood can be eminently walkable and still contain many unwalkable streets. In fact, many great downtowns alternate good streets with bad ones. All that matters is that the good streets connect into a continuous network so that, while you may have to walk across a "C" street, you never have to walk along one.[3] This phenomenon occurs in every American city that is graced with rear alleys.

Even more surprising is how small a network of walkability can be while still giving the impression of a walkable city. Some smaller cities that are known for their walkability, like Greenville, South Carolina, owe much of their reputation to just one great street. Less important than the size of a walkable district is its quality. This was a lesson that we were taught most convincingly by Denver.

In 1993, the city-planning world was abuzz with stories about Denver. "You've got to get to Denver," people kept telling us. "It's amazing what they're doing there."

So we went to Denver, and what we found there was not Denver, but Denver's Lower Downtown, LoDo. In fact, it wasn't LoDo, really; it was just a few blocks of LoDo, blocks that happened to hold John Hickenlooper's Wynkoop brewery, pool hall, and comedy club, across the street from the (empty) beaux arts Union Station, surrounded by some industrial lofts that had just begun to attract urban pioneers. The urbanism wasn't perfect, but it was close enough, although only a few acres of it showed much promise at all. Most of the district was unchanged from decades prior when, according to sportswriter Rick Reilly, "it was full of druggies and brutes and three-toothed thieves. And those were the women."[4]

But those few almost-perfect blocks were enough. Like us, other people were hearing these stories and had begun investing in LoDo and in Denver at large. Within ten years, the whole city was experiencing a powerful renaissance. Denver's population has grown 28 percent since 1990.

Did all those people come to Denver because of the Wynkoop brewery? Clearly not. But it only takes a few blocks to create a reputation. The lesson of LoDo is to start small with something that is as good as you can make it. That is the beauty of urban triage.

DOWNTOWNS FIRST

As much sense as it makes logically, urban triage can be a challenge politically. First, there is the name, which aptly conveys the presence of winners and losers and, for that reason, requires a lot of explanation. I am always quick to point out how the automotive strip can actually demand higher rents than Main Street, and that this is merely a discussion about walkability, not property value. That said, maybe the name *urban triage* needs to be replaced by something less trenchant.

Second, and a bigger problem, is the way that public servants think about distributing resources. Most mayors, city managers, and municipal planners feel a responsibility to their entire city. As a result, they tend to sprinkle the walkability fairy dust indiscriminately. They are also optimists—they wouldn't be in government otherwise—so they want to believe that they can someday attain a city that is universally excellent. This is lovely, but it is counterproductive. By trying to be universally excellent, most cities end up universally mediocre. Walkability is likely only in those places where all the best of what a city has to offer is focused in one area. Concentration, not dispersion, is the elixir of urbanity.

This discussion is a loaded one, as it quickly raises questions of equity, and not just from street to street, but from neighborhood to neighborhood. In most American cities, realistic planning for walkability starts downtown, where most of the key ingredients are already in place. But not many people may actually live there yet. So, who are the efforts for, and are they justified? This is one of the toughest questions a city planner can face. In Baton Rouge, it was phrased this way: "Why are you working on downtown, when it's in such better shape than where we live? Why aren't you doing a plan for our community instead?"

The answer to this question is simple. The downtown is the only part of the city that belongs to everybody. It doesn't matter where you may find your home; the downtown is yours, too. Investing in the downtown of a city is the only place-based way to benefit all of its citizens at once.

And there's more. Every relocation decision, be it a college graduate's or a corporation's, is made with an image of place in mind. That image is palpable and it is powerful. It is resolutely physical: a picture of buildings, streets, squares, cafés, and the social life that those places engender. Whether good or bad, that image is hard to shake. And, with rare exception, that image is downtown.

Each city's reputation therefore rests in large part on its downtown's physical attributes. If the downtown doesn't look good, the city doesn't look good. People won't want to move there, and it will be that much harder for citizens to feel good about the place where they have chosen to live. A beautiful and vibrant downtown, in contrast, can be the rising tide that lifts all ships. As in LoDo, a little bit of great downtown can help push a whole city into the great category. That is the place to begin.

As I ponder the concept of city image, there is one image in particular that I can't get out of my head. I am ten years old, gathered in front of the television with my parents and brother, and we are watching the title credits to *The Mary Tyler Moore Show*. In stark distinction to most American cities portrayed on TV at the time, Mary's Minneapolis is sparkling, lively, and brimming with opportunity. A thirty-year-old woman has broken off her engagement and moved to the big city to start afresh. We don't know what awaits her, but share in her wide-eyed embrace of the infinite possibility of urban life. Surrounded by fellow pedestrians, she pirouettes joyfully in the street and lofts her wool cap into the air. We never see it come down.

ACKNOWLEDGMENTS

This is the first book on design that I have written without Andres Duany or Elizabeth Plater-Zyberk, but don't be fooled: it would not have been possible, or at least any good, without them. Not only are a significant percent of this book's ideas theirs; so too is the strategy of organizing those ideas into a ruthlessly instrumental framework, one that I can only hope is up to their standard.

When this book was almost finished, I sent it along to Andres so he could call my attention to any of their ideas that I had not properly credited. He declined to take on this task, a choice that embodies two of his dominant personality traits: a violent allergy to wasting time, and an intellectual generosity of truly historic proportion. For that reason, if you read something you like, there is a good chance that I got it from Andres—not that he would want the credit.

I first heard Andres lecture in 1988, and I had a very specific reaction: Oh My God, this has to be a book. The result was *Suburban Nation.* More than twenty years later, I was fortunate enough to have that scenario play out in reverse when, after my lecture to her former organization, CEOs for Cities, Carol Coletta thanked me with the same words. Unlike my suggestion to Andres, Carol was not offering to write the book for me; that would still be my job. But without Carol this book would not have been written.

In addition to their encouragement, Carol and CEOs for Cities can be thanked for securing a grant that allowed me to take the time off to write. That grant came from the Fund for the Environment and Urban Life, whose founder, Richard Oram, had made the mistake of asking me: "Is there anything interesting out there we should be supporting?" I hope that I can be forgiven for responding so selfishly.

With the promise of a grant, I created a proposal for my brilliantly skeptical agent, Neeti Madan She demanded three rewrites, and just as I was about to give up, she sold it to Farrar, Straus and Giroux, the publishers of *Suburban Nation*. Given our wholly positive experience creating that book, I was unsurprised to learn that I had been assigned no less an editor than Sean McDonald, who, in addition to being famously smart about books, is probably the one person on earth who cares more about city planning than I do. He also has zero tolerance for TMI, so, if you find any of this book boring, it is because I overruled some of his cuts. Then again, if you wish the book were longer, please call him repeatedly on his home phone.

Four additional editors, unpaid, contributed heavily to this effort, all of them Specks. Father Mort provided executive-level direction. Mother Gayle and brother Scott, essayists of the first rank, pored over every sentence and improved many. And wife Alice served as a daily sounding board, not to mention source of inspiration. She also carved out a space for me to write by miraculously corralling two young children in an unchildproofed country.

That country was Italy, where I was generously hosted by two tremendously supportive organizations: the American Academy in Rome, and the Bogliasco Foundation's Liguria Study Center. I am personally grateful to Adele Chatfield-Taylor and the Harrison family for their enthusiastic encouragement, and also for overlooking the baby damage.

I have dozens of people to thank for the information and stories that make up this book. As the text and notes suggest, certain chapters depend heavily on the thought leaders in their subjects, roughly as follows: economics: Chris Leinberger and Joe Cortright; health: Richard Jackson, Howie Frumkin, and Lawrence Frank; parking: Donald Shoup; transit: Yonah Freemark; safety: Dan Burden; biking: Jeff Mapes and Robert Hurst; and urban triage: Andres Duany.

While this list is by no means complete, I also received important help from Adam Baacke, Kaid Benfield, Scott Bernstein, Ron Bogle, Tom Brennan, Amanda Burden, Norman Garrick, Robert Gibbs, Alex Gorlin, Vince Graham, Charlie Hales, Blake Kreuger, Bill Lennertz, Matt Lerner, Todd Litman, Mike Lydon, Michael Mehaffy, Charles Marohn, Paul Moore, Wes Marshall, Eileen McNeil, Darrin Nordahl, Brian O'Looney, Eva Otto, David Owen, Jay Primus, Shannon Ramsay, Ginny Seyferth, Christian Sottile, Boo Thomas, Brent Toderian, John Torti, Harriet Tregoning, and Sam Zimbabwe.

Finally, it was mayors who helped me understand the need for this book, the issues that it had to address, and the requirement that its recommendations be both reality-based and actionable now. These include Steve Bellone (Babylon, NY), Jim Brainard (Carmel, IN), John Callahan (Bethlehem, PA), Mick Cornett (Oklahoma City), Frank Cownie (Des Moines, IA), Manny Diaz (Miami), A C Wharton (Memphis), and the incomparable Joe Riley (Charleston, SC), who has demonstrated over ten consecutive terms that city design matters more than most of us can imagine.

NOTES

A GENERAL THEORY OF WALKABILITY

1. Andres Duany, Elizabeth Plater-Zyberk, and Jeff Speck, *Suburban Nation*, 164.
2. Andres Duany and Jeff Speck, *The Smart Growth Manual*, Point 10.7.

I: WHY WALKABILITY?

1. Andres Duany, Elizabeth Plater-Zyberk, and Jeff Speck, *Suburban Nation*, 217.

WALKING, THE URBAN ADVANTAGE

1. Jack Neff, "Is Digital Revolution Driving Decline in U.S. Car Culture?"
2. J. D. Power press release, October 8, 2009.
3. Richard Florida, "The Great Car Reset."
4. The Segmentation Company, "Attracting College-Educated, Young Adults to Cities," 7.
5. Patrick C. Doherty and Christopher B. Leinberger, "The Next Real Estate Boom."
6. Ibid.
7. Christopher B. Leinberger, *The Option of Urbanism*, 89.
8. Ibid.
9. Ibid., 90.
10. David Byrne, *Bicycle Diaries*, 283.
11. Carol Morello, Dan Keating, and Steve Hendrix, "Census: Young Adults Are Responsible for Most of D.C.'s Growth in Past Decade."
12. Christopher B. Leinberger, "Federal Restructuring of Fannie and Freddie Ignores Underlying Cause of Crisis."

13. Christopher B. Leinberger, "The Next Slum."
14. Leinberger, *Option*, 96–98.
15. Ibid., 101, and Anton Troianovski, "Downtowns Get a Fresh Lease."
16. Leinberger, *Option*, 91, 8–9.
17. Joe Cortright, "Walking the Walk: How Walkability Raises Home Values in U.S. Cities," 20.
18. Belden Russonello & Stewart, "What Americans Are Looking for When Deciding Where to Live," 3, 2.
19. Joe Cortright, "Portland's Green Dividend," 1.
20. Ibid., 1–2, and Joe Cortright, "Driven Apart."
21. Ibid., 3.
22. Poster, Intelligent Cities Initiative, National Building Museum.
23. Leinberger, *Option*, 20.
24. Barbara J. Lipman, "A Heavy Load: The Combined Housing and Transportation Costs of Working Families," iv.
25. Ibid., 5.
26. Doherty and Leinberger, "The Next Real Estate Boom."
27. Ibid.
28. Leinberger, "Federal Restructuring."
29. Catherine Lutz and Anne Lutz Fernandez, *Carjacked*, 207.
30. Leinberger, *Option*, 77–78, and "Here Comes the Neighborhood"; Jeff Mapes, *Pedaling Revolution*, 143.
31. Jon Swartz, "San Francisco's Charm Lures High-Tech Workers."
32. David Brooks, "The Splendor of Cities."
33. Mapes, 268.
34. Jonah Lehrer, "A Physicist Solves the City," 3.
35. Ibid., 4.
36. Hope Yen, "Suburbs Lose Young Whites to Cities"; Leinberger, *Option*, 170.
37. Ibid.

WHY JOHNNY CAN'T WALK

1. Jim Colleran, "The Worst Streets in America."
2. Jeff Speck, "Our Ailing Communities: Q&A: Richard Jackson."
3. Ibid.
4. Lawrence Frank, Lecture to the 18th Congress for the New Urbanism.
5. Molly Farmer, "South Jordan Mom Cited for Neglect for Allowing Child to Walk to School."
6. Howard Frumkin, Lawrence Frank, and Richard Jackson, *Urban Sprawl and Public Health*, xii.
7. Thomas Gotschi and Kevin Mills, "Active Transportation for America," 27.

8. Jan Gehl, *Cities for People*, 111.

9. Neal Peirce, "Biking and Walking: Our Secret Weapon?"

10. Gotschi and Mills, 44.

11. Jeff Mapes, *Pedaling Revolution*, 230.

12. Elizabeth Kolbert, "XXXL: Why Are We So Fat?"

13. Christopher B. Leinberger, *The Option of Urbanism*, 76.

14. Catherine Lutz and Anne Lutz Fernandez, *Carjacked*, 165.

15. Frumkin, Frank, and Jackson, 100.

16. Ibid.

17. Erica Noonan, "A Matter of Size."

18. American Dream Coalition website.

19. Richard Jackson, "We Are No Longer Creating Wellbeing."

20. Kevin Sack, "Governor Proposes Remedy for Atlanta Sprawl," A14.

21. Lutz and Lutz Fernandez, 172–73; American Lung Association, "State of the Air 2011 City Rankings"; Lutz and Lutz Fernandez, 173.

22. Asthma and Allergy Foundation of America, "Cost of Asthma"; John F. Wasik, *The Cul-de-Sac Syndrome*, 68.

23. WebMD slideshow, "10 Worst Cities for Asthma."

24. Charles Siegel, *Unplanning*, 30.

25. Lutz and Lutz Fernandez, 182.

26. Frumkin, Frank, and Jackson, 110.

27. All traffic fatality data collected by Drive and Stay Alive, Inc.

28. Frumkin, Frank, and Jackson, 112.

29. Speck, "Our Ailing Communities."

30. Jane Ford, "Danger in Exurbia: University of Virginia Study Reveals the Danger of Travel in Virginia," *University of Virginia News*, April 30, 2002.

31. Doug Monroe, "The Stress Factor," 89.

32. Mapes, 239.

33. Deborah Klotz, "Air Pollution and Its Effects on Heart Attack Risk," *The Boston Globe*, February 28, 2011.

34. Frumkin, Frank, and Jackson, 142; Lutz and Lutz Fernandez, 156; Alois Stutzer and Bruno S. Frey, "Stress That Doesn't Pay," as described in Joe Cortright, "Portland's Green Dividend," 2.

35. Mainstreet.com, quoted in "Survey Says" by Cora Frazier, *The New Yorker*, March 19, 2012.

36. Dan Buettner, *Thrive*, 189.

37. Frumkin, Frank, and Jackson, 172.

38. Dom Nozzi, http://domz60.wordpress.com/quotes/.

THE WRONG COLOR GREEN

1. Terry Tamminen, *Lives per Gallon*, 207.
2. Michael T. Klare, quoted in Catherine Lutz and Anne Lutz Fernandez, *Carjacked*, 90.
3. Josh Dorner, "NBC Confirms That 'Clean Coal' Is an Oxymoron."
4. Bill Marsh, "Kilowatts vs. Gallons."
5. Firmin DeBrabander, "What If Green Products Make Us Pollute More?"
6. Ibid.
7. Michael Mehaffy, "The Urban Dimensions of Climate Change."
8. David Owen, *Green Metropolis*, 48, 104.
9. *A Convenient Remedy*, Congress for the New Urbanism video.
10. Witold Rybczynski, *Makeshift Metropolis*, 189.
11. The study was prepared by Jonathan Rose Associates, March 2011.
12. New Urban Network, "Study: Transit Outperforms Green Buildings."
13. Kaid Benfield, "EPA Region 7: We Were Just Kidding About That Sustainability Stuff."
14. Ibid.
15. Dom Nozzi, http://domz60.wordpress.com/quotes/.
16. Owen, 19, 23.
17. Andres Duany, Elizabeth Plater-Zyberk, and Jeff Speck, *Suburban Nation*, 7–12.
18. Edward Glaeser, "If You Love Nature, Move to the City."
19. Owen, 2–3, 17.
20. Peter Newman, Timothy Beatley, and Heather Boyer, *Resilient Cities*, 7, 88.
21. Ibid., 92.
22. John Holtzclaw, "Using Residential Patterns and Transit to Decrease Auto Dependence and Costs."
23. "2010 Quality of Living Worldwide City Rankings," Mercer.com.
24. Newman, Beatley, and Boyer, 99.

STEP 1: PUT CARS IN THEIR PLACE

1. Dom Nozzi, http://domz60.wordpress.com/quotes/.
2. Ralph Waldo Emerson, "Experience" (1844), quoted in Cotton Seiler, *Republic of Drivers*, 16; Walt Whitman, "Song of the Open Road" (1856).
3. Seiler, 94.
4. David Byrne, *Bicycle Diaries*, 8.
5. Patrick Condon, "Canadian Cities American Cities: Our Differences Are the Same," 16.
6. Ibid., 8.
7. Witold Rybczynski, *City Life*, 160–61.

8. Donald Shoup, *The High Cost of Free Parking*, 65.

9. Bob Levey and Jane Freundel-Levey, "End of the Roads," 1.

10. Ibid., 2–3.

11. Ibid., 2–4.

12. Terry Tamminen, *Lives per Gallon*, 60–61.

13. Christopher B. Leinberger, *The Option of Urbanism*, 164.

14. Randy Salzman, "Build More Highways, Get More Traffic."

15. Charles Siegel, *Unplanning*, 29, 95.

16. Federal Highway Administrator Mary Peters, Senate testimony, quoted in Nozzi, http://domz60.wordpress.com/quotes/.

17. Peter Newman, Timothy Beatley, and Heather Boyer, *Resilient Cities*, 102.

18. Texas Transportation Institute, Texas A&M University, "2010 Urban Mobility Report."

19. Nozzi, op. cit.

20. Andres Duany, Elizabeth Plater-Zyberk, and Jeff Speck, *Suburban Nation*, 16.

21. Information from an e-mail exchange with Dan Burden.

22. Jane Jacobs, *Dark Age Ahead*, 73.

23. Ibid., 74–79.

24. Yonah Freemark and Jebediah Reed, "Huh?! Four Cases of How Tearing Down a Highway Can Relieve Traffic Jams (and Save Your City)."

25. Kamala Rao, "Seoul Tears Down an Urban Highway, and the City Can Breathe Again," *Grist*, November 4, 2011.

26. Ibid.

27. Ibid.

28. Siegel, 102; William Yardley, "Seattle Mayor Is Trailing in the Early Primary Count."

29. "Removing Freeways—Restoring Cities," preservenet.com.

30. Jan Gehl, *Cities for People*, 9.

31. Ibid., 13.

32. Newman, Beatley, and Boyer, 117.

33. Jeff Mapes, *Pedaling Revolution*, 81.

34. Witold Rybczynski, *Makeshift Metropolis*, 83.

35. Jeff Speck, "Six Things Even New York Can Do Better."

36. Ken Livingstone, winner commentary by Mayor of London, World Technology Winners and Finalists.

37. Data taken alternately from two sources: Ibid., and Wikipedia, "London Congestion Charge."

38. Ibid.

39. Stewart Brand, *Whole Earth Discipline*, 71.

40. Wikipedia, "New York Congestion Pricing."

41. Ibid.

42. Ibid.
43. Nozzi, op. cit.
44. Bernard-Henri Lévy, *American Vertigo.*
45. Ivan Illich, *Toward a History of Needs.*
46. Ibid., 119.
47. Duany, Plater-Zyberk, and Speck, 91n.
48. Catherine Lutz and Anne Lutz Fernandez, *Carjacked*, 145.

STEP 2: MIX THE USES

1. Andres Duany, Elizabeth Plater-Zyberk, and Jeff Speck, *Suburban Nation*, 10.
2. Conversation with Adam Baacke, June 14, 2011.
3. Nicholas Brunick, "The Impact of Inclusionary Zoning on Development," 4.
4. Judy Keen, "Seattle's Backyard Cottages Make a Dent in Housing Need."
5. Data from the City of Seattle Department of Planning and Development.
6. Tim Newcomb, "Need Extra Income? Put a Cottage in Your Backyard," time.com, May 28, 2011.

STEP 3: GET THE PARKING RIGHT

1. Martha Groves, "He Put Parking in Its Place."
2. Ibid.
3. Eric Betz, "The First Nationwide Count of Parking Spaces Demonstrates Their Environmental Cost."
4. Donald Shoup, *The High Cost of Free Parking*, 189.
5. Catherine Lutz and Anne Lutz Fernandez, *Carjacked*, 8.
6. Ibid.
7. Shoup, 83.
8. Ibid., 591.
9. Ibid., 2.
10. Ibid., 208–14.
11. Ibid., 24.
12. Ibid., 559.
13. Philip Langdon, "Parking: A Poison Posing as a Cure."
14. Ibid.
15. Langdon.
16. Betz.
17. Shoup, 81.
18. Sarah Karush, "Cities Rethink Wisdom of 50s-Era Parking Standards."

19. Washington, D.C., Economic Partnership (2008), "2008 Neighborhood Profiles—Columbia Heights."
20. Interview with architect Brian O'Looney of Torti Gallas and Partners.
21. Paul Schwartzman, "At Columbia Heights Mall, So Much Parking, So Little Need."
22. Ibid.
23. Shoup, 43.
24. Ibid., 8.
25. Andres Duany, Elizabeth Plater-Zyberk, and Jeff Speck, *Suburban Nation*, 163n.
26. Shoup, 131.
27. Ibid., 157.
28. Langdon; Shoup, 146.
29. Langdon.
30. Shoup, 150.
31. Ibid.
32. Noah Kazis, "NYCHA Chairman: Parking Minimums 'Working Against Us.'"
33. Wikipedia, "Carmel-by-the-Sea, California."
34. Shoup, 102–103, 230, 239.
35. Ibid., 239.
36. Ibid., 262.
37. Ibid., 498.
38. Ibid., 122.
39. Ibid., 327, 310, 14, 359.
40. Ibid., 328.
41. Ibid., 400.
42. Ibid., 380–81.
43. Douglas Kolozsvari and Donald Shoup, "Turning Small Change into Big Changes."
44. Shoup, 299.
45. Ibid., 383.
46. Ibid., 391–92.
47. Groves.
48. Bill Fulton, mayor of Ventura, blog posting, September 14, 2010.
49. Ibid.
50. Groves.
51. Shoup, 309.
52. Rachel Gordon, "Parking: S.F. Releases Details on Flexible Pricing."
53. Ibid.
54. Kolozsvari and Shoup; Shoup, 417.
55. Kolozsvari and Shoup.

56. Shoup, 417, 434, 415.
57. Ibid., 348–53.
58. Kolozsvari and Shoup; Shoup, 417.
59. Kolozsvari and Shoup.
60. Langdon.
61. Kolozsvari and Shoup.
62. Shoup, 397.
63. Ibid., 275.
64. Ibid., 299.
65. Alex Salta, "Chicago Sells Rights to City Parking Meters for $1.2 Billion."
66. Ibid.

STEP 4: LET TRANSIT WORK

1. Yonah Freemark, "Transit Mode Share Trends Looking Steady." Data from U.S. Census Bureau's American Community Survey, October 13, 2010.
2. Donald Shoup, *The High Cost of Free Parking*, 2.
3. Peter Newman, Timothy Beatley, and Heather Boyer, *Resilient Cities*, 86–87.
4. Freemark, "Transit Mode Share Trends Looking Steady."
5. Daniel Parolec, presentation to the Congress for the New Urbanism, June 2, 2011.
6. Terry Tamminen, *Lives per Gallon*, 112.
7. David Owen, *Green Metropolis*, 127.
8. Ibid., 121.
9. Andres Duany and Jeff Speck, *The Smart Growth Manual*, Point 3.2.
10. Newman, Beatley, and Boyer, 109.
11. Christopher B. Leinberger, *The Option of Urbanism*, 166.
12. John Van Gleson, "Light Rail Adds Transportation Choices on Common Ground," 10.
13. Todd Litman, "Raise My Taxes, Please!"
14. Yonah Freemark, "The Interdependence of Land Use and Transportation."
15. dart.org, 2008.
16. Wendell Cox, "DART's Billion Dollar Boondoggle."
17. Yonah Freemark, "An Extensive New Addition to Dallas' Light Rail Makes It America's Longest."
18. Van Gleson, 10.
19. Freemark, "An Extensive New Addition."
20. San Miguel County Local Transit and Human Service Transportation Coordination Plan, LSC Transportation Consultants in association with the URS Corporation, Colorado Springs, 2008, pages III-6 through III-7.

21. Charles Hales, presentation at Rail-Volution, October 18, 2011.
22. American Public Transportation Association Transit Ridership Report, 1st quarter 2011. Washington, D.C.
23. D.C. Surface Transit, "Value Capture and Tax-Increment Financing Options for Streetcar Construction."
24. Ibid.
25. Ibid.
26. American Public Transportation Association Transit Ridership Report, 1st quarter 2011.
27. D.C. Surface Transit.
28. Equilibrium Capital, "Streetcars' Economic Impact in the United States," PowerPoint presentation.
29. D.C. Surface Transit.
30. Ibid.
31. Andres Duany, Elizabeth Plater-Zyberk, and Jeff Speck, *Suburban Nation*, 202–203.
32. Darrin Nordahl, *My Kind of Transit*, ix.
33. Ibid., 126–43.
34. Mark Jahne, "Local Officials Find Fault with Proposed Hartford–New Britain Busway."
35. U.S. Government Accounting Office, "Bus Rapid Transit Shows Promise."
36. Morgan Clendaniel, "Zipcar's Impact on How People Use Cars Is Enormous."

STEP 5: PROTECT THE PEDESTRIAN

1. Wesley Marshall and Norman Garrick, "Street Network Types and Road Safety," table 1.
2. Andres Duany, Elizabeth Plater-Zyberk, and Jeff Speck, *Suburban Nation*, 160n.
3. Dan Burden and Peter Lagerwey, "Road Diets: Fixing the Big Roads."
4. Reid Ewing and Eric Dumbaugh, "The Built Environment and Traffic Safety," 363.
5. Robert Noland, "Traffic Fatalities and Injuries," cited in Catherine Lutz and Anne Lutz Fernandez, *Carjacked*, chapter 9, note 19.
6. "Designing Walkable Urban Thoroughfares."
7. NCHRP Report 500, "Volume 10: A Guide for Reducing Collisions Involving Pedestrians," 2004.
8. 20splentyforus.org.uk.
9. Duany, Plater-Zyberk, and Speck, 36–37.
10. Malcolm Gladwell, "Blowup," 36; also in Duany, Plater-Zyberk, and Speck, 37n.
11. Tom McNichol, "Roads Gone Wild."

12. Tom Vanderbilt, *Traffic*, 199.
13. McNichol.
14. Jeff Mapes, *Pedaling Revolution*, 62.
15. McNichol.
16. David Owen, *Green Metropolis*, 186.
17. McNichol.
18. Ibid.
19. Duany, Plater-Zyberk, and Speck, 64.
20. Christian Sottile, "One-Way Streets: Urban Impact Analysis," commissioned by the city of Savannah (unpublished).
21. Ibid.
22. Melanie Eversley, "Many Cities Changing One-Way Streets Back."
23. Alan Ehrenhalt, "The Return of the Two-Way Street."
24. Ibid.
25. Ibid.
26. Duany, Plater-Zyberk, and Speck, 71.
27. Jan Gehl, *Cities for People*, 186.
28. Mapes, 85.
29. Michael Grynbaum, "Deadliest for Walkers: Male Drivers, Left Turns."
30. Damien Newton, "Only in LA: DOT Wants to Remove Crosswalks to Protect Pedestrians."
31. Owen, 185.

STEP 6: WELCOME BIKES

1. Ron Gabriel, "3-Way Street by ronconcocacola," Vimeo.
2. Hayes A. Lord, "Cycle Tracks."
3. Jan Gehl, *Cities for People*, 105.
4. Allison Aubrey, "Switching Gears: More Commuters Bike to Work."
5. Jeff Mapes, *Pedaling Revolution*, 24.
6. Robert Hurst, *The Cyclist's Manifesto*, 176.
7. Gehl, 104–105.
8. Mapes, 14.
9. John Pucher and Ralph Buehler, "Why Canadians Cycle More Than Americans," 265.
10. Jay Walljasper, "The Surprising Rise of Minneapolis as a Top Bike Town."
11. Pucher and Buehler, "Why Canadians," 273.
12. Ibid., 265.
13. Mapes, 65, 70.
14. Jay Walljasper, "Cycling to Success: Lessons from the Dutch."
15. Mapes, 71; John Pucher and Lewis Dijkstra, "Making Walking and Cycling Safer: Lessons from Europe," 9.
16. Mapes, 62.

17. Russell Shorto, "The Dutch Way: Bicycles and Fresh Bread."
18. Ibid.
19. Gehl, 185–87.
20. Mapes, 81.
21. Wikipedia, "Modal Share," data from urbanaudit.org.
22. Mia Burke, "Joyride."
23. Mapes, 155.
24. Burke.
25. bikerealtor.com.
26. Mapes, 158, 143.
27. Ibid., 139.
28. Noah Kazis, "New PPW Results: More New Yorkers Use It, Without Clogging the Street"; Gary Buiso, "Safety First! Prospect Park West Bike Lane Working."
29. Gary Buiso, "Marty's Lane Pain Is Fodder for His Christmas Card."
30. Ibid.
31. Andrea Bernstein, "NYC Biking Is Up 14% from 2010; Overall Support Rises."
32. Lord.
33. Hurst, 81.
34. Ibid., 175.
35. Bernstein.
36. Thomas Gotschi and Kevin Mills, "Active Transportation for America," 28.
37. Ibid., 24.
38. Ibid., 225.
39. Children's Safety Network, "Promoting Bicycle Safety for Children."
40. John Forester, *Bicycle Transportation*, 2nd ed., 3.
41. Hurst, 90.
42. John Pucher and Ralph Buehler, "Cycling for Few or for Everyone," 62–63.
43. Mapes, 40.
44. Tom Vanderbilt, *Traffic*, 199.
45. Hurst, 94.
46. Steven Erlanger and Maïa de la Baume, "French Ideal of Bicycle-Sharing Meets Reality."
47. Wikipedia, "Bicycle Sharing System."
48. Clarence Eckerson, Jr., "The Phenomenal Success of Capital Bikeshare."
49. Christy Goodman, "Expanded Bike-Sharing Program to Link D.C., Arlington."
50. "Capital Bikeshare Expansion Planned in the New Year," D.C. DOT, December 23, 2010.
51. Wendy Koch, "Cities Roll Out Bike-Sharing Programs."

52. David Byrne, *Bicycle Diaries*, 278.
53. Lord.

STEP 7: SHAPE THE SPACES

 1. Thomas J. Campanella, *Republic of Shade*, 135.
 2. Jan Gehl, *Cities for People*, 4.
 3. Ibid., 120, 139, 34.
 4. Ibid., 50.
 5. Christopher Alexander, *A Pattern Language*, 115.
 6. Gehl, 42.
 7. Ibid., 171–73.
 8. Jane Jacobs, *The Death and Life of Great American Cities*, 203.
 9. Andres Duany and Jeff Speck, *The Smart Growth Manual*, Point 10.5.
10. Gehl, 146.

STEP 8: PLANT TREES

 1. R. S. Ulrich et al., "View Through a Window May Influence Recovery from Surgery."
 2. "The Value of Trees to a Community," arborday.org/trees/benefits.cfm.
 3. Dan Burden, "22 Benefits of Urban Street Trees."
 4. Howard Frumkin, Lawrence Frank, and Richard Jackson, *Urban Sprawl and Public Health*, 119.
 5. Eric Dumbaugh, "Safe Streets, Livable Streets," 285–90.
 6. Burden.
 7. U.S. Department of Agriculture, Forest Service Pamphlet #FS-363.
 8. Burden.
 9. Henry F. Arnold, *Trees in Urban Design*, 149.
10. Zoe G. Davies, Jill L. Edmondson, Andreas Heinemeyer, Jonathan R. Leake, and Kevin J. Gaston, "Mapping an Urban Ecosystem Service: Quantifying Above-Ground Carbon Storage at a City-Wide Scale."
11. David Whitman, "The Sickening Sewer Crisis in America."
12. Greg Peterson, "Pharmaceuticals in Our Water Supply Are Causing Bizarre Mutations to Wildlife."
13. "Rainfall Interception of Trees, in Benefits of Trees in Urban Areas," coloradotrees.org.
14. Burden.
15. Kim Coder, "Identified Benefits of Community Trees and Forests."
16. Charles Duhigg, "Saving US Water and Sewer Systems Would Be Costly."
17. Whitman.
18. Thomas J. Campanella, *Republic of Shade*, 89.

19. Ibid., 75–77.
20. Anthony S. Twyman, "Greening Up Fertilizes Home Prices, Study Says."
21. Geoffrey Donovan and David Butry, "Trees in the City."
22. Ibid.
23. Jan Gehl, *Cities for People*, 180.
24. See milliontreesnyc.org.

STEP 9: MAKE FRIENDLY AND UNIQUE FACES

1. Jan Gehl, *Cities for People*, 88.
2. Ibid., 137.
3. Ibid., 77.
4. Ibid., 151.
5. Andres Duany, Elizabeth Plater-Zyberk, and Jeff Speck, *Suburban Nation*, 175–78.
6. Chris Turner, "What Makes a Building Ugly?"
7. James Fallows, "Fifty-Nine and a Half Minutes of Brilliance, Thirty Seconds of Hauteur."
8. Ethan Kent, "Guggenheim Museum Bilbao," Project for Public Spaces Hall of Shame.
9. Léon Krier, *The Architecture of Community*, 70.
10. Jane Jacobs, *The Death and Life of Great American Cities*, 291.
11. David Owen, *Green Metropolis*, 178.
12. Ibid., 181.
13. Jacobs, 91.
14. Ibid., 91n.

STEP 10: PICK YOUR WINNERS

1. Andres Duany, Elizabeth Plater-Zyberk, and Jeff Speck, *Suburban Nation*, 166.
2. Blair Kamin, "Ohio Cap at Forefront of Urban Design Trend."
3. Andres Duany and Jeff Speck, *The Smart Growth Manual*, Point 7.8.
4. Rick Reilly, "Life of Reilly: Mile-High Madness."

WORKS CITED

BOOKS

Alexander, Christopher. *A Pattern Language*. New York: Oxford University Press, 1977.

Arnold, Henry F. *Trees in Urban Design*, 2nd ed. New York: John Wiley, 1992.

Brand, Stewart. *Whole Earth Discipline: Why Denser Cities, Nuclear Power, Transgenic Crops, Restored Wetlands and Geoengineering Are Necessary*. New York: Penguin, 2009.

Buettner, Dan. *The Blue Zones: Lessons for Living Longer from the People Who've Lived the Longest*. Washington, D.C.: National Geographic, 2008.

———. *Thrive: Finding Happiness the Blue Zones Way*. Washington, D.C.: National Geographic, 2010.

Byrne, David. *Bicycle Diaries*. New York: Viking, 2009.

Campanella, Thomas J. *Republic of Shade: New England and the American Elm*. New Haven: Yale University Press, 2003.

Designing Walkable Urban Thoroughfares: A Context-Sensitive Approach: An ITE Recommended Practice. Institute of Transportation Engineers and Congress for the New Urbanism, Washington, D.C., 2010.

Duany, Andres, Elizabeth Plater-Zyberk, and Jeff Speck. *Suburban Nation: The Rise of Sprawl and the Decline of the American Dream*. New York: North Point Press, 2000.

Duany, Andres, and Jeff Speck. *The Smart Growth Manual*. New York: McGraw-Hill, 2010.

Forester, John. *Bicycle Transportation*, 2nd ed. Cambridge, Mass.: MIT Press, 1994.

Frumkin, Howard, Lawrence Frank, and Richard Jackson. *Urban Sprawl and Public Health: Designing, Planning, and Building for Healthy Communities*. Washington, D.C.: Island Press, 2004.

Gehl, Jan. *Cities for People*. Washington, D.C.: Island Press, 2010.

Hart, Stanley I., and Alvin L. Spivak. *The Elephant in the Bedroom: Automobile Dependence and Denial: Impacts on the Economy and Environment*. Pasadena, Calif.: New Paradigm Books, 1993.

Higham, Charles. *Trading with the Enemy: An Exposé of the Nazi-American Money Plot, 1933–1949*. New York: Delacorte Press, 1983.

Hurst, Robert. *The Cyclist's Manifesto: The Case for Riding on Two Wheels Instead of Four*. Helena, Mont.: Globe Pequot Press, 2009.

Illich, Ivan. *Toward a History of Needs*. New York: Pantheon, 1977. First published in 1973.

Jacobs, Alan. *The Boulevard Book*. Cambridge, Mass.: MIT Press, 2002.

———. *Great Streets*. Cambridge, Mass.: MIT Press, 1993.

Jacobs, Jane. *Dark Age Ahead*. New York: Random House, 2004.

———. *The Death and Life of Great American Cities*. New York: Vintage, 1961.

Koolhaas, Rem, Hans Werlemann, and Bruce Mau. *S,M,L,XL*. New York: Monacelli Press, 1994.

Krier, Léon. *The Architecture of Community*. Washington, D.C.: Island Press, 2009.

Leinberger, Christopher B. *The Option of Urbanism: Investing in a New American Dream*. Washington, D.C.: Island Press, 2009.

Lévy, Bernard-Henri. *American Vertigo: On the Road from Newport to Guantanamo*. London: Gibson Square, 2006.

Lutz, Catherine, and Anne Lutz Fernandez. *Carjacked: The Culture of the Automobile and Its Effect on Our Lives*. New York: Palgrave Macmillan, 2010.

Mapes, Jeff. *Pedaling Revolution: How Cyclists Are Changing American Cities*. Corvallis: Oregon State University Press, 2009.

Newman, Peter, Timothy Beatley, and Heather Boyer. *Resilient Cities: Responding to Peak Oil and Climate Change*. Washington, D.C.: Island Press, 2009.

Nordahl, Darrin. *My Kind of Transit: Rethinking Public Transportation in America*. Chicago: The Center for American Places, 2008.

Owen, David. *Green Metropolis: Why Living Smaller, Living Closer, and Driving Less Are the Keys to Sustainability*. New York: Penguin, 2009.

Rybczynski, Witold. *City Life: Urban Expectations in a New World*. New York: Scribner, 1995.

———. *Makeshift Metropolis: Ideas About Cities*. New York: Scribner, 2010.

Seiler, Cotton. *Republic of Drivers: A Cultural History of Automobility in America*. Chicago: University of Chicago Press, 2008.

Shoup, Donald. *The High Cost of Free Parking*. Chicago: Planners Press, 2004.

Siegel, Charles. *Unplanning: Livable Cities and Political Choices*. Berkeley, Calif.: The Preservation Institute, 2010.

Tamminen, Terry. *Lives per Gallon: The True Cost of Our Oil Addiction*. Washington, D.C.: Island Press, 2006.

Vanderbilt, Tom. *Traffic: Why We Drive the Way We Do (and What It Says About Us)*. New York: Knopf, 2008.

Wasik, John F. *The Cul-de-Sac Syndrome: Turning Around the Unsustainable American Dream*. New York: Bloomberg Press, 2009.

Whyte, William. *City: Rediscovering the Center*. New York: Doubleday, 1988.

ARTICLES AND REPORTS

AAA. "Your Driving Costs," 2010. aaa.com.

American Lung Association. "State of the Air 2011 City Rankings." stateoftheair.org/2011/city-rankings.

American Public Transportation Association. "Transit Ridership Report, 1st Quarter 2011."

"America's Top-50 Bike Friendly Cities." bicycling.com, undated.

Asthma and Allergy Foundation of America. "Cost of Asthma." aafa.org, undated.

Belden Russonello & Stewart Research and Communications. 2004 National Community Preference Survey, November 2004.

———. "What Americans Are Looking for When Deciding Where to Live." 2011 Community Preference Survey, March 2011.

Benfield, Kaid. "EPA Region 7: We Were Just Kidding About That Sustainability Stuff." sustainablecitiescollective.com, April 18, 2011.

Bernstein, Andrea. "NYC Biking Is Up 14% from 2010; Overall Support Rises." transportationnation.org, July 28, 2011.

Berreby, David. "Engineering Terror." *The New York Times*, September 10, 2010.

Betz, Eric. "The First Nationwide Count of Parking Spaces Demonstrates Their Environmental Cost." *The Knoxville News Sentinel*, December 1, 2010.

Branyan, George. "What Is an LPI? A Head Start for Pedestrians." ddotdish.com, December 1, 2010.

Brooks, David. "The Splendor of Cities." Review of *Triumph of the City* by Edward L. Glaeser (New York: Penguin, 2011). *The New York Times*, February 7, 2011.

Brunick, Nicholas. "The Impact of Inclusionary Zoning on Development." Report of Business and Professional People for the Public Interest, bpichicago.org, 2004, 4.

Buiso, Gary. "Marty's Lane Pain Is Fodder for His Christmas Card." *The Brooklyn Paper*, December 12, 2010.

———. "Safety First! Prospect Park West Bike Lane Working." *The Brooklyn Paper*, January 20, 2011.

Burden, Dan. "22 Benefits of Urban Street Trees." ufei.org/files/pubs/22benefitsofurbanstreettrees.pdf, May 2006.

Burden, Dan, and Peter Lagerwey. "Road Diets: Fixing the Big Roads." Walkable Communities Inc., 1999. walkable.org/assets/downloads/roaddiets.pdf.

Burke, Mia. "Joyride: Pedaling Toward a Healthier Planet." planetizen.com, February 28, 2011.

"Call for Narrower Streets Rejected by Fire Code Officials." New Urban News. bettercities.net, December 1, 2009.

Chen, Donald. "If You Build It, They Will Come . . . Why We Can't Build Ourselves Out of Congestion." *Surface Transportation Policy Project Progress* VII: 2 (March 1998): 1, 4.

Children's Safety Network. "Promoting Bicycle Safety for Children," 2. childrenssafetynetwork.org, 2011.

Clendaniel, Morgan. "Zipcar's Impact on How People Use Cars Is Enormous." fastcompany.com, July 19, 2011.

Coder, Rim D. "Identified Benefits of Community Trees and Forests." University of Georgia study, October 1996. warnell.forestry.uga.edu/service/library/for96=039/for96=039.pdf.

Colleran, Jim. "The Worst Streets in America." planetizen.com, March 21, 2001.

Condon, Patrick. "Canadian Cities American Cities: Our Differences Are the Same." Smart Growth on the Ground Initiative, University of British Columbia, February 2004. jtc.sala.ubc.ca/newsroom/patrick_condon_primer.pdf.

Cortright, Joe: "Driven Apart: Why Sprawl, Not Insufficient Roads, Is the Real Cause of Traffic Congestion." CEOs for Cities, White Paper, September 29, 2010.

———. "Portland's Green Dividend." CEOs for Cities White Paper, July 2007.

———. "Walking the Walk: How Walkability Raises Home Values in U.S. Cities." CEOs for Cities White Paper, August 2009.

Cortright, Joe, and Carol Coletta. "The Young and the Restless: How Portland Competes for Talent." Portland, Ore: Impresa, Inc., 2004.

Cox, Wendell. "DART's Billion Dollar Boondoggle." *Dallas Business Journal*, June 16, 2002.

Davies, Zoe G., et al. "Mapping an Urban Ecosystem Service: Quantifying Above-Ground Carbon Storage at a City-Wide Scale." *Journal of Applied Ecology* 48 (2011): 1125–34.

D.C. Surface Transit. "Value Capture and Tax-Increment Financing Options for Streetcar Construction." Report commissioned by D.C. Surface Transit from the Brookings Institution, HDR, Re-Connecting America, and RCLCO, June 2009.

DeBrabander, Firmin. "What If Green Products Make Us Pollute More?" *The Baltimore Sun*, June 2, 2011.

District Department of Transportation, Washington, D.C. "Capital Bikeshare Expansion Planned in the New Year," December 23, 2010.

Doherty, Patrick C., and Christopher B. Leinberger. "The Next Real Estate Boom." *The Washington Monthly*, November/December 2010.

Doig, Will. "Are Freeways Doomed?" salon.com, December 1, 2011.

Donovan, Geoffrey, and David Butry. "Trees in the City: Valuing Trees in Portland, Oregon." *Landscape and Urban Planning* 94 (2010): 77–83.

Dorner, Josh. "NBC Confirms That 'Clean Coal' Is an Oxymoron." Huffington Post, November 18, 2008.

Duhigg, Charles. "Saving US Water and Sewer Systems Would Be Costly." *The New York Times*, March 14, 2010.

Dumbaugh, Eric. "Safe Streets, Livable Streets." *Journal of the American Planning Association* 71, no. 3 (2005): 283–300.

Duranton, Gilles, and Matthew Turner. "The Fundamental Law of Road Congestion: Evidence from U.S. Cities." *American Economic Review* 101 (2011): 2616–52.

Durning, Alan. "The Year of Living Car-lessly." daily.sightline.org, April 28, 2006.

Eckerson, Clarence, Jr. "The Phenomenal Success of Capital Bikeshare." streetfilms.org, August 2, 2011.

Ehrenhalt, Alan. "The Return of the Two-Way Street." governing.org, December 2009.

El Nasser, Haya. "In Many Neighborhoods, Kids Are Only a Memory." *USA Today*, June 3, 2011.

Erlanger, Steven, and Maïa de la Baume. "French Ideal of Bicycle-Sharing Meets Reality." *The New York Times*, October 30, 2009.

Eversley, Melanie. "Many Cities Changing One-Way Streets Back." *USA Today*, December 20, 2006.

Ewing, Reid, and Robert Cervero. "Travel and the Built Environment: A Meta-Analysis." *Journal of the American Planning Association* 76, no. 3 (2010): 11.

Ewing, Reid, and Eric Dumbaugh. "The Built Environment and Traffic Safety: A Review of Empirical Evidence." *Journal of Planning Literature* 23, no. 4 (2009): 347–67.

Fallows, James. "Fifty-Nine and a Half Minutes of Brilliance, Thirty Seconds of Hauteur." theatlantic.com, July 3, 2009.

Farmer, Molly. "South Jordan Mom Cited for Neglect for Allowing Child to Walk to School." *The Deseret News*, December 15, 2010.

Florida, Richard. "The Great Car Reset." theatlantic.com, June 3, 2010.

Ford, Jane. "Danger in Exurbia: University of Virginia Study Reveals the Danger of Travel in Virginia." *University of Virginia News*, April 30, 2002.

Freemark, Yonah. "An Extensive New Addition to Dallas' Light Rail Makes It America's Longest." thetransportpolitic.com, December 5, 2010.

———. "The Interdependence of Land Use and Transportation." thetransportpolitic.com, February 5, 2011.

———. "Transit Mode Share Trends Looking Steady." thetransportpolitic.com, October 13, 2010.

Freemark, Yonah, and Jebediah Reed. "Huh?! Four Cases of How Tearing Down a Highway Can Relieve Traffic Jams (and Save Your City)." infrastructurist.com, July 6, 2010.

Fremont, Calif., City of. "City Council Agenda and Report," May 3, 2011.

Fried, Ben. "What Backlash? Q Poll Finds 54 Percent of NYC Voters Support Bike Lanes." streetsblog.org, March 18, 2011.

Garrett-Peltier, Heidi. "Estimating the Employment Impacts of Pedestrian, Bicycle, and Road Infrastructure. Case Study: Baltimore." Political Economy Research Institute, University of Massachusetts, Amherst, December, 2010.

Gerstenang, James. "Cars Make Suburbs Riskier Than Cities, Study Says." *The Los Angeles Times*, April 15, 1996.

Gladwell, Malcolm. "Blowup." *The New Yorker*, January 22, 1996.

Glaeser, Edward. "If You Love Nature, Move to the City." *The Boston Globe*, February 10, 2011.

Goodman, Christy. "Expanded Bike-Sharing Program to Link D.C., Arlington." *The Washington Post*, May 23, 2010.

Gordon, Rachel. "Parking: S.F. Releases Details on Flexible Pricing." sfgate.com, April 2, 2011.

Gotschi, Thomas, and Kevin Mills. "Active Transportation for America: The Case for Increased Federal Investment in Bicycling and Walking." railstotrails.org, October 20, 2008.

Gros, Daniel. "Coal vs. Oil: Pure Carbon vs. Hydrocarbon." achangeinthewind.com, December 28, 2007.

Groves, Martha. "He Put Parking in Its Place." *The Los Angeles Times*, October 16, 2010.

Grynbaum, Michael. "Deadliest for Walkers: Male Drivers, Left Turns." *The New York Times*, August 16, 2010.

Haddock, Mark. "Salt Lake Streets Have Seen Many Changes over Past 150 Years." *Deseret News*, July 13, 2009.

Hansen, Mark, and Yuanlin Huang. "Road Supply and Traffic in California Urban Areas." *Transportation Research*, part A: *Policy and Practice* 31, No. 3 (1997): 205–18.

Heller, Nathan. "The Disconnect." *The New Yorker*, April 16, 2012.

Holtzclaw, John. "Using Residential Patterns and Transit to Decrease Auto Dependence and Costs." Natural Resources Defense Council, 1994. docs.nrdc.org/SmartGrowth/files/sma_09121401a.pdf.

Jackson, Richard. "We Are No Longer Creating Wellbeing." dirt.asla.org, September 12, 2010.

Jahne, Mark. "Local Officials Find Fault with Proposed Hartford–New Britain Busway." mywesthartfordlife.com, January 18, 2010.

J. D. Power and Associates. Press release, October 8, 2009.

Johnson, Kevin, Judy Keen, and William M. Welch. "Homicides Fall in Large American Cities." *USA Today*, December 29, 2010.

Kamin, Blair. "Ohio Cap at Forefront of Urban Design Trend." *The Chicago Tribune*, October 27, 2011.

Karush, Sarah. "Cities Rethink Wisdom of 50s-Era Parking Standards." *USA Today*, September 20, 2008.

Kazis, Noah. "East River Plaza Parking Still Really, Really Empty, New Research Shows." streetsblog.org, April 20, 2012.

———. "New PPW Results: More New Yorkers Use It, Without Clogging the Street." streetsblog.org, December 8, 2010.

———. "NYCHA Chairman: Parking Minimums 'Working Against Us.'" streetsblog.org, October 17, 2011.

Keates, Nancy. "A Walker's Guide to Home Buying." *The Wall Street Journal*, July 2, 2010.

Keen, Judy. "Seattle's Backyard Cottages Make a Dent in Housing Need." usatoday.com, May 26, 2010.

Kent, Ethan. "Guggenheim Museum Bilbao." Project for Public Spaces Hall of Shame, pps.org.

Klotz, Deborah. "Air Pollution and Its Effects on Heart Attack Risk." *The Boston Globe*, February 28, 2011.

Koch, Wendy. "Cities Roll Out Bike-Sharing Programs." *USA Today*, May 9, 2011.

Kolbert, Elizabeth. "XXXL: Why Are We So Fat?" *The New Yorker*, July 20, 2009.

Kolozsvari, Douglas, and Donald Shoup. "Turning Small Change into Big Changes." *Access*, no. 23 (2003). shoup.bol.ucla.edu/SmallChange.pdf.

Kooshian, Chuck, and Steve Winkelman. "Growing Wealthier: Smart Growth, Climate Change and Prosperity." Washington, D.C.: Center for Clean Air Policy, January 2011.

Kruse, Jill. "Remove It and They Will Disappear: Why Building New Roads Isn't Always the Answer." *Surface Transportation Policy Project Progress* VII: 2 (March 1998): 5, 7.

Kuang, Cliff. "Infographic of the Day: How Bikes Can Solve Our Biggest Problems." Co.Design, 2011. fastcodesign.com/1665634/infographic-of-the-day-how-bikes-can-solve-our-biggest-problems.

Langdon, Philip. "Parking: A Poison Posing as a Cure." *New Urban News*, April/May 2005.

———. "Young People Learning They Don't Need to Own a Car." *New Urban News*, December 2009.

Lehrer, Jonah. "A Physicist Solves the City." *The New York Times Magazine*, December 17, 2010.

Leinberger, Christopher B. "Federal Restructuring of Fannie and Freddie Ignores Underlying Cause of Crisis." *Urban Land*, February 1, 2011.

———. "Here Comes the Neighborhood." *The Atlantic Monthly*, June 2010.

———. "Now Coveted: A Walkable, Convenient Place." *The New York Times*, May 25, 2012.

———. "The Next Slum." *Atlantic Monthly*, March 2008.

Levey, Bob, and Jane Freundel-Levey. "End of the Roads." *The Washington Post*, November 26, 2000.

Lipman, Barbara J. "A Heavy Load: The Combined Housing and Transportation Costs of Working Families." Center for Housing Policy, October 2006.

Litman, Todd. "Economic Value of Walkability." Victoria Transport Policy Institute, May 21, 2010.

———. "Rail in America: A Comprehensive Evaluation of Benefits." Victoria Transport Policy Institute, December 7, 2010.

———. "Raise My Taxes, Please! Evaluating Household Savings from High-Quality Public Transit Service." Victoria Transport Policy Institute, February 26, 2010.

———. "Smart Congestion Reductions: Reevaluating the Role of Highway Expansion for Improving Urban Transportation." Victoria Transport Policy Institute, February 2, 2010.

———. "Terrorism, Transit, and Public Safety: Evaluating the Risks." Victoria Transport Policy Institute, December 2, 2005.

———. "Whose Roads? Defining Bicyclists' and Pedestrians' Right to Use Public Roadways." Victoria Transport Policy Institute, November 30, 2004.

Lord, Hayes A. "Cycle Tracks: Concept and Design Practices." The New York City Experience. New York City Department of Transportation, February 17, 2010.

LSC Transportation Consultants. "San Miguel County Local Transit and Human Service Transportation Plan. Colorado Springs, 2008."

Lyall, Sarah. "A Path to Road Safety with No Signposts." *The New York Times*, January 22, 2005.

Marohn, Charles. "Confessions of a Recovering Engineer." Strong Towns, November 22, 2010. strongtowns.org/journal/2010/11/22/confessions-of-a-recovering-engineer.html.

Marsh, Bill. "Kilowatts vs. Gallons." *The New York Times,* May 28, 2011.

Marshall, Wesley, and Norman Garrick. "Street Network Types and Road Safety: A Study of 24 California Cities." *Urban Design International,* August 2009.

Mayer, Jane. "The Secret Sharer." *The New Yorker*, May 23, 2011.

McNichol, Tom. "Roads Gone Wild." *Wired*, December 12, 2004.

Mehaffy, Michael. "The Urban Dimensions of Climate Change." planetizen .com, November 30, 2009.

Meyer, Jeremy P. "Denver to Eliminate Diagonal Crossings at Intersections." denverpost.com, April 6, 2011.

Miller, Jon R., M. Henry Robison, and Michael L. Lahr. "Estimating Important Transportation-Related Regional Economic Relationships in Bexar County, Texas." VIA Metropolitan Transit, 1999. vtpi.org/modeshift .pdf.

Monroe, Doug. "Taking Back the Streets." *Atlanta* magazine, February 2003, 85–95.

———. "The Stress Factor." *Atlanta* magazine, February 2003.

Morello, Carol, Dan Keating, and Steve Hendrix. "Census: Young Adults Are Responsible for Most of D.C.'s Growth in Past Decade." *The Washington Post*, May 5, 2011.

Nairn, Daniel. "New Census Numbers Confirm the Resurgence of Cities." discoveringurbanism.blogspot.com, December 15, 2010.

NCHRP Report 500, "Volume 10: A Guide for Reducing Collisions Involving Pedestrians." NCHRP, 2004.

Neff, Jack. "Is Digital Revolution Driving Decline in U.S. Car Culture?" *Advertising Age*, May 31, 2010.

Newcomb, Tim. "Need Extra Income? Put a Cottage in Your Backyard." time.com, May 28, 2011.

Newton, Damien. "Only in LA: DOT Wants to Remove Crosswalks to Protect Pedestrians." la.streetsblog.org, January 23, 2009.

New Urban Network. "Study: Transit Outperforms Green Buildings." bettercities.net/article/study-transit-outperforms-green-buildings-14203, undated.

Noland, Robert. "Traffic Fatalities and Injuries: The Effect of Changes in Infrastructure and Other Trends." Center for Transport Studies, London, 2002.

Noonan, Erica. "A Matter of Size." *The Boston Globe*, March 7, 2010.

"Off with Their Heads: Rid Downtown of Parking Meters." *Quad City Times* editorial, August 8, 2010.

Peirce, Neal. "Biking and Walking: Our Secret Weapon?" citiwire.net, July 16, 2009.

———. "Cities as Global Stars." Review of *Triumph of the City* by Edward Glaeser. citiwire.net, February 18, 2011.

Peterson, Greg. "Pharmaceuticals in Our Water Supply Are Causing Bizarre Mutations to Wildlife." alternet.com, August 9, 2007.

Pucher, John, and Ralph Buehler. "Cycling for Few or for Everyone: The Importance of Social Justice in Cycling Policy." *World Transport Policy and Practice* 15, no. 1 (2009): 57–64.

———. "Why Canadians Cycle More Than Americans: A Comparative Analysis of Bicycling Trends and Policies." Institute of Transport and Logistics Studies, University of Sydney, Newtown, NSW, Australia. *Transport Policy* 13 (2006): 265–79.

Pucher, John, and Lewis Dijkstra. "Making Walking and Cycling Safer: Lessons from Europe." *Transportation Quarterly* 54, no. 3 (2000): 25–50.

"Rainfall Interception of Trees, in Benefits of Trees in Urban Areas." coloradotrees.org, undated.

Rao, Kamala. "Seoul Tears Down an Urban Highway, and the City Can Breathe Again." *Grist*, November 4, 2011.

"Recent Lessons from the Stimulus: Transportation Funding and Job Creation." Smart Growth America report, February 2011.

Reilly, Rick. "Life of Reilly: Mile-High Madness." si.com, October 23, 2007.

"Removing Freeways—Restoring Cities." preservenet.com, undated.

"Research: Trees Make Streets Safer, Not Deadlier." *New Urban News*, bettercities.net, September 1, 2006.

Reynolds, Gretchen. "What's the Single Best Exercise?" *The New York Times Magazine*, April 17, 2011.

Rogers, Shannon H., John M. Halstead, Kevin H. Gardner, and Cynthia H. Carlson. "Examining Walkability and Social Capital as Indicators of Quality of Life at the Municipal and Neighborhood Scales." *Applied Research in the Quality of Life* 6, no. 2 (2010): 201–53.

Sack, Kevin. "Governor Proposes Remedy for Atlanta Sprawl." *The New York Times*, January 26, 1999: 14.

Salta, Alex. "Chicago Sells Rights to City Parking Meters for $1.2 Billion." ohmygov.com, December 24, 2008.

Salzman, Randy. "Build More Highways, Get More Traffic." *The Daily Progress*, December 19, 2010.

Schwartzman, Paul. "At Columbia Heights Mall, So Much Parking, So Little Need." *The Washington Post*, October 8, 2009.

Shorto, Russell. "The Dutch Way: Bicycles and Fresh Bread." *The New York Times*, July 30, 2011.

Smiley, Brett. "Number of New Yorkers Commuting on Bikes Continues to Rise." *New York*, December 8, 2011. With link to New York City Department of Transportation press release.

Smith, Rick. "Cedar Rapids Phasing Out Back-In Angle Parking." *The Gazette*, June 9, 2011.

Snyder, Tanya. "Actually, Highway Builders, Roads Don't Pay for Themselves." dc.streetsblog.org, January 4, 2011.

Sottile, Christian. "One-Way Streets: Urban Impact Analysis." Commissioned by the City of Savannah, as yet unpublished.

Speck, Jeff. "Our Ailing Communities: Q&A: Richard Jackson." metropolismag.com, October 11, 2006.

"Status of North American Light Rail Projects." lightrailnow.org, 2002.

Stutzer, Alois, and Bruno S. Frey. "Stress That Doesn't Pay: The Commuting Paradox." Institute for Empirical Work in Economics, University of Zurich, Switzerland, ideas.repec.org/p/zur/iewwpx/151.html.

Summers, Nick. "Where the Neon Lights Are Bright—and Drivers Are No Longer Welcome." *Newsweek*, February 27, 2009.

Swartz, Jon. "San Francisco's Charm Lures High-Tech Workers." *USA Today*, December 6, 2010.

The Segmentation Company, "Attracting College-Educated, Young Adults to Cities." Prepared for CEOs for Cities, May 8, 2006.

Transportation for America. *Dangerous by Design 2011*. Undated.

Troianovski, Anton. "Downtowns Get a Fresh Lease." *The Wall Street Journal*, December 13, 2010.

Turner, Chris. "The Best Tool for Fixing City Traffic Problems? A Wrecking Ball." Mother Nature Network, mnn.com, April 15, 2011.

———. "What Makes a Building Ugly?" Mother Nature Network, mnn.com, August 5, 2011.

"2010 Quality of Living Worldwide City Rankings." Mercer.com.

"2010 Urban Mobility Report." Texas Transportation Institute, Texas A&M University, 2010.

Twyman, Anthony S. "Greening Up Fertilizes Home Prices, Study Says." *The Philadelphia Inquirer*, January 10, 2005.

Ulrich, R. S., et al. "View Through a Window May Influence Recovery from Surgery." *Science* 224, 420 (1984): 420–21.

U.S. Department of Agriculture. "Benefits of Trees in Urban Areas." Forest Service Pamphlet #FS-363.

U.S. Environmental Protection Agency. "Location Efficiency and Housing Type—Boiling It Down to BTUs." USEPA Report prepared by Jonathan Rose Associates, March 2011.

U.S. Government Accounting Office. "Bus Rapid Transit Shows Promise." September 2001.

"The Value of Trees to a Community." Arbor Day Foundation, arborday.org/trees/benefits.cfm.

Van Gleson, John. "Light Rail Adds Transportation Choices on Common Ground." National Association of Realtors (2009): 4–13.

Vlahos, James. "Is Sitting a Lethal Activity?" *The New York Times Magazine*, April 14, 2011.

Walljasper, Jay. "Cycling to Success: Lessons from the Dutch." citiwire.net, September 23, 2010.

———. "The Surprising Rise of Minneapolis as a Top Bike Town." citiwire.net, October 22, 2011.

Washington, D.C., Economic Partnership. "2008 Neighborhood Profiles—Columbia Heights."

Whitman, David. "The Sickening Sewer Crisis in America." aquarain.com, undated.

Wieckowski, Ania. "The Unintended Consequences of Cul-de-Sacs." *Harvard Business Review*, May 2010.

Yardley, William. "Seattle Mayor Is Trailing in the Early Primary Count." *The New York Times*, August 19, 2009.

Yen, Hope. "Suburbs Lose Young Whites to Cities: Younger, Educated Whites Moving to Urban Areas for Homes, Jobs." Associated Press, May 9, 2010.

RADIO, TELEVISION, FILM, AND SLIDESHOWS

A Convenient Remedy. Congress for the New Urbanism video.

Aubrey, Allison. "Switching Gears: More Commuters Bike to Work." NPR *Morning Edition*, November 29, 2010.

Barnett, David C. "A Comeback for Downtown Cleveland." NPR *Morning Edition*, June 11, 2011.

Equilibrium Capital. "Streetcars' Economic Impact in the United States." PowerPoint presentation, May 26, 2010.

Gabriel, Ron. "3-Way Street by ronconcocacola." Vimeo.

WebMD. "10 Worst Cities for Asthma." Slideshow. webmd.com/asthma /slideshow-10-worst-cities-for-asthma.

LECTURES AND CONFERENCES

Brooks, David. Lecture. Aspen Institute, March 18, 2011.

Frank, Lawrence. Lecture to the 18th Congress for the New Urbanism, Atlanta, Georgia, May 20, 2010.

Gladwell, Malcolm. Remarks. Downtown Partnership of Baltimore Annual Meeting, November 17, 2010.

Hales, Charles. Presentation at Rail-Volution, October 18, 2011.

Livingstone, Ken. Winner commentary by Mayor of London. World Technology Winners and Finalists, World Technology Network, 2004.

Parolec, Daniel. Presentation to the Congress for the New Urbanism, June 2, 2011.

Ronkin, Michael. "Road Diets." PowerPoint presentation, New Partners for Smart Growth, February 10, 2007.

Speck, Jeff. "Six Things Even New York Can Do Better." Presentation to New York City Planning Commission, January 4, 2010.

WEBSITES

20's Plenty for Us: 20splentyforus.org.uk.

American Dream Coalition: americandreamcoalition.org.

Better! Cities & Towns: Walkable Streets (source of many quotes): bettercities
.net/walkable-streets.
Brookings VMT Cities Ranking: scribd.com/doc/9199883/Brookings-VMT
-Cities-Ranking.
Dallas Area Rapid Transit: dart.org.
Dom's Plan B Blog: http://domz60.wordpress.com/quotes/.
Jane's Walk: janeswalk.net.
Kaufman, Kirsten: bikerealtor.com.
Lonely Planet readers poll: Top 10 Walking Cities. lonelyplanet.com/blog/2011
/03/07/top-cities-to-walk-around/.
Mercer.com: Quality of Living Worldwide City Rankings 2010.
Million Trees NYC: milliontreesnyc.org.
Urban Audit: urbanaudit.org.
Walk Score: walkscore.com.

IMAGES
Poster, Intelligent Cities Initiative, National Building Museum, Washington,
D.C.

GEOGRAPHIC INDEX

GENERAL INDEX